THE PARADOX OF DEMOCRACY

THE PARADOX OF DEMOCRACY

Free Speech, Open Media, and
Perilous Persuasion

ZAC GERSHBERG AND SEAN ILLING

The University of Chicago Press CHICAGO AND LONDON

The University of Chicago Press, Chicago 60637
The University of Chicago Press, Ltd., London
© 2022 by Zac Gershberg and Sean Illing
Published 2022
Paperback edition 2023
Printed in the United States of America

32 31 30 29 28 27 26 25 24 23   1 2 3 4 5

ISBN-13: 978-0-226-68170-2 (cloth)
ISBN-13: 978-0-226-82941-8 (paper)
ISBN-13: 978-0-226-81890-0 (e-book)
DOI: https://doi.org/10.7208/chicago/9780226818900.001.0001

Library of Congress Cataloging-in-Publication Data

Names: Gershberg, Zachary, 1980– author. | Illing, Sean D., author.
Title: The paradox of democracy : free speech, open media, and perilous persuasion / Zac Gershberg and Sean Illing.
Description: Chicago : University of Chicago Press, 2022. | Includes bibliographical references and index.
Identifiers: LCCN 2021047957 | ISBN 9780226681702 (cloth) | ISBN 9780226818900 (ebook)
Subjects: LCSH: Mass media and public opinion. | Democracy—Philosophy. | Journalism—Political aspects.
Classification: LCC P95.8 .G47 2022 | DDC 302.23—dc23/eng/20211110
LC record available at https://lccn.loc.gov/2021047957

♾ This paper meets the requirements of ANSI/NISO Z39.48-1992 (Permanence of Paper).

To Karen & Lauren, without whom not

It is to be regretted the world does not discriminate more justly in its use of political terms.

JAMES FENIMORE COOPER, *The Bravo* (1831)

CONTENTS

INTRODUCTION

This book makes an unconventional claim about democracy. In almost every major work on the subject, democracy is reduced to a body of institutions and practices. We are told, time and again, that the touchstone of any democratic society is the universal right to vote and a government that enshrines the law. This description isn't wrong so much as narrow; it identifies the core features of democracy, but it doesn't capture the constitutive condition of this type of society. Moreover, it's better to think of democracy less as a government type and more as an open communicative culture. Democracies can be liberal or illiberal, populist or consensus based, but those are potential outcomes that emerge from this open culture. And the direction any democracy takes largely depends on its tools of communication and the passions they promote. This is more than an academic distinction. To see democracy as a culture of free expression is to foreground its susceptibility to endless evolution, even danger.

We call this the paradox of democracy: a free and open communication environment that, because of its openness, invites exploitation and subversion from within. This tension sits at the core of every democracy, and it can't be resolved or circumnavigated. To put it another way, the essential democratic freedom—the freedom of expression—is both ingrained in and potentially harmful to democracy. We state this at the outset because it helps frame everything that follows. More than a regime or a governing philosophy, democracy is both a burden and a challenge. Like the Greek mythological hero Sisyphus, who was condemned by the gods to roll a rock up a hill for all eternity, democracy is an unwieldy boulder continually throwing us back into an absurd situation. No matter what we do or how hard we push, the boulder persists. Democracy is dangerous for precisely this reason, which presents not just a collective-action problem but a genuine existential dilemma: it demands that we take responsibility for the situation in which we find ourselves. Democracy has no defined purpose, and it is shaped in real time by the communicative choices of individual citizens and politicians. But it offers no guarantees of good governance or just outcomes.

The belief that democracy is a fixed system with inherent features has led to a lot of confusion. Most people still hold what's often called the folk theory of democracy: ordinary citizens have preferences about what the government ought to do; they elect leaders who will carry out those preferences and vote against those who will not. In the end, we're left with a government that more or less serves the majority. And all this is supposed to take place in a culture of rules and norms that privileges minority rights, respects the rule of law, and welcomes peaceful transitions of power. But that culture is precisely what we call liberalism—it's not democracy as such. Confusion on this point has obscured the nature and demands of democratic life.

So this book is largely our attempt to see democracy with clear and unforgiving eyes. It is descriptive. We linger on democracy's weaknesses and contradictions while insisting it remains the best form of politics because it affords freedom of expression and the possibility of confronting power in all its forms—that's democracy's claim to superiority over all other political cultures. Citizens no less than politicians have a voice through what they say and publish, how they assemble and mobilize, and how they vote. But democratic freedom can be self-negating because persuasion is the operative variable. Governments, even democratic governments, can elect to constrain the voice of the people and limit who gets to count as a citizen. New media open up new rhetorical styles in political discourse, and bad politics ensue.

The ancient Greeks understood this long before us, and they even developed two frameworks for free speech that highlighted the problem. *Isegoria* described the right of citizens to equal participation in public discourse; *parrhesia* described the right of individuals to say anything they wanted, whenever they wanted, and to whomever they wanted. As chapter 2 explains, isegoria created the political environment of democracy, while parrhesia actualized it. But the right to say anything opened the door to all manners of subversion, which has been a challenge to every democracy ever since. The emergence of isegoria in Athens, for instance, was accompanied by the joint rituals of ostracism and tribalism. In today's language, you might say that Socrates was the first democratic citizen to be "canceled" by the same democratic forces that made his speech free in the first place. This is the defining tension of any democratic society, and citizens and politicians alike are forced to navigate it. Just as Sisyphus makes that rock meaningful by owning it, so we propel democracy by freely communicating with others. But the paradox we're going to outline makes this task enormously difficult. Our communicative environment, which lays the foundation for shared meaning, is unruly and continually upended by media innovation and treacherous politics that send the boulder of democracy rolling back down the hill.

Citizens, philosophers, and politicians have always fretted about democracy for exactly this reason. Although it facilitates a culture in which deliberative discourse and collective judgment are possible, it can also be gamed, prompting crises from within. The panic today over democracy is no different. Since 2016, a whole genre of literature has emerged in books and essays seeking to explain how democracies fall or why Western liberalism is in retreat. The consensus is that if democracy isn't quite dead, it's certainly under attack. We are surely living through a period of intense democratic disruption. All over the world, from India to Hungary to Turkey to Brazil to the United States, democratic cultures have been disordered. What we're witnessing is a convergence of various forces unleashed by novel media and populist rhetorical styles that implode democracy from within.

Our goal is not to diminish the reality of the crisis before us. Liberal democracy, as a culturally dominant time, has died. So have many of the norms and institutions that undergirded it. But the discourse around this problem is far too circumscribed. To read many of the current books about democracy is to walk away with the impression that we're in the midst of something new, something unique to our moment. It's as though the default state of democracy is stability, and periods of disruption are the exception. But the reverse is much nearer the truth. At the very heart of democracy is a contradiction that cannot be resolved, one that has affected free societies from ancient Greece to contemporary America. To function, democracies require more than just voting. Citizens are afforded access to information and an open system of debate. But throughout history, when new forms of communications arrive—from the disingenuous use of sophistic techniques developed in Athens to the social media–enabled spread of propaganda we see today—they often undermine the practices of democratic politics. The more widely accessible the media of a society, the more susceptible that society is to demagoguery, distraction, and spectacle. We see this time and again: media continually evolve faster than politics, resulting in recurring patterns of democratic instability.

Classical rhetoric was a necessity for the early democratic cultures of Athens and Rome—but sophistry, a form of deceptive, crowd-pleasing speech, overwhelmed both societies and hastened their collapse. The printing press allowed for the mass production of books and the creation of newspapers, which ushered in the Enlightenment and the democratic revolutions of the eighteenth century—yet these public networks also sowed chaos in the aftermath of the American and French Revolutions. The former was able to negotiate a deeply partisan press that threatened the viability of the United States in its infancy, but France exploded into the violent Reign of Terror. In the nineteenth century, the penny press and the telegraph's speedy dissemination of news collapsed geographic distances and helped spread the norms of liberal society across Europe—but it also fomented nationalist discourses. Political leaders and news outlets generated narratives full of nativist fears and petty resentments to gain traction in place of deliberative debate, and the appeals of this mediated rhetoric would eventually lead Europe toward World War I. While cinema and radio further opened media and created a more accessible mass culture, they also provided essential platforms for European fascists to overwhelm democracy into totalitarianism. Television transformed politics so citizens could directly see and listen to their representatives, with many positive results, but the imperatives of the medium also shaped politics as much as covered it. To succeed, politicians in the televisual era needed to adapt to a new incentive structure, in which superficial branding, sound bites, and optics predominated.

And now the paradox of democracy has reached its zenith with a flood of new digital communication platforms inundating free societies with instantaneous information and nonstop networked dialogue. The public sphere of the twenty-first century is more democratic and open than ever before. Political leaders communicate directly with their publics en masse; citizens provide immediate feedback and can publish or broadcast to mass audiences on their own. Yet the democratic openness of communication in the twenty-first century has destabilized democratic politics. There are no longer any controls on the flow of information. The public is now angry, distrustful of whether their representatives can even make sound decisions. That may be healthy from a democratic perspective, but with so much noise on social media and so many news outlets disseminating contradictory information, citizens are justifiably confused and cynical. Many find it easier to retreat into echo chambers and share misinformation than discern what's real amid the chaos of the public sphere.

It's hard to see a way out of this mess. The very instruments of democracy have been turned against it. Before groping for solutions, we must situate our current predicament in a broader historical context and realize we're facing the same precipice confronted by ancient democratic societies like Athens and Rome. Whereas they tipped over, unable to control the runaway momentum of their forms of communication, we still have time to back away from the edge. But first we must see democracy with clear eyes.

It helps to remember that there is no golden age. Democratic systems, by their very nature, are always unstable, always imperiled, which is why the Trump era's flurry of books about democracy's demise is misleading. Many of them, especially Steven Levitsky and Daniel Ziblatt's How Democracies Die, help explain why and how democracies "backslide" into authoritarian systems, and why key liberal-democratic norms like "mutual tolerance" and "forbearance" are important safeguards against illiberalism.[1] Yascha Mounk's The People vs. Democracy is equally useful in reminding us that paradoxically enough, it is the people who most often threaten democracy, not heavy-handed tyrants from above.[2] The true guardians of democracy, Mounk insists, are the institutions and values that constrain the popular will. Anne Applebaum's *Twilight of Democracy* is another deeply instructive study of the illiberal drift of so many democracies across the globe.[3] However, like so many others, Applebaum's view proceeds from a default assumption that democracy is a discrete system. But that assumption prevents us from understanding democracy as a constantly evolving culture, with liberalism as one potential outcome among many. We must recognize that democracy and illiberalism are as compatible as democracy and liberalism. Then the focus turns naturally to democratic culture and the forces that push it one way or the other. Still, each of the aforementioned analyses are indispensable, and they highlight different dimensions of the same problem. But we need to zoom back and take a much broader view of democracy. It's not that Levitsky and Ziblatt, Mounk, and Applebaum are wrong; we are in the midst of a crisis. The question for us is the precise nature of that crisis and whether it is a crisis of democracy at all.

If we reduce democracy to a bundle of institutions or a set of rules, like regular elections or universal suffrage or the legal protection of civil rights, we miss what is most essential to democratic order: an open culture of persuasion. To say that a state is democratic is to say little about how it is actually governed. Political theorists like Italy's Norberto Bobbio have argued that liberalism and democracy are interchangeable on account of their mutual dependence. But just because "liberalism provides those liberties necessary for the proper exercise of democratic power," as Bobbio wrote, does not mean that liberalism is essential to or indistinguishable from democracy.[4] A properly liberal state is one in which individual rights are paramount; it protects the individual not only against the abuses of a tyrant but also against the abuses of democratic majorities. Think of liberal democracy as democracy with moral and legal buffers. It's what you get when the Hellenic ideal of individual freedom is buttressed by the Roman devotion to rule of law, or what some today would call constitutionalism. Liberal democracy, in other words, is the form of democracy most of us have come to prefer, but it is by no means the only form of democracy. We need only look to modern-day Hungary, whose populist leader, Viktor Orbán, has championed "illiberal democracy."

Liberal democracies have long been sustained by traditional mass media such as newspapers and radio and television. Citizens remained somewhat passive while media gatekeepers and politicians hashed out a norms-driven discourse of information and debate in the public sphere. Citizens absorbed what they read, listened to, and watched, registering their approval or disapproval at the polls. Then something changed. The rise of polarizing cable television news, the blogosphere, and the outrageous flows of social networking, now hooked to our palmed smartphones, let citizens in on the act of forging discourses and choosing what news they prefer. The result is a more democratic and less liberal world. The belief that the democratic experiment was destined to end in something like liberal democracy was just that: a belief. It turns out there is nothing inexorable about the logic of democracy; it is just as likely to culminate in tyranny as it is freedom. And the rise of illiberalism highlights a crucial point: our present crisis is as much about culture as it is politics. Despite all our assumptions about the inherent value of democracy, a democratic culture guarantees no outcome. Democratic cultures can support liberal-democratic governments, or they can just as easily spawn plutocratic or authoritarian systems. It might seem counterintuitive to think of democracies as breeding grounds for tyranny, but it's no contradiction at all.

A long tradition of democratic skeptics, from Plato to Walter Lippmann, understood the challenges of democratic life. Some of these skeptics were too pessimistic, too willing to abandon the project altogether, but their criticisms are as relevant as ever. If we want to navigate the paradox today, we'll have to grapple with these critiques and be honest about the possibilities and limitations of democracy. In *The Republic*, Plato asks readers to consider all the political regimes side by side. Oligarchy, democracy, and tyranny, in that order, are said to be the worst forms of government. Oligarchies become democracies for predictable reasons: inequality and corruption spread so pervasively that the social conditions become intolerable. "Democracy comes into power," Plato says, "when the poor are the victors, killing some and exiling some, and giving equal shares in the government to all the rest."[5] But democracy is a poor substitute for oligarchy. While it's full of freedom of speech and spangled with every kind of liberty imaginable, over time this boundless freedom can degenerate. A spirit of excess takes hold, and eventually the state falls sick and the people pine for order and stability. Thus emerges the tyrannical strongman.

Plato was arguably the first theorist to reckon with the paradox as we understand it, though he never quite expresses it in those terms. His critique of democracy was precisely that it can't be controlled, that the open rhetorical culture on which it depends would be exploited repeatedly by would-be tyrants. The people, he insisted, would happily throw in their lot with demagogic firebrands if things got bad enough or when they simply grew tired of the plodding pace of democratic politics. So concerned was Plato about the unruliness of mobs that he capped the number of citizens capable of self-government at just over five thousand. In the end, his pessimism got the better of him. He abandoned democracy as a noble but ultimately flawed pursuit. But it's telling that he couldn't offer anything like a viable alternative. The best he could muster is a vision of the quasi dictatorship of philosopher-kings in which the wisest are trained to rule over the lowly masses.

Walter Lippmann, the great twentieth-century journalist, offered perhaps the next best critique of democracy. Unlike Plato, Lippmann does not toss out the baby with the bathwater. But like Plato, he doubts the capacity of everyday citizens to live up to the demands of democratic politics. In his 1922 opus, *Public Opinion*, Lippmann poses a straightforward question: Can citizens achieve a basic knowledge of public affairs and then make reasonable choices about what to do? If the answer is no, then the entire democratic project is at best a folly. Lippmann considers the romanticized vision of democracy espoused by the American Founders. Does it square with the reality of our world today? The Founders imagined that citizens, no matter how sprawling the state became, would still function much as they did in the small, self-contained communities that existed in the eighteenth century. Which is to say, they would be asked to make decisions about issues with which they had direct experience. Of course, the Founders were thinking of white male property-owning farmers who understood their local environment, knew their neighbors, and didn't live in a highly industrialized society. For Thomas Jefferson, as Lippmann wrote, the democratic ideal consisted of "an ideal environment and a selected class."[6] That environment looks nothing like ours, and the range of issues voters are expected to know something about today far exceeds the demands at the time of the nation's founding. The key question for Lippmann wasn't whether the average person was intelligent enough to make decisions about public policy; it was whether the average person could ever know enough to choose intelligently.

Lippmann helped create propaganda to gin up support for World War I. That experience taught him how susceptible the public is to manipulation. We're told about the world before we see it, we imagine things before we experience them, and we become hostages to these preconceptions. These narratives give us an ordered picture of the world, to which our tastes and stereotypes and values are anchored. Which is why it's so hard to separate people from their dogmas. "No wonder, then," as Lippmann says, "that any disturbance of the stereotypes seems like an attack upon the foundations of the universe. It is an attack upon the foundations of *our* universe."[7]

Lippmann was right that most voters lack anything like a direct knowledge of political affairs. They are forced, by dint of circumstances, to rely on pictures painted by the news media. So if journalism can provide accurate pictures of the world, citizens ought to have the information they need to perform their democratic duties. Lippmann says this works in theory but not in practice. The world, he argues, is large and fast moving. Consequently, the speed of communication in the age of mass media forces journalists to speak through slogans and simplified interpretations. This critique was challenged by John Dewey, who nevertheless conceded Lippmann's point about the folly of public opinion. "As matters now stand," he wrote in a review of Lippmann's *Public Opinion*, "every issue is hopelessly entangled in a snarl of emotions, stereotypes and irrelevant memories and associations."[8] Still, he rejected Lippmann's call for a technocratic elite that would effectively govern on behalf of the masses. Dewey insisted that in a democracy, political knowledge can only come about through conversation among citizens. The only reality that matters is the reality that citizens collectively construct. If you accept, as Lippmann does, that the public is atomized and permanently cut off from the conversation about public affairs, then you've undercut the very possibility of democracy.

Together, Plato, Lippmann, and Dewey provide a useful frame for the story we tell in this book. All three of them understood, with unusual clarity, just how difficult democracy is. Plato throws in the towel, rejecting democracy as an agreeable form of anarchy. Lippmann believes in it, but he can't figure out how to make it work. Dewey acknowledges all the challenges, but he insists that viable alternatives are nonexistent. Our approach is to judge democracy on its own terms, to accept and trace its structural weaknesses and ask how we might live in a world in which those weaknesses are maximally exposed.

So many accounts of democracy emphasize legislative processes or policy outcomes, but these often miss the depth of connection between communication and political culture. When culture is discussed, it's often in the context of liberal-democratic values. But the question we're asking is: What determines the valence of those values? If a democracy stands or falls on the quality of the culture propping it up, then we ought to know under what conditions those values are affirmed and rejected. We believe those conditions are determined by a society's tools of communication, facilitated through media, to persuade. Indeed, we'll go a step further: democracies are defined by their cultures of communication. If a democracy consists of citizens deciding, collectively, what ought to be done, then the manner through which they persuade one another determines nearly everything else that follows. And that privileges media ecology as the master political science. Some of its foremost practitioners, like Marshall McLuhan and Neil Postman, sensed, far better than political scientists or sociologists, that our media environment decides not just what we pay attention to but also how we think and orient ourselves in the world. For every form of media possesses its own epistemology, a series of biases and disruptions that shape how we, as citizens, come to know things. Each medium also offers an ontology, a construction of reality that guides our being and interaction with others. Whereas print media makes demands of our time and ability to read, television insists on the passive consumption of entertaining images. The costs and technological equipment associated with publishing and broadcasting ensured some level of scarcity, thereby limiting communications. Then along came digital media, which armed everyone with a computer or smartphone with an opportunity to publish or broadcast mass communications themselves. While Plato, Lippmann, and even Dewey recognized how difficult it is to control public discourse in a democracy, none of them could have imagined anything like the media environment before us today. We're now confronting the greatest structural challenge to democracy we've ever seen: a truly open society. Without gatekeepers, there are no constraints on discourse. Digital technology has changed everything. Consequently, reality is up for grabs in a way it never has been before.

To understand how we got here, let us restate the paradox: democracies exist through an open communication environment, but this condition of freedom invites political actors to exploit novel media technologies and draw from demagogic rhetorical styles. Democracies are thus constantly undermined by their constitutive conditions of communication. There is no way out of this dilemma: either a society is free or it isn't. If it isn't free, it's not a democracy. And if it is, that means everything, rhetorically, ought to be permitted.

Democratic societies thus exist in a state of permanent tension. The freedom on which they depend poses a continual existential threat, and the only bulwark against the implications of the paradox is an active, discerning citizenry. The peculiar tyranny of today is harder to see because it is so pervasive. We are not under the yoke of ideological terror or state-sanctioned oppression. On the contrary, we've watched our deliberative culture be transformed by radical changes in the modes of public conversation. It has changed how we think, live, and relate to one another. Our ideology *is* our technology; our technology *is* our culture; and culture always precedes politics. This does not leave us in the most enviable of positions. Since we can't put the technological genie back in the bottle, we must learn to live in the world we've made. But there are reasons for optimism despite our gloomy tone. First, although something is different about the current period of disruption, we've been here before. The history of democracy is the history of communicative innovation, disruption, and adaptation. The pace of change today is far quicker, and the convergence of media more intense, but recognizing the chaos we inherit is the first, best step toward mitigating the challenges.

From Robert Putnam's famous 2000 book, *Bowling Alone*, to Patrick Dineen's 2018 tract, *Why Liberalism Failed*, scholars have lamented the loss of civic bonds in America. People aren't involved in their communities anymore, in part because they don't have to be. We've got smartphones and Netflix and a thousand other diversions. No wonder social capital has been on the decline for several decades. At the same time, local newspapers are dying out and political discourse is becoming increasingly nationalized, which means most issues are abstract and dominated by tribal allegiances and caricatured Right-Left narratives. To the extent that citizens think and talk about politics, they think and talk about national politics. In our current mediascape, that means whatever cable news is covering, whatever narratives are driving traffic on the internet. Our attentional bandwidth is incessantly occupied with party politics or congressional and parliamentary drama. Elections are reduced to simplistic referendums on, say, the presidency, rather than on concrete issues. Ideally, democracy would be heavily rooted in a sense of place. But we have reached the point where mediated space has fully dislocated our lived realities. If citizens can only engage with local politics by relating them to national politics, nearly every issue becomes a binary choice between my team and your team, between Republicans and Democrats or Tories and Labour.

A recurring theme in this book is that democracy is much more than a form of government. It is, as Dewey said, "a mode of associated living, of conjoint communicated experience."[9] We must therefore rethink the basic questions of political life. What does it mean to be a citizen? What obligations do we have to each other? What values do we share, and how do we affirm them collectively? The paradox demands that these questions be asked and considered over and over again without the benefit of a final answer. All democratic communities are held together not by a shared conception of truth but by a commonly recognized experience and a commitment to active dialogue. Because of the paradox, democracy is always suspended between chaos and order, just as Sisyphus's boulder is always perilously close to tumbling back down the hill. There is no avoiding this existential dilemma; it defines every democratic culture.

It's not easy to live in this state of tension, especially in a wide-open rhetorical culture like the one we have today. Novel media technologies have altered our social and psychic environment—and, by extension, the values and institutions that ground society. There is no going back; the winds of technological change will keep blowing whether we want them to or not. But, as McLuhan observed, we are lucky in that the pace of change today is so fast, so instantaneous, that we might well be able to take control of our destiny and steer it in the most fruitful direction possible. That we can at least see what is happening to us is already a tremendous advantage over previous eras. But make no mistake: the revolution has already occurred, and our present task is to regain our footing in the world it has wrought.

The real challenge before us is not an absence of democracy. On the contrary, we're confronting the true face of democracy: a totally unfettered culture of open communication. Nearly all democracies up until now have been democracies in name only; they've been mediated by institutions designed to check popular passions and control the flow of information. But those institutional walls were weakened by the electronic revolution and later shattered by digital technology. It's no longer possible to limit access to information or curate what is and isn't news. The test is whether our democratic institutions can withstand this kind of pressure, whether we can, somehow, keep pushing that democratic boulder up the hill.

And that remains an open question.

THE BIAS AND THE DISRUPTION

After the natural disaster, people came together for a short time. The whole world was one, in perfect harmony. One family whose ingenuity had helped them survive built a massive structure to honor human progress. People from across the world would be interconnected like never before as a result of their efforts. But then the real tragedy hit, and its effects far outweighed the initial damage. This time, the flood was permanent. God was ambivalent about the rebuilding process. If all persons spoke the same language, God surmised, then nothing they planned to do would be impossible. And so, according to the Old Testament, God destroyed the Tower of Babel, scattered people across the earth, and confused their languages to imperil human understanding.

This biblical tale from Genesis captures the conditions in which we find ourselves. We dream the dream of perfect communication through novel technologies, like the Tower of Babel, but the goal of universal harmony eludes us. Great structures are erected, and the distance of geographic space collapses through media invention and innovation. Yet no matter how hard we try, discord persists. We are forever divided.

The Tower of Babel lives on as tragic myth. Its destruction haunts us, and we can't but inhabit the struggle left in its wake. That was clearly God's intention or a result of our social evolution. Either way, the technological progress of communication, from the early alphabet to the smartphone, dangles the promise of perfect cooperation and communication, but that day never comes. Cuneiform tablets, papyrus, the alphabet, rhetoric and the categories of speech, parchment and the codex, paper and the printing press, newspapers and the telegraph, radio and television, cable and satellite, the internet and social networking: they'll never be enough, despite the dramatic changes new media offer. Efforts in mathematics and philosophy to perfect a language that clarifies meaning once and for all have failed, and the horizons of AI and robotics will undoubtedly prove chimerical as well. Humans have continually sought "the task of winning for themselves the full and reconciled mastery of the Tower of Babel," as Umberto Eco once observed,[1] yet communication remains permanently fraught. The word spelled *t-r-e-e* can never fully approach the actual tree itself, and the gulf between signifier and signified reflects the demarcation between self and other, cultural harmony and political disquiet.

The biblical story offers a useful metaphor for who we are and what we face, and the fall of Babel had anticipated the problems of democracy long before democracy was conceived. Democracy is flawed not because it fails as political theory but because it relies on imperfect tools; it is permanently condemned to the freedom of communication, which requires persuasion. It *should* feature a well-informed citizenry and a responsible public sphere of accurate information and a reasonable exchange of debate. In practice, the liberty democracy supplies is largely rhetorical in scope. We can persuade one another about whom to support and what to do. It's only natural that demagoguery and misinformation follow in such a state of open communication.

It would be easier to find solace in the wisdom of a philosopher-king, or in the stability of totalitarian systems, or in the monarch governing through divine right. But if we choose democracy—and we absolutely should—then we must accept its plodding, sclerotic nature. We must live with the chaos of open society and the cynicism and demagoguery that accompany it. We must tolerate bullshit from politicians who pander to the fickle tastes of public opinion as well as from our neighbors who recirculate false information on Facebook. No democratic system is immune to imperfect communication.

That the world's longest-running democracy could elect Donald Trump, a tabloid celebrity with no political experience, shows that the range of potential outcomes in a democracy is far wider than we ever imagined. His presidency reflected the paradox in all its chaotic glory. Democracy only guarantees that we communicate freely. The decisions of whom to appoint and what shall be done follow. But since we communicate through a variety of media, there are no epistemological guardrails, no limits to discourse. Such restrictions are beyond the paradoxical structure of democracy. Noble ideals may emerge, of course, and when they do democracies can deliver satisfying history. We mustn't confuse the verdict with the trial, however. Democracy only affords that contest of communication, and even then the constraints are far fewer, in terms of evidence and rules, than those of a courtroom presided over by a judge. In a court of law, someone must present a logical argument with evidence; in democracies, anything goes.

That's the terrifying freedom of democracy writ large. We do ourselves a disservice by attaching sentimental idealism to democracy and overlooking the predominance of communication it entails. As John Dewey once observed, communication is not simply the pipe through which water flows. It locates humans squarely in the realm of meanings, and that struggle over meaning is always where democracy can be found. To extend Dewey's metaphor, think of the open communication that democracy provides, and the media innovation it galvanizes, as the base elements of hydrogen and oxygen. Just as water can be mediated in its liquid, solid, and gaseous forms, so it is with discourse: verbal and nonverbal, visual and textual, and now, with added complexity, digital enhancements. Democratic politics aren't a battle of ideas so much as a competition of communication where style can always be substance, no matter how often we complain or pretend otherwise. Add in the technological maelstrom that saturates our own cultural environment and you've got perhaps the greatest challenge to democratic order in human history. At the same time, democratic culture reigns supreme. We're more connected than ever before, freer and more prosperous than at any time in human history. Facebook and its ilk, spread diffusely across social networking, come as close to erecting the worldwide Tower of Babel as can be imagined, and yet we know too well the disruption they have wrought.

Hence the paradox: the more open the communication we enjoy, the more endangered democracy finds itself. In the perpetual fallout from the disintegrating Tower of Babel, we are flung scattered across space and continually struggle to achieve clarity through communication, which reflects our divisions as much as our ability to secure agreement. Every manner of sophistry and rabble-rousing is possible. Democracy necessitates hard work precisely because it is facilitated through the imperfect means of communication. There's no guarantee of fair or wise decision-making, and no new medium can transcend this singular, flawed basis of human interaction.

And yet democracy still reflects a genuine index of human liberty through the struggle over meaning in communication. It sanctifies our freedom to speak, to publish, to assemble, and—perhaps most important—to criticize those in positions of power. In doing so, democracy also allows for communication innovation to enhance the connections between people. Nonetheless, it's also true that new communication styles and media technologies offer more opportunities for manipulation. So goes democracy, marching along this fragile, paradoxical state of affairs—always at the mercy of its own genesis. What does it mean, then, to be condemned to communication? Why anchor this aspect of human interaction as the point of departure for an inquiry into democracy?

Communication is how we create and exchange meaning. Our experiences are filtered through an interactive sensorium of symbolic forms of communication, beginning with oral language, the first media technology, up through the digital environments of social networking today. Consciousness itself, as Friedrich Nietzsche put it, "is really only a net of communication between human beings."[2] Reality may seem more augmented now, but its texture—the thick muck of experience— has always been mediated by communication. We dwell with one another mediated through language, texts, and images as well as sight, sound, and touch. Communication, in all its forms, plays a defining role in the panoply of human existence. And what's most notable about communication, according to the theorist Kenneth Burke, is that we can't help but foster identification with one another, hoping to ultimately transcend that struggle for meaning. We continually try to build that Tower of Babel but fail to recognize how we aren't meant to complete it, that it will always be dashed to bits.

Philosophically, we may quibble with this perspective. Perhaps such a framework of communication is too broad. A review of the literature can be cited both for and against. Our goal is not to enter the debate or insist that the reader adopt a position. But any inquiry into the paradox of democracy must concede the importance of communication. If communication could be practiced with perfect clarity, democracy would be easy. There would be no trouble because there would be no need for persuasion, the ultimate arbiter of meaning. Democracy throws us squarely into the imperfections of communication, but that becomes an opportunity to cooperate with others. It is the fount of human collaboration. Through communication we form groups and decide what can and should be done. That is accomplished easily enough, up to a limit. According to British anthropologist Robin Dunbar, generating social cohesion, egalitarianism, and stability among humans is possible—for groups numbering no more than 150 people.[3] The Dunbar Number marks the capacity for developing and sustaining equitable relationships in a social network. The implication is that hunter-gatherer societies may have been better equipped to handle the conditions of democracy than the agrarian societies replacing them, let alone more modern societies with complex forms of media. The important thing is that 150 persons represent the limit of our ability to achieve cooperative reasonableness in communication. Exceed the Dunbar Number and we're no longer dealing in such richness, directness, and honesty. The Tower of Babel falls as meaning is lost or abused in translation.

This is important to keep in mind amid the panic over "alternative facts" in our "post-truth" world. We certainly face an epistemic crisis as journalism and other institutions of knowledge—from schools and government agencies to respected scientific bodies—are dismissed and overwhelmed by the volume of communication that flourishes in digital culture. But the epistemic problems we encounter are tied to, even preceded by, the fundamental imperfections of our communications environment more generally. "Part of the problem stems from the fact that facts, even a lot of facts, do not constitute reality," writes Brooke Gladstone. "Reality is what forms after we filter, arrange, and prioritize those facts and marinate them in our values and traditions."[4]

Gladstone, a media reporter, is among the few journalists who seem to grasp that the problems of objectivity are threatened not just by bad-faith politicians and their supporters who undermine the press. Something larger is at stake, something that allows for, even encourages, the inhibition of facts before its own purposeful deception. Before we were ever *wired*, this is how we were wired: unable to actualize the emergence of a perfect harmony of shared, collective truth.

In gesturing to these structural concerns about truth, the point isn't to excuse those who knowingly propagandize. But we should be realistic about how reality is forged and realize that that process will always be exploited. An open and free system of communication permits this sort of corruption of social interaction. One advisor to President George W. Bush knew this well when he boasted in 2004 to the *New York Times*, "When we act, we create our own reality. And while you're studying that reality—judiciously, as you will—we'll act again, creating other new realities."[5] A quote on background may never have been uttered more genuinely. Limiting our concerns to the loss of facts is far too narrow as a moral directive. We can complain about the collapse of truth, or we can accept the mediated flux of reality and chart what's really going on. As Lee McIntyre, who literally wrote the book on post-truth, admits, "What seems new in the post-truth era is a challenge not just to the idea of *knowing* reality but to the existence of reality itself."[6] In fairness, the manipulation of reality did not begin with Donald Trump or obfuscation over climate change or weapons of mass destruction. Reality has always been mediated to filter experience, consciousness always subject to interaction. As such, we'll never share a perfect epistemological grounding whereby a "real debate" can begin because how we experience the world is always up for grabs. Revolutions in communications prompt shifts in human consciousness, as the media ecologist Elizabeth Eisenstein so thoroughly documented.[7] This could be said of early cuneiform tablets, the invention of the alphabet, the introduction of rhetorical style, the codex, the printing press, the telegraph, cinema, radio, and television. Likewise, as Nicholas Carr has demonstrated in his book *The Shallows*, the internet has shifted our consciousness once again, fragmenting our perceptions and limiting concentration.[8]

Media carve out reality and structure human experiences because they negotiate meaning through time and across space. Since the perfected clarity of meaning can never be achieved, there is always a mediated remainder of communication, and it is this remainder that sows discord. As another media ecologist, Joshua Meyrowitz, once observed, media create "certain types of social environments that include and exclude, unite or divide people in particular ways."[9] Different cultural understandings of reality and knowledge thus arise, depending on the media employed. New media introduce shifts not just to technology but to communicative style, and how we create and absorb information changes. Our interactions assume new relational forms. As such, the political impact on the practices of democracy can be profoundly unsettling.

This, more than any journalistic preference, is what constitutes media bias. "The media is biased" may be the single most misunderstood phrase, or statement, in the English language. The sentence is also grammatically incorrect: media are plural. Any sentence prefaced with "the media" is likely to retard our understanding of media, culture, and society. "The media" does not exist. A particular medium carries particular characteristics, which should be assessed. Media truly are biased and in different ways, but not in the manner the phrase has been invoked—that "the media" prefer(s) one side or another and slant(s) reporting accordingly. To the extent that that actually occurs, it is a problem of journalism ethics. News reporting should be accurate, its methods transparent. That journalism covers "both sides" is a secondary concern in terms of ethics. Journalism is intended to describe events and furnish news; when practiced at its highest, most distinguished form, it provides a democratic service by informing the public about institutions and persons of power. If there are political implications to reporting, so be it. When journalism fails to live up to such standards, news outlets and reporters should be criticized. That is healthy democratically and should be encouraged.

Cries of media bias have been wielded as a political sledgehammer. From the standpoint of democracy, that's fine. Free societies provide a cultural environment to devise and implement persuasive political strategies through mediated channels of communication. The success of the allegation has been enormous, as confidence in journalism has eroded to all-time lows. Reality has been disrupted, since what matters is not how many citizens believe the news media are actually biased but how much journalists and news outlets are hectored into performing fairness. For several decades, the American mainstream press endeavored to satisfy the political demand of neutrality, sacrificing even objectivity itself to avoid labels of bias. And yet the press will never escape accusations of liberal bias so long as its reporting fails to endorse "conservative" causes.

This is rather unfortunate too. The world—and not just the United States—desperately needs conservatism right now. Not the conservatism that concerns itself solely with power and wealth, but one that insists on measured continuity to slacken the velocity of communication that threatens to envelop the globe, one that provides spaces of repose and reflection. Only conservatism can offer this, but its pursuit of power results in heat, not light. While conservatives should concern themselves with media bias, they do so as a cynical political strategy rather than a thoughtful engagement with the dynamism of culture. Luckily, this ongoing political hustle might be seen as a moment for reflection, a clear glimpse at the awesome contingencies of democratic environments. If nothing else, the campaign against "bias" opens a space to explore the interplay of actual biases, which form an important part of the paradox that has been obscured.

In examining American television, we might say that Fox News, MSNBC, and CNN all suffer from the same bias: that of twenty-four-hour cable news. The medium rewards sensationalism and punditry, not comprehensive reporting. The real target demographic is your nervous system, with the goal of fomenting perpetual agitation. The political "slant" does not matter so much as the format—talking heads chatter away about the latest outrage in culture and politics, then move on to something else. Television news features an endless cycle of talk amid a blur of images, incapable of informing an audience or even facilitating reasonable dialogue. But media bias is not just limited to television, and it exists independent of the contemporary charges against journalistic slanting. Media are biased insofar as they are steered to particular styles of discourse. A culture is the product of its media, for politics as well as arts and entertainment. Environmental conditions, not singular acts of bias, can change how we learn as well as disrupt the patterns of our lives.

For Marshall McLuhan, media bias could be grouped into the categories of hot and cool. Hot media such as film, radio, and books were considered absorbing experiences, filled with high definition. What that meant for McLuhan was that such media offer intensity: reading books, you are alone, focused; watching films in a movie theater, you are dominated by the big, dark space and the images emanating from the towering projection screen; listening to the radio at home or in the car, the acoustic space surrounds your person, compelling your attention. As a result, hot media have a high propensity for persuasion, as bodies are disciplined through the form of communication. Cool media, by contrast, were considered lower in definition but facilitate a more interactive experience for the user. Newspapers function this way, because your hands crinkle through the sections and your eye skips from story to story, reading only the headlines or ledes for some and ignoring others, but then maybe reading fully through those that interest you. Television is also cool, as it is controlled through touch; and though we certainly have high-definition television now, it doesn't dominate the space of one's domicile. We might remember McLuhan for his expression "The medium is the message," but his real contribution is how media bias dictates ideological forms. His work suggests that changes to media do not just affect how the politics of democracy are covered by journalists; it suggests that changes to media transform politics in and of themselves.

The distinctions between hot and cool media have now collapsed. Look no further than ex-president Trump, who mixed the heated rhetoric of partisan radio host with the cool, interactive approach of a celebrity on Twitter. McLuhan had accounted for this in part by observing how the content of any one medium is always another medium. That goes for film, which adopted the novel and the theater as its content, and the television, which combined radio programming and cinema. The challenge of the digital interface, including both the internet at large and social networking in particular, is that the online world embodies all previous media as its content. Through smartphone or computer or tablet, we can instantaneously access the rhetorical engagements of political speech, the spot news of the daily press, the long form of the magazine, filmmaking, and television programming, from news to entertainment. The bias of the digital is thus all-encompassing, rendering some of McLuhan's categories obsolete.

Yet McLuhan also understood that beyond bias, one of the results of the impact of novel media was disruption. "Mental breakdown of varying degrees," he wrote, "is the very common result of uprooting and inundation with new information and endless new patterns of information."[10] Disruption, in other words, did not begin with the tech industry. The digital upending of print journalism, cable television, and retail, among other industries, is simply the latest in a long line of media-driven changes to culture, economics, and politics. Facebook may define itself by the motto Move Fast and Break Things, but it's par for the course in human history. Media have biases that determine a society's characteristics, and the biases of novel media disrupt those characteristics to create new political norms and affiliations, new cultural values, and new economic opportunities. The printing press was the forerunner to the Industrial Revolution, just as the internet was to our own digital economy of today. McLuhan's ability to discern this pattern of disruption makes his contributions valuable, more than any specific category or term he developed.

The same could be said for McLuhan's mentor, a fellow Canadian by the name of Harold Innis. In *The Bias of Communication*, Innis demonstrated how media influence cultures through a preference for time or space. Heavy, durable media, going back to stone tablets, privileged time. Oral cultures that relied on face-to-face communication and passed down epic tales from generation to generation also concerned themselves with time. Such societies valued tradition and continuity. In the ancient world, for example, the Egyptians devised an early monopoly on papyrus, which was biased toward an elaborate style that elevated and isolated a priestly class of knowledge workers. The Babylonians and the Sumerians developed cuneiform to write on clay with a stylus, a simpler process that facilitated contact and trade with others. The Greeks improved on the Phoenician alphabet by adding vowels to create a flexible oral tradition with written laws, essential in the development of democracy. The Romans preserved the Greek oral tradition but trained slaves to write and copy books, expanding their republic into an empire. Judaism persevered through all manner of rulers by sustaining rich cultural traditions of oral and written works. Though Jesus, like Socrates, did not write anything down, the rise of Christianity benefited from utilizing new media such as parchment, which was superior to papyrus, and the codex, which bound books. Paper and the first printing presses had been created in China well before their appearance in Europe. The unique system of characters in its writing and printing biased Chinese civilization toward time, however, which did not feature mass dissemination. Chinese media innovation was thus not as disruptive. The Islamic civilization that stretched from India to Spain could effectively manage both time and space for hundreds of years. Its learned culture—including, but not limited to, pioneering innovations in architecture and mathematics and the preservation of Western thought—relied heavily on paper, marshaled from the Chinese and eventually exported to Europe.

A scribal manuscript culture had begun to take root in Europe before Gutenberg's printing press. This, too, was biased toward time. But the object of modern communications, beginning with the printing press, is space. Vernacular languages established themselves more prominently, leading to nationalistic expressions of art, heritage, and law. New maps prompted an interest in discovery, leading to trade with other continents and colonization of the Americas. Innis also detected disruption in the way we experience reality by negotiating time and space. "Shifts to new media of communication," he wrote ominously, "have been characterized by profound disturbances."[11] The Roman Catholic Church managed time, and its enforcement of Latin left it vulnerable to cultural changes throughout Europe. In 1522 alone, King Francis I issued laws in French, not Latin, while Martin Luther printed copies of the New Testament in German. Whereas the original Gutenberg Bible is said to have exceeded the cost of a home when it was first released, Luther's was affordable to commoners. Religious wars consumed Europe as a fallout of the schism. In 1580, Montaigne's essays were published, offering an intimate account of the self which anticipates the Facebook humble-brag. In 1605, the first newspaper was circulated in Strasbourg; *Don Quixote*, the first modern novel, appeared in Spain. Technologies changed media that changed communicative styles that changed culture that changed thinking and interaction. How we centered ourselves as individuals and the relationships we had to culture, institutions, and the nation-state all transformed.

As nationalism and colonialism and trade spread, information—to create it, to disseminate it, and to receive it—was power. The American colonies and the French revolutionaries well understood this spatial dynamic, while monarchies, like the church before them, were concerned with time and underestimated space. The Americans and the French effectively mobilized thanks to thriving print networks. Early newspapers decentralized space, and the telegraph helped create the modern newspaper by organizing that space. News is ephemeral, but it can travel; as a result, it became a commodity that could be trafficked. Time had been locally relevant before the telegraph, often by county or parish. The telegraph created the uniformity of standard time, shaping reality once more. Before the advent of that message transmission system, the very term *communication* had been synonymous with transportation. Now that information could exceed the velocity of human travel, our understanding of communication assumed a spatial texture. The Confederacy, concerned with time to ensure slavery's permanence, failed to build a sound communications infrastructure, seeing information as a threat. President Lincoln's war room, outfitted with a telegraph to communicate with generals in the field, controlled the spatial dimensions of the war.

In Europe around the same time, the telegraph proved instrumental in founding the nation-states of Germany and Italy through language and nationalism. Liberal reforms were introduced as parliaments gained power in European monarchies. However, the bias of time proved fateful for the Austro-Hungarian Empire in the early twentieth century as World War I broke out amid public fervor advanced by newspapers and breakdowns in telegraphic diplomacy. The Bolsheviks benefited from a chaotic public sphere during the last years of the tsar and the brief interlude of a liberal government. Democracies gained a foothold in the aftermath of World War I, but cinematic newsreels and radio, which started as wireless telegraphy, possessed a bias for space that facilitated fascism, another world war, and genocide. Whereas the early newspaper was decentralized, radio and cinema contracted space, which allowed for organized propaganda. The destruction of Europe was terrifying and owes much to the continual disruptions of media innovation.

Innis died in 1952 just as television became a mass medium. TV negotiated space in the same manner as radio, with an added visual dimension. The speed of media, along with the impact of images, would accelerate nonstop from there. In one of his last writings, Innis issued "a plea for time," hoping for a return to the richness of oral cultures that privileged continuity through a focus on time. Here we can begin to see what we're up against. The horizon of time in a democracy is always the next election, which is partly why it's so difficult to deal with monumental challenges like climate change. The biases of a global media culture make it very difficult to think about the continuity of time. The problem is, as Innis recounted in his final plea, that every modern media innovation has been focused on dissemination through space at the expense of time. Effectively tackling the subject of climate change would require the introduction of either a new medium geared toward time or a new social movement to orient people to time. Moreover, these cultural innovations would need to be global in scope. As of now, only magazines, books, and scholarly journals afford an appreciation for time given their weekly, monthly, quarterly, or annual publishing schedules.

The problems of democracy, then, are both massive and structural. While this has always been the case, the endless media innovations of the past two centuries have been unusually disruptive. We may think that the Tower of Babel has been erected for interaction on our smartphones, but the underlying problems of communication remain. The good news is that bias and disruption aren't new. Democracy has always been imperiled by these sorts of challenges. And while democratic perfection may elude us, thinking carefully about the past can at least help us navigate the present and the future.

2

MERE RHETORIC
FROM FREE SPEECH TO BREAD
AND CIRCUSES

An elderly man stood to defend himself. With a weary humility, he confessed to the jury that his eloquence paled in comparison with his accusers. He would not try to absolve himself of guilt. Instead, he trusted that his words would ring true and that that would be enough. "Pay no attention to my manner of speech," he implored the jury.[1]

Unfortunately, as retold in Plato's *Apology*, the truth failed. Despite his clear refutation of the allegations, the defendant, Socrates, was found guilty and condemned to death. The verdict was ordained throughout the works of Plato, who anticipates the tragic fate to befall his great mentor. As Socrates proclaims in another dialogue of Plato's, the *Gorgias*, "But I know this well, that if I do come into court involved in one of those perils ... it wouldn't be at all strange if I were to be put to death."[2] Socrates dedicated his life to a solemn quest for directing the soul to truth. Yet he had the misfortune to live through the chaotic democratic culture of Athens, which was overrun by crass politics and boisterous drama.

Socrates was a victim of a democracy. The Athenian court system featured no lawyers and existed as an extension of civic participation. Political leaders, let alone citizens, could be ostracized or sentenced to death for matters trivial as well as serious. Assemblies for political deliberation and legal cases were composed of citizens from the demos. There was no guarantee that the people would possess truth, achieve justice, or cultivate virtue. The demos, it turns out, does not necessarily make for a good polis.

Democracy—in theory and practice—is always unstable. For one thing, it relies on open communication between citizens, not the sturdiness of institutions or the wisdom of law. From the time of Solon's initial democratic reforms in the early sixth century BCE to Cleisthenes' securing of Athenian democracy from Sparta and the tyrants later that century, democracy was defined through its association with *isegoria*, which translates as the freedom and equality of speech. Cleisthenes recognized ten tribes within Attica, all to meet at an assembly (the *ecclesia*) on the Pnyx, a windy hill nearby. Democracy has implied free speech and tribalism ever since, for better or worse. Herodotus, the ancient historian, employed the terms *democracy* and *isegoria* synonymously. He would observe, moreover, that "Athens increased in greatness" because "equality and free speech are clearly good."[3] Those first meetings of self-government began with an open-ended call from a herald: "Who wishes to address the assembly?" From there, anything could happen because everything, rhetorically, was permitted.

Democracy proceeds from the freedom and equality to raise one's voice among others in public. *Isonomia*, or the equality before the law, comes later. The liberty of isegoria is how democracy can furnish the right of *isonomia*. Isegoria provides the communicative and cultural environment of democracy. Its most important characteristic, as one scholar of antiquity has noted, can be found in "rousing a sense of community, a sense that the polis is not a tyrant's possession but every citizen's property."[4] So long as any one citizen among the demos can address others, society can proceed openly—allowing for the people and their representatives to talk and consider what to do.

But the Greeks had two distinct ways of expressing free speech. If isegoria developed the political environment of democracy, the second understanding, *parrhesia*—which translates as the right to say anything—actualized it. So while isegoria ensured that citizens could offer public discourse in a democracy, parrhesia encouraged the kinds of bold, unencumbered expression that enriched democratic life. What isegoria develops in theory, parrhesia constructs in practice. Most often, that meant critical and daring acts of communication: "To speak with parrhesia," writes one scholar, "was to confront, oppose, or find fault with another individual or a popular view in a spirit of concern for illuminating what is right or best."[5] The meanings for isegoria and parrhesia can be seen as distinct, but they are also symbiotic. Free speech does not guarantee truth or virtue; it simply allows for the confrontation of persuasive communication. Isegoria thus enables parrhesia, which can be simultaneously divisive and refreshing.

The French philosopher Michel Foucault admired parrhesia and the fact that the Greeks accepted parrhesia despite their awareness that it was dangerous for democracy, opening the door to demagogues. For parrhesia, in Foucault's view, fostered a courageous foundation for individual liberty. It created the space for discourse and civic participation, and it was essential to any free society. The problem with parrhesia is that it turns not just on boldness of speech but on truth telling. To Foucault, this was a game that relied on the audience's ability to decide who had the moral qualities to possess and convey the truth. One person's virtue is another's outrage, however. Some may feel that Malcolm X delivered vital truths to the American people when they most needed to hear them; others considered him a subversive radical who fomented violence. A portion of the American electorate found in Donald Trump a tribune of the people, someone who spoke inconvenient truths and upended the status quo in Washington. Those who rejected Trump saw a populist huckster preying on the resentments of alienated voters. In both cases, parrhesia was revealed as a type of truth.

What this shows us is that truth is not the dominant metaphor or quality on which free speech and democracy are forged. That would be rhetoric, which in Aristotle's formation constituted the ability of finding the best possible means of persuasion in any given situation. Rhetoric drives public opinion and the gamesmanship that necessarily follows. As Pericles, the Athenian statesman and democratic reformer, observes in his famous funeral oration during the Peloponnesian War, "But since it was judged by those of long ago, that this speech is a fine thing, I too must follow the custom and try to conform with the wishes and opinions of each one of you as far as is possible."[6] Only because of isegoria and rhetoric is democracy, according to Pericles, "administered in the interest not of the few but the many."[7] Yet our suspicions of persuasion predate democracy, stretching all the way back to the story of Eve in the Garden of Eden. For many, persuasion still signals coercion or manipulation, yet the persuasion of rhetoric is the fundamental medium of democracy—a medium that, like all other communication technologies, opens itself to exploitation. The fate of Socrates reflects this. His death sentence marks democracy's original sin. As I. F. Stone wrote, "The paradox and shame in the trial of Socrates is that a city famous for free speech prosecuted a philosopher guilty of no other crime than exercising it."[8]

Isegoria continually throws democracy into an agonistic encounter. The concept of the agon was essential to Attic society, nurtured as contests of sport in the Olympic Games as well as in the democratic assemblies. Both rhetoric and athletics are competitive, and citizens were trained in each in the ancient *gymnasia* of the time. Whereas sport allowed citizens to wrestle athletically, democracy allowed anyone (considered a citizen) to battle politically. The agon of democracy and sport affords a contested gathering of equals.[9] But just as the healthy qualities of athletics are corrupted by a win-at-all-costs mentality, so democracies similarly buckle under the pressure of bad-faith rhetorical strategies to win. Sport doesn't breed character any more than democracy does; both simply reveal it. In each instance of democratic politics and sport, the virtues of the underlying practices are compromised in the public spectacle of pursuing victory. To the Sophist Gorgias, one of the foremost practitioners of rhetoric, this was obvious: "For surely speech, like the summons at the Olympic games, calls him who will, but crowns him who can."[10] The connection was not lost on Plato either; he dismissed Sophists like Gorgias as "athlete[s] in verbal combat."[11] For the Athenians, athletic competition was a wholly appropriate way to consider political rhetoric.

We observed in the previous chapter that humans are condemned to the freedom of communication. That means democracy is condemned to the freedoms of isegoria and rhetoric. A society that privileges free expression will necessarily rely on persuasion. There is no democracy without an open process of deliberation, and there is no democracy whose processes of deliberation escape the hazards of persuasive rhetoric. Nothing is predetermined for democracy; there is no purpose, or telos, other than how people communicate and make decisions. Richard Weaver, a twentieth-century rhetorician, understood this, observing that "equalitarian democracy takes its counsel without point of reference."[12] Hence all those frustrating aspects of politics we despise. Yet the outrageous charlatan, the conniving cynic, and the inspirational leader all peddle rhetoric one way or the other. It is the chief tool of free speech around which democracy is based. Rhetoric is a feature of democracy, not a bug. Free speech is open to the public, and speakers may abuse the right, just as the public may fail to support wise leaders or sound policies.

The term *rhetoric* has taken on a pejorative hue as "mere rhetoric." To engage in rhetoric is to offer nothing of value except to win through deception or manipulation. Rhetoric is thus employed only by those selling us something rotten. But there's no way to engage the practices of democracy without practicing rhetoric. To consider any specific act of communication as "mere rhetoric" is to deny the very possibility of a democratic culture. It's satisfying to denounce the rhetoric of our opponents, nevertheless. For that we can thank Plato, who introduced it into our cultural lexicon over two thousand years ago. To him, rhetoric always amounted to *mere* rhetoric. It was little more than a knack for duping others. Rhetoric, he argued, could offer no more than a facsimile of true wisdom. Plato, of course, still took the threat of rhetoric seriously. In the *Phaedrus*, he—through Socrates—defines rhetoric as the power of language to "make small things appear great and great things small."[13] What offends Socrates here is that rhetoric is concerned with appearances, while he pursues truth. This concern with appearances over truth emerges as a key theme in the *Republic*, where Plato attacks the poets as imitators and deceivers uninterested in the reality of truth.

In Plato's Allegory of the Cave in book 7, Socrates imagines prisoners chained up in the dark. All they can see are shadows projected on a wall, created by the light of a fire located behind them. That becomes their reality; it's all they know. If one were to be freed, he would meet the harsh light of a new reality. He would see the truth. Should that former prisoner then return to the cave, it would be a struggle to convince those left behind of the reality above. The prisoners prefer the safety of shadows, and they resent the liberation from ignorance. The cave allegory is not just a metaphor for human perception and truth; it speaks to the problems inherent in democracy. The plight of the Platonic philosopher is that citizens are prisoners, overwhelmed by shadows. Socrates hopes that philosophers might descend back into the cave, anyway, leading the people into the light of truth. This dream of pure truth functions as a desire to transcend our humanity. It is ultimately incompatible with democracy as a contest of persuasion to win the crowd. Yet as we know, the crowd can be led astray by those saying what people want to hear.

Plato's critique of democracy is flawed but convincing. As a political system, democracy is chaotic and foundationless. The second president of the United States of America, John Adams, knew this well: "Democracy never lasts long. It soon wastes, exhausts, and murders itself. There never was a democracy yet that did not commit suicide."[14] Yet conflating democracy with good government would be an intellectual and historical mistake. Democracy, from the Athenians to today, has never promised good government. It has only promised—*it can only promise*—a freedom of deliberation among citizens and their representatives, with rhetoric as the key tool with which to exercise such freedom. This shocked Socrates, who wondered how "anyone can stand up and advise [the assembly], carpenter, blacksmith, shoemaker, merchant, ship-captain, rich man, poor man, well-born, low-born—it doesn't matter—and nobody blasts him for presuming to give counsel without any prior training under a teacher."[15] That is likely why Athenian democracy, for the two centuries it lasted, continually dissolved and reorganized itself. At one point, following democratic support for a botched invasion of Sicily in 415 BCE, the assembly voted itself out of existence. It was the first democracy to implode from within: the demos was tempted by an oligarchical elite to waste and exhaust itself. It wouldn't be the last time. The government of the Thirty Tyrants was installed after the Peloponnesian War, in 404 BCE. Socrates and his followers, it should be remembered, supported both oligarchical interludes. In each case, democracy recovered soon after, but in general the Athenian experience of democracy was a series of stops and starts. That's consistent with the whole history of democracy.

Truth and justice may reflect the highest virtues of democracy, but the paradoxical qualities of isegoria and rhetoric mean they are never guaranteed in advance. Unwise decision-making is not just possible but probable as the self-serving desires of *plethos* (the mass), *hoi polloi* (the many), and *ho ochlos* (the mob) can be unleashed. To stand for democracy means accepting that free and equal speech can easily succumb to unruly passions. And before the age of lawyers, as Socrates discovered in the Athenian courts, juries themselves had been a deeply unreliable lot. Socrates could have appealed to the Athenian tradition of isegoria in his defense. Given the close vote that convicted him, a tally of 280–220, adopting such a strategy would have been the wise choice. But Socrates could not invoke isegoria. Strategically, he was trapped. To do so would have implied that isegoria was good for Athenian society. Had he been acquitted on those grounds, his philosophical legacy would have been tarnished. To his credit, Socrates was fearless. He accepted his fate with courage and equanimity, and he made history by bowing to bogus charges and inviting the outrage of his star pupil, Plato.

We shouldn't quibble with Plato's decision to transform Socrates into a tragic hero. Indeed, Plato was accurate in diagnosing the problems of democracy and rhetoric. He successfully deployed the character of Socrates as a weapon against the Sophists, those teachers of rhetoric found throughout Attica. They trained the newfound citizens of democracy in the arts of rhetoric and statesmanship. Socrates ridicules them constantly in Plato's dialogues. The Sophists were interested in cultivating not truth but rather rhetoric, *doxa* (public knowledge), and *phronesis* (practical wisdom). All three categories are focused on the here and now, negotiating the cultural conflicts that exist in a democratic society. They sold their teaching services for money, and their offerings centered on influencing the demos. As one modern scholar of Socrates has written, "Sophists glorify pleasure, power, honor, wealth, and reputation, feeding their clients a steady diet of spiritual poison."[16] In Plato's *Sophist*, they are referred to specifically as "hired hunter[s] of rich young men."[17]

In their defense, the Sophists were necessary for Athenian democracy. Otherwise, who would help citizens—elected to positions of political power by lottery and serving as their own lawyers and jurists—

negotiate this fledgling public sphere? Rhetoric was an essential tool, not some cosmetic prop. Plato, in this sense, was unkind, relying on straw man arguments to belittle the Sophists. Yet they were also their own worst enemy, and Plato identified how their teaching and thinking encouraged a kind of relativism. The Sophists openly admitted that there was no moral or truthful foundation for rhetoric, or democracy for that matter. They thought we could only proceed with the imperfect resources of communication, which is fundamentally about persuasion. Training exercises focused on debating equally from both sides of the argument and not caring for the underlying truth, or rightness, of a situation. Gorgias, the Sicilian Sophist who lived past one hundred years of age and helped orchestrate the disastrous Athenian invasion of his homeland, was perhaps the most notorious. "All who have and do persuade people of things do so by molding a false argument," he once boasted, glorifying rhetoric as "the power of drugs over the nature of bodies."[18] Gorgias would dare a crowd to throw out any subject and promised to deliver the best speech on the subject that anyone had ever heard. It was the dawn of bullshit, and it coincided neatly with the world's first democracy. No wonder sophistry was met by Plato with such scorn.

Protagoras, a friend and counselor to the statesman Pericles, was more respected as a Sophist, but he was criticized by Socrates in two separate dialogues for his humanistic excess. Man is the measure of all things, Protagoras remarked. Elsewhere, he added that he could not *say* whether the gods existed, as such epistemological certainty existed beyond the scope of human speech. Although these statements can be dismissed as the heresies of a political operator, they also forge a practical philosophy of democracy. The very nature of self-government requires the awesome responsibilities of citizenship, divorced from the heavens. Hence, the scope of democracy is necessarily secular. We can be inspired by a god or gods to guide our thinking and moral purpose, but democracy is an existential affair among persons in the here and now. We talk, we argue, we make decisions. Those choices may be wise or foolish, but they're all too human in any case. A god can't anoint a democratic leader or pass legislation. Matters must be discussed among citizens and their political representatives through communicative media, first and foremost. Another Sophist, Thrasymachus, once said, "Since our fortune has reserved us for this later time ... the work neither of gods nor of chance but of the administration of persons, one really has to speak."[19] Since democracy relies on open communication, it can't but expose our biases, foibles, and weaknesses; the Sophists merely helped facilitate the interactions of a free and flawed society. But Plato relentlessly mocked them. In the *Theaetetus*, Socrates says, "I was astonished that [Protagoras] did not state that 'Pig is the measure of all things' or 'Baboon' or some yet more out-of-the-way creature with the power of perception."[20] Protagoras would earn his comeuppance as well, as he was later charged with impiety. When he fled to Sicily to avoid trial, he drowned at sea. As it turned out, neither philosopher nor Sophist was immune from ostracism and condemnation in Athenian democracy.

Yet the Platonic Socrates is perhaps most engaging about rhetoric when avoiding the Sophists altogether. In the conclusion to the *Phaedrus*, we find a sterling treatise on media. After critiquing rhetoric for its lack of concern with truth and the soul, Socrates transitions to a consideration of the mediated effects of texts: "When it has once been written down, every discourse roams about everywhere, reaching indiscriminately those with understanding no less than those who have no business with it."[21] This is prescient, anticipating the rise of printing and publishing, radio waves and television broadcasts, and the internet in all its networked glory. The dissemination of mediated communication is located as the far greater threat than mere rhetoric and the relativism of Sophists. Plato evinces a sharp sensitivity to the forms of communication as media and how they complicate our experience of reality. As we noted above, the *Phaedrus* prefigures the turn in the *Republic*, where it's poets who come under attack. The lesson is that a medium of communication always dissembles, collapsing the distinction between reality and rhetoric. Not only are democracy and truth rendered incompatible, but Plato suggests that democratic cultures, with their penchant for freedom of political and artistic expression, are ill equipped to sustain a society of rationally minded souls. A true rhetoric, Socrates concludes in the *Phaedrus*, would have to be shared between souls, not address people in public through speech and writing with the goal of persuasion. But that would render democracy impossible, since democracy is grounded in communication among persons, not the noumenal spaces of pure form. Should we dismiss the whole thing, then, and acquiesce to rule by a philosophically gifted elite? Is there a way to bridge these ancient divides between rhetoric and philosophy, democracy and good governance?

Though Plato could never tie them together, his most distinguished pupil attempted to do so. Aristotle synthesized rhetoric as a rational pursuit of public discourse. While he admitted that *ethos*, the character of a speaker, and *pathos*, the arousal of audience emotions, play a supplemental role in the persuasion of audiences, he sought to privilege *logos*, the exercise of reason, as its driving force. Aristotle hoped that rhetoric would furnish a model for virtuous behavior. Thus, he denounced the Sophists and their style of expression, as did another more responsible rhetorician of the time, Isocrates. But there are no reliable checks on rhetoric in a truly democratic culture. This became increasingly clear to Aristotle, and it was one of the reasons he remained skeptical of democratic regimes. He joked that when rabbits talk about equality in the assembly, lions coolly respond by asking them to show their claws. Democracy, in his view, was also likely to give rise to demagogues. Still, he considered democracy a form of balanced freedom. It opposes oligarchy, which is preoccupied with the wealth of the few, and tyranny, which revolves around the protection and prerogatives of a tyrant. Yet the most direct endorsement Aristotle could muster was fairly muted: "Democracy is the worst, but the best when all are bad."[22]

Such is the paradox. And not even Aristotle could live up to this qualified praise of democracy. After tutoring Alexander of Macedonia, the son of King Philip II, he approved of Macedonian control of Attica—as did Isocrates. The Athenians would view Aristotle as a traitor to their experiment in self-government. Following the death of Alexander and retaining an assembly with nominal powers, they made one last democratic push, and among the items they chose to pursue was charging Aristotle with impiety, much like his mentor's mentor. Rather than stand trial, Aristotle willingly ostracized himself to the island of Chalcis. Shortly before his death, he had supposedly remarked that he would not allow the Athenians to sin twice against philosophy.

Ancient Athens is often held up as a model of democracy, but the reality is more complicated than that. The city purged two of its greatest intellectual lights, denied citizenship to women, maintained a system of slavery and pederasty, and botched multiple war efforts. And yet Athens helps clarify what democracy is and what it isn't. It begins and ends with isegoria, from which a culture of freedom can emerge. Isegoria generates creative cultural practices of communicative liberty, the value from which all others—democracy, architecture, theater, sculpture, poetry, sport—flow. In Sparta, citizens could vote but not freely express themselves. In Athens, it was different precisely because of isegoria, whose cultural richness demanded public spaces for politics, the marketplace, dramatic performance, and visual artistic exhibition. Democracy is not limited to government but rather promotes a culture of interactivity. It does not automatically translate into wise counsel or fair treatment.

At the same time, two of the greatest statesmen to arise from Athenian democracy were gifted orators trained by Sophists. Both Pericles in the fifth century BCE and then Demosthenes in the fourth exhibited a talent for speech and influencing public opinion. Each man opposed powers that threatened to engulf Athens—Pericles opposed the Peloponnesians; Demosthenes, the Macedonians. Each combined political popularity with a respect for the limits of power. That is, both stood for and expanded democratic ideals and practiced what they preached, neither fearing nor uncorking the unruly freedoms that make democracy so combustible. Contrast that with Socrates and Plato, and later Aristotle and Isocrates: these thinkers abandoned democracy as an unworkable mess. In the end, they concluded that self-rule was incompatible with human nature. The tug of emotion and identity, they feared, would always supplant the light of truth.

Then there are the questions of who gets to exercise the liberties of citizenship in a democracy and who has the right to speak. Over twenty centuries later, democracies continue to struggle with these. The Athenians, for their part, did not extend the franchise of isegoria far enough. We moderns have done better on this front, though we could certainly do better. What remains, however, is the freedom and equality of speech. To have a democracy requires not only establishing isegoria but accepting that isegoria relies on rhetoric—which necessitates not only persuasion among persons but the pernicious aspects of sophistry. While Thucydides attempted to distinguish the good political rhetoric of Pericles from the bad rhetoric of the demagogues, the distinction shouldn't matter. That we use rhetoric at all is the point of departure for democracy. To wish away "mere rhetoric" is to deny the practice of politics altogether. The wager of democracy is precisely this: that a free society must allow for isegoria no matter how unseemly the results.

Another man in another trial in another democracy stood to defend himself. This time, the facts were clear: he had committed war crimes as a military leader. After an opposing force surrendered, he attacked and killed the defenseless, then profited from selling the survivors into slavery. The man brought dishonor on himself and his country and was charged with treason. Curiously, despite being a trained orator, he chose not to speak in his defense. Instead, he turned to his children, who wept beside him. The pathos of the moment was overwhelming. With the children carrying on, the jury was convinced that the man deserved acquittal.

Years later, this man, Servius Sulpicius Galba, would be elected to serve the highest office in the Roman Republic—that of consul. If Athenian democracy can't shake the stain of Socratic guilt, the legacy of republican Rome can't escape Galba's exculpation and rehabilitation. The two trials of democracy are inverse images of each other, with Socrates' refusal to engage in rhetoric like that of Galba's chief opposition, Cato the Elder. Also known as Cato the Censor, he represented the Stoic ideal of dignity and hated the Greek influence of rhetoric. Under his leadership, the Romans tried and failed to nix the teaching of rhetoric altogether in 161 BCE.

Yet any democratic society will be shaped by rhetoric. In Rome, as in Athens, rhetoric became a necessity for education and politics alike. Cato the Elder was a fine public speaker in his own right. He was considered by Quintilian, a later Roman rhetorician, to be the first exemplary orator in the country's history. Cato's career met with many successes, including pushing Rome to wage a battle against Carthage, which expanded its influence and riches. But Cato insisted that oratorical success should be natural and flow from one's inborn dignity. The Hellenic rhetorical influence was pure gloss, he felt. The Galba trial would prove him wrong. His anger at Galba invoked rage but failed at the level of persuasion. This was not lost on Marcus Tullius Cicero, who in the next century would develop rhetoric as a theorist, lawyer, and statesman. Cicero had studied in Greece and developed a respect for the power and responsibility of rhetoric, writing, "This particular art has constantly flourished above all others in every free state."[23] The Romans built on the Greek foundation of rhetoric, focusing on delivery. Early in his legal career, Cicero shouted and gesticulated almost uncontrollably; he adopted a workout regimen to avoid physical exhaustion. As a politician, he provided a calm presence in the chaos of the last years of the republic—at least until Antony ordered his murder and paraded his head and hands on the Roman rostrum, the platform from which orators addressed the public. It was a tragic premonition for what was to come, as Cicero had hoped his martyrdom would preserve the freedom of his country.

Conventional wisdom holds that Roman society was more disciplined than Athens, that the republican system the Romans crafted was less combustible. But the idea that a republican system of government and a democratic society are mutually exclusive is silly. It's true that the American Founders preferred Rome to Athens. And yes, the Roman system was more structured, with a senate and two co-consuls balancing power against the people's tribunals. Yet the Roman Republic was certainly a democracy in that it deliberated to make decisions, and its citizens enjoyed freedom of expression. Whereas Athens elected its political leaders by lottery, Rome held elections. Its polls literally amounted to the counting of heads. Rome, in the traditional sense of voting, was even more democratic.

Yet this system did not provide clear structure in deliberation, as the republic experienced the paroxysms of a raucous public culture just as Athens did. Rome was flush with open communication, in the rhetorical arts as well as in media innovations in writing and public spectacle. Early forerunners of written newspapers, such as the *Annals* and later the *Acta diurna*, were posted and read aloud. The former were straightforward accounts of senate proceedings; the latter included legislative details but widened to include all manner of cultural trivia. *Librarii* were slaves skilled in reading and writing, copying books and newsletters to be disseminated throughout the extensive Roman network of roads. With control of Egypt, Rome had access to the world's chief source of papyrus. Meanwhile, political leaders were expected to furnish celebratory entertainments, from religious festivals and triumph parades to chariot races and gladiator combats. The position of *aedile* was tasked with public works, investing in infrastructure such as aqueducts as well as the throwing of spectacles. For those aspiring to higher political office, such as becoming a senator or a consul, serving as *aedile* was a necessary stepping-stone. Public figures were expected to donate to the public coffers in a process known as *euergetism*, which covered both bread and circuses. Parades lasted for several days, and politicians chucked money into crowds. Roman citizens expected this, encouraged this, even demanded this. Politicians exhibited their magnificence as well as their munificence, and the thirty-five tribes considered such generosity in allocating their votes. It was a coherent strategy. As the historian Paul Veyne recounted, "The senators of the Republic, who were engaged in very high politics, gave games in order to show the people that, even if they did little *through* the people, they did a lot *for* the people."[24]

The politics of Roman democracy were overwhelmed by this atmosphere of spectacle. Though citizenship expanded throughout most of Italy, Rome was riddled with widespread political violence, civil wars, and devious political intrigues. The Gracchi brothers of the second century BCE were two political reformers who served as tribunes. They represented a *populares* party whose actions inspired recriminations from supporters of the senate. Their rhetoric was populist, opposing the elite. One brother, Tiberius, was clubbed to death; Gaius, a decade afterward, chose suicide when cornered by opponents. After civil wars that broke out in the early first century BCE, consuls such as Sulla devised a dictatorship with the approval of the senate and people's tribunes. Sulla invoked emergency powers to rule as an authoritarian, and he sentenced his political enemies to death. Though he stepped down eventually, he attenuated the scope of the republic by transferring power from the people's assembly to the senate. More chaos was to come as violent battles broke out among those jockeying for political office. As consul, Cicero exposed a plot by Catiline, who had hatched a revolutionary campaign to murder leading officials. Those responsible for the conspiracy were sentenced to death, but then Clodius, a tribune, exiled Cicero and confiscated his properties for not affording Catiline a proper trial. Clodius was later killed in a street battle with the forces of Milo, another politician seeking the consulship. Cicero unsuccessfully defended Milo at the ensuing trial, after the razing of the senate grounds by Clodius's supporters. The final decades of the republic would feature civil wars between the forces of Pompey and Caesar; the apotheosis and then the assassination of the latter; and a final battle between Octavian and Antony, who had absconded to Egypt. The conspirators Brutus and Cassius wagered that they could return the republic to its norms by killing Caesar, but the jig was up. Norms, once shattered, can be lost forever. Julius Caesar died, but not in vain: Caesarism would enjoy a long half-life.

To suggest that democratic passions were tempered by the republican structure of Rome as compared with Athens is inaccurate. They were both outrageous, and each was ensconced in the paradox of open and innovative communication that unraveled their governments. By 27 BCE, the republic had exhausted itself. Octavian became Augustus, serving both as emperor and as the tribune of the people. The senate was pleased with this sheen of representation, as now the bread and circuses were no longer its responsibility. Its members had willingly abdicated their role and now focused on their own private interests, not those of the public. Augustus, for his part, reigned for over forty years. As the richest man in the world at the time, he could afford to be both magnificent and munificent. He supplied endless entertainments and administered the government effectively, even fairly. Bread and circuses did not represent the public sphere of politics but formed the basis of society itself. How can democracy compete with authoritarian rule that keeps the populace well fed, entertained, and cohesive?

For a while, that held. As Augustus died in 14 CE, he supposedly gasped, "Have I played my part well? Then applaud as I exit." The cheers were warranted. Government was good, and Augustus had implemented a postal service to connect the far-flung empire with a standardized system of news. Postcards made of wood, inscribed with wax, were used as far away as Hadrian's Wall, which marked the northernmost reach of Rome, in England. Unfortunately, not many of Augustus's successors would play the part well. Tiberius, his heir, retreated to Capri and cared nothing for popular entertainments, generating resentment. Future emperors like Caligula, Nero, and Commodus swung in the other direction, participating directly as theatrical actors, chariot racers, and gladiators, respectively. They exercised power arbitrarily and cruelly. Caligula had crowds of spectators slaughtered at the Circus, Nero forced senators to battle as gladiators. The line between reality and image would collapse as Caligula was murdered backstage following a pantomime performance of a murder. The crowd struggled to distinguish the spilling of fake blood from the regicide.

In transitioning from a republic to an empire, Rome thought it could transcend the paradox through a Caesar who would stand in for the people, with rhetoric used exclusively for ceremonial purposes. Free speech was allowed, provided that political matters regarding the current emperor were not discussed. The senate had many opportunities to seize on imperial instability to return Rome to republican rule but elected not to. As an oligarchical elite, it preferred public focus on the emperor. The term *suffragium* transformed from referring to the rights of citizens to vote, as it had during the republic, to the widespread practice of patronage under the empire. The senators may have willingly limited their power, but absent a democratic public they were beyond accountability. They considered it a justifiable trade-off—one that would anticipate a feudalist future.

During the imperial period, Rome would win several more military victories. The task then became one of management, in terms of both government administration and media. Some emperors, like Marcus Aurelius in the second century CE, ruled wisely and fostered a sense of openness. Others did not. But beyond the emperors, media, as spectacle and as news, calcified the culture. Gladiator events were formalized as the Colosseum was erected. They had no basis in political exchange, as before. The Acta, or gazettes, trailed off in the third century CE. The postal network collapsed as well. Rome ceased to be a site of politics, as emperors often traveled with their retinues in the

East. From a boisterous population of one million inhabitants in the Eternal City during the last days of republic, fewer than one hundred thousand had been dwelling there by the time the barbarians reached the gates. Roman redoubts began walling cities rather than inviting openness, and the network of communication collapsed.

There were no Ciceros to save the day. Seneca came close. A fearless orator in the senate, he attacked Caligula and lobbied for a return of the republic. But after a period of exile, the famed Stoic returned to offer guidance to the young Nero, who ascended to the throne as his mother poisoned his stepfather, Claudius. Seneca is credited with piloting the good governance of the emperor's early tenure, though at a high cost: the philosopher debased himself by rationalizing the emperor's cold-blooded murder of his half-brother. In his writings, Seneca comes off as disciplined and wise, yet taming authoritarian power would prove difficult in the long run. Nero spiraled out of control, ordering the deaths of both his mother and later Seneca, who was (falsely) accused of a treasonous assassination. The age of the statesman was over.

Humor, from Juvenal to Lucian to the *Satyricon*, was the last gasp of artistic invention as democracy was snuffed out in Rome. Rhetoric as a practice was chiefly confined to ceremony in what was known as the Second Sophistic under imperial rule. The primary goal of oratory was no longer political deliberation but declamation, the ability to speak extemporaneously on hypothetical and imaginary topics. Declamation had been used as teaching exercises for the older Sophists, but now it was cemented as a detached, self-centered practice. Instead of communicating for a public purpose, the confines of rhetoric narrowed to those which pleased the crowd for sheer entertainment. Longinus, one of the key rhetoricians of the period, encouraged only those forms of oratory that could arouse feelings of the sublime in audiences: "For grandeur produces ecstasy rather than persuasion in the hearer," he wrote, "and the combination of wonder and astonishment always proves superior to the merely persuasive and pleasant."[25] Rhetoric, and the public sphere along with it, was defanged. Oratorical excellence was featured in speaking contests glorifying the emperor, not arguments for elections and policy. To the extent that the senate convened on public matters, and not its own concentration of wealth, it was often to adjudicate charges of treason against those who might criticize the emperor. The primary basis of democracy—freedom of political expression—had been fully co-opted. The proper place of "mere rhetoric" in the ancient world can thus be located in the last vestiges of imperial Rome, not the volatile debates of the assemblies.

While the legacy of Greek Sophists remains complicated, we can at least say that they promoted rhetoric at the behest of democracy under the protection of isegoria, or free speech. By contrast, the Second Sophistic under Roman imperial rule offered rhetoric as a retreat from democratic politics in a public sphere that was slowly contracting. We might abhor the role of sophistry and consider it inimical to the practices of democracy. But again, rhetoric and sophistry will exist in any culture—as government propaganda, cultural spectacles, movements of social resistance, political debate, corporate advertising, and so on. The difference for democracies is that citizens can be educated in discernment and trained in the art of persuasion. And if the public is purged from the sphere of deliberative communication, those in power will monopolize it. The cultural shift of losing rhetoric as a public forum of exchange ultimately doomed whatever traces of democracy the ancient world had left and in many ways sealed Rome's fate.

That rhetoric was revivified at all during this period can be credited to the early Christians in the fourth century CE, who pioneered new forms of communication. In terms of oratory, they developed forms of sermons, panegyrics, homiletics, and apologia to spread, extol, and defend the new faith. The early church also harnessed the newfound power of bookbinding to agree to publish the canonical works of what became the New Testament. Though some Christians blanched at the connection between rhetoric and its association with relativism, Saint Augustine, who had studied rhetoric as a student, argued that employing it in the service of faith was acceptable. His belief was strong enough to acknowledge the disconnect between the signs of language and religious truth. Absent any civic culture, the communicative power of the church strengthened, from the oratory of the pulpit to the creation of illuminated manuscripts, whose painstaking process curtailed the ability of reproduction. Monasteries possessed libraries, but the church was a closed cultural system; it could foster deliberation only in a controlled communicative environment. There was, in the thousand years since the collapse of Rome, little in the way of free speech, and not much of public spectacle (save for the autos-da-fé of the Inquisition).

The character of a culture is determined by its conditions of communication. The Greek and Roman experiences show that democracies must be grounded in isegoria. But we also know that any culture promoting open communication renders itself vulnerable to the manipulative powers of persuasion, and persuasion is facilitated through media innovation. In the ancient world, rhetorical speech acts in the assembly should have always been diligent, logical, and serious, yet there was no guard against pure sophistry to coerce the assent of others. News, as with the *Acta diurna*, should have informed citizens of political deliberations so they could soundly exercise their judgment. However, that was no brake on the trivia or power politics into which it degenerated. Mass spectacles should have been reserved for celebrating the religious fervor of the people, the nobility of accomplished public leaders, and excellence in sport. Instead, the people were showered with money and baubles, public leaders sought to deify themselves, and athletic contests appealed to a lust for senseless violence.

Socrates encouraged his fellow citizens to pay no heed to the manner of his speech, but that's unrealistic. Appearances matter, and style frequently triumphs over substance. For that reason, demagogues will always rise to the surface in democratic societies. The question is, Can the many use their speech to counteract the concentration of power by the few? Democracy, in theory, answers this question affirmatively, but its practices ultimately proved unreliable in the ancient world. Consequently, democracy fell into disrepute for more than a thousand years—until another medium came along to expedite freedom of expression once more.

3

THE NEWS-PRINT REVOLUTION

The old man was weak. He admitted as much, telling the jury his body had been weighed down by years of hard labor. This man, a lawyer, was an immigrant in colonial territory, and he was representing another immigrant. An acquittal would not be easy. The prosecutor was clear that there was nothing left to argue. The judge would go on to compel the jury to return a guilty verdict. Yet the lawyer—Andrew Hamilton, a Philadelphian by way of Scotland serving as counsel in New York that summer of 1735—asked the jury to consider a higher purpose. Acquitting the defendant, he said, would erect "a noble foundation for securing to ourselves, our posterity, and our neighbors, that, to which nature and the laws of our country have given us a right—the liberty—both of exposing and opposing arbitrary power (in these parts of the world, at least) by speaking and writing truth."[1]

The jury withdrew for its deliberations. After a short time, it returned. John Peter Zenger, the German printer at trial, was found not guilty. Three huzzahs immediately rang out in the crowded courtroom. That night in New York City, a feast was thrown for Hamilton, and the next day cannons were fired in his honor as Zenger was freed.

Crown v. Zenger exposed the "the germ of American freedom" and "revolutionized America," as Gouverneur Morris later reflected. For Morris, who composed the preamble to the Constitution of the United States that memorably begins with "We the People," the trial was a family affair. His grandfather, a judge, was an investor in Zenger's publication, the *New-York Weekly Journal*, which dared to criticize the new

royal governor. Zenger hadn't even written the article in question; a coterie of local lawyers and politicians drafted criticisms of the governor
after he impeached Judge Morris from office. Zenger merely printed
the work.

The Zenger trial is now recalled as imbuing American jurisprudence
with the idea that the truth can protect an individual against a libel suit.
Hamilton had asked the prosecution to identify false, defamatory prose
in the publication, thereby shifting the burden of proof, but he also
stretched the case to its democratic limits. The trial became a debate
about free expression as such, not merely the litigation of criminal libel.
Hamilton declared that citizens "have a right to publicly remonstrate
against the abuses of power in the strongest terms." Not only did the
jury render a verdict strengthening the practices of a free press; it also
affirmed the right of citizens to discuss matters of public interest and,
more specifically, criticize their superiors.

While the ancient world founded democratic freedoms on the persuasion of oratory, the age of revolution that shook the eighteenth century realized freedom in the persuasion of print media—specifically,
the force and periodicity of newspapers and pamphlets. After the
British imposed a modest stamp tax on its American colonies in 1765,
a successful protest led by newspapers secured its quick repeal. Colonial printers would not stop there, though. The solitary germ of
Hamilton's arguments spread from the defense of print in a court of
law to arouse the colonial political body at large. Newspapers sparked a
revolutionary fervor that encouraged the colonists to resent the British
as occupiers, declare independence, and fight as rebels against one of
the great military powers of the time. As a result, the right to political
advocacy through speech, print, and association would be granted in
the First Amendment to the US Constitution.

In the spirit of a similar openness, the French people were summoned
for an Estates General. Clergy, nobility, and commoners alike were to
deliberate over legislation during that fateful summer of 1789, and the
king relaxed laws on publishing leading up to the event. The year prior,
Paris enjoyed but four newspapers, and the French state's *Gazette de
France* enjoyed something of a monopoly on royal propaganda. By
the time of the Estates General, close to two hundred newspapers had

cropped up, and thousands of opinionated news pamphlets had flooded the streets of Paris. The country's newspaper circulation soon reached three hundred thousand per day. After the heroic popularizing of the storming of the Bastille—which liberated all of seven prisoners—the French Revolution was under way thanks to an energized public sphere of free expression. The Declaration of the Rights of Man and of the Citizen would affirm, in Article XI, that the free communication of ideas and opinions is one of the most precious liberties.

Newspapers thus inspired and facilitated a democratic surge in this age of revolution. Print, a medium known for organizing rational thought, came to be seen as the machinery of the Enlightenment. It defended reason against the irrational power of aristocratic, religious, and royal hierarchy. But the mediated texture of newspapers and pamphlets—news-print, for short—also exhibited a set of biases and sophistic strategies that resuscitated the paradox of democracy and ignited a wave of democratic distrust. America's first newspaper, *Publick Occurrences Both Forreign and Domestick*, foreshadowed this. Appearing in 1690 and promising monthly publication, except for such cases when a "Glut of Occurrences happen oftener," Benjamin Harris, the enterprising Boston journalist and publisher, vowed to "obtain a Faithful Relation of all such things" in order to combat "that Spirit of Lying which prevails among us." The paper led with a happy account of the "Christianized Indians" who were celebrating Thanksgiving and then quickly devolved into a screed against "barbarous Indians," whom Harris accused of kidnapping white children and later called "miserable savages."[2] Massachusetts authorities promptly shut down the publication within twenty-four hours—for publicizing military maneuvers, not for promoting racism—and another newspaper would not appear in the colonies for more than a decade. This pattern of the early press before the advent of democracy was familiar to Harris. He had started a paper in London years before, leading to his imprisonment for trafficking in conspiracies of a popish plot.

Marshall McLuhan called this tumultuous period the Gutenberg Galaxy, and it's easy to consider *print* an umbrella term encompassing everything from books to newspapers and pamphlets. The changes with respect to the speech and orality of ancient times were certainly clear. Yet over three hundred years passed between the invention of the printing press and the American and French Revolutions, and the production, distribution, and effects of a book differ greatly from the politically charged ephemera of a newspaper or pamphlet. Both printed media enjoy the Gutenbergian gift of reproduction that increased literacy rates. However, the sequential logic, individualism, and reason so often attributed to books do not necessarily apply to news-print, since the latter emphasizes place and speed. While books can race to publication and solicit changes, they're also subject to serious demands of time and space: the isolation and care with which someone must read or write a book in solitude and the expense and logistics of production demand a particular discipline of individual experience. In contrast, news-print collapses time, because its content must be written quickly and distributed with haste. Its form, unlike that of the book, encourages immediate collective consumption, only to be discarded soon afterward. Whereas the content of news-print is dashed off, that of books is thought out by authors and drawn out during the publishing process. The American colonial experience was a democratic advantage in this regard, as it featured a bevy of independent publishers who focused only on news-print.

Johannes Gutenberg, the man himself—not the legend—affords us an example. Although he's remembered for printing the first Bible, which sparked the Reformation, his own press wasn't nearly as revolutionary as many suppose. Rather than challenge the papal issue of indulgences, which was anathema to Martin Luther, Gutenberg made good business by printing them. To the extent he influenced the print revolution to come, it wasn't so much in book form as in political pamphlets. Soon after he published his famous Bible in 1455, for instance, Gutenberg disseminated *A Warning to Christendom against the Turks*, encouraging the pope and the Holy Roman Emperor to embark on a new crusade. The papal authorities were happy to oblige, as a bull was issued in agreement. The new technology of print served as an immediate supplicant to power—at least for its first half century.

It's misguided, then, to speak of an inherent "logic" to print. Rather, we ought to distinguish the biases and disruptive qualities of news-print, a medium enabling a rhetoric of attention. This ideology of publicity proved resourceful for Luther and his followers. It wasn't Luther's simple act of defiant protest that mattered but his foresight to send copies of his theses to sympathetic friends. They possessed the where-withal to have those printed and circulated, launching the first shots of the Reformation. Luther's sermons also benefited from being printed in German, not Latin. News-print demanded the development of in-formal vernacular languages, and Luther employed the lowest, most common form of dialect he could at the time. His allies would not be the only friends to help him either. Lucas Cranach, a local Wittenberg painter, composed a famous woodcut portrait of him that was deployed in printing as a standardized cover. Luther's face was literally every-where as millions of pamphlets flooded Europe to spread the news. Luther himself was not very charismatic, but he didn't have to be. His mediated presence, as Andrew Pettegree shows in *The Invention of News*, caused a sensation.

This publicity power belies the inherent rationality of print. Books may have developed a fashion of private repose, but the cacophonous world of news-print revived what Walter Ong called an "oral residue" of the rhetoric of Athens and Rome. News-print carved out a social space for the public to register cultural and political judgment. Mass media disseminate; various publics respond by rendering a verdict through enthusiasm, anger, or indifference. But news was not the chief beneficiary of news-print, as it had long existed, even thrived, during democracy's great interregnum. Elite cultural politics were dominated by script-based communication, an exclusive medium that had little to offer the public. The Roman Catholic Church, along with powerful city-states like Nuremberg and Venice, sustained power through networks of private, handwritten correspondence. Venice formalized this process through *avvisi*, exclusive newsletters that necessitated the accuracy of information for commerce. The historical irony here is how the private, script-based news of avvisi was far more reliable than various print me-dia as organs of public opinion. When information is exclusively col-lected and distributed, power can concentrate, as elite networks enjoy an advantage. From this angle, truth occludes the liberty of the public.

The danger of news-print—and that of a democratic public sphere more generally—is that it encourages imperfect information and the fickle exercise of public taste. Freedom of expression, from isegoria to the First Amendment, does not lead inexorably to truth. To believe otherwise is to deny the paradox. The open communication of democracy reveals difference, not unanimity. From the standpoint of maintaining order in a society or sustaining the culture of a civilization, we might prefer private networks of information limited to oligarchical elites or authoritarian lackeys or totalitarian bureaucrats. Venice demonstrated this; so did ancient Egypt's priestly caste, which controlled information through its exclusive jurisdiction over hieroglyphics and the nilometer, a structure for measuring the clarity and height of the Nile River during flood season; and the Han, T'ang, and Sung dynasties of China held a similar advantage with *tipao*, private newsletters similar to avvisi. The real question concerning news-print and mass-mediated technologies more generally, then, becomes whether the unruly, chaotic freedom of democratic discourse is preferable to monopolies of information managed by a select few.

The contours of news-print played a role in the agitations of the seventeenth century, whose disruptions anticipated the democratic revolutions of the eighteenth. The Dutch Republic threw off the yoke of the Habsburg monarchy thanks to a conflagration of published pamphlets. Some of the world's first consistent newspapers were published there as single-page broadsheets, such as *Tidings from Various Quarters*. In addition, the Dutch developed the stop press, which allowed newspapers to add updates from late-breaking reports. News-print was formalized and played a decisive role in the cultural and economic success of the Netherlands, but newspapers were also confined to pursuing mercantile ends. The first trappings of a capitalist, modern economy of finance developed as futures markets could be initiated by virtue of accurate information. An early financial bubble, in the market for tulips, inflated and burst based on this traffic of news. While it did not cause a broader economic crisis, tulipmania demonstrated the uneasy dependence of markets on reliable news sources. Even the most honest practices of journalistic objectivity rarely equate to perfectly predictable human behavior. The hope that markets achieve economic equilibrium or that democracy ensures good governance is just that—a hope. Like script correspondence, Dutch publications chose not to facilitate political debate or legislative deliberation, only news of foreign events that affected commerce. The Dutch model limited news to service the market, not democracy.

The desire to live in a democracy without a turbulent public sphere is understandable but ultimately illusory. Pretending otherwise leads to frustration and resignation. The English Revolution, or Civil War, provides a case in point. The Crown enjoyed a monopoly on the press in the early seventeenth century, but after Charles I called forth the Long Parliament in 1640 to negotiate a financial crisis, news-print soon overwhelmed English politics. One of the first acts of the new parliament was to abolish the Star Chamber, a court of absolute monarchical prerogative which had controlled publishing. Some twenty thousand copies of Parliament's "Grand Remonstrance" were published as the House of Commons permitted formal debate to be publicized for the first time.

The battlefield engagements over the course of the 1640s—which would only be resolved in 1649, with the execution of the king—were mirrored by the pamphlet wars between royalists and republicans. At first, these disputes were mediated by public exchanges between citizens. After Henry Walker, an ironmonger, published a pamphlet in support of Parliament in 1641, John Taylor, a sailor, responded with a vociferous denunciation. Entitled "A Reply as true as Steele, To A Rusty, Rayling, Ridiculous, Lying, Libel," the pamphlet's cover features a winged satanic devil defecating on a man holding an iron pitchfork, clearly intended to be Walker.[3] The Long Parliament issued a Licensing Act to control print in 1643, but supporters of the Crown and of its foes continued with competing propaganda organs like *Marcus aulicus* (in support of the king) and *Marcus Britannicus* (favoring Parliament). The former was overseen by Marchamont Nedham, an expert sophistic printer. At one point he stretched republicanism to an uncomfortable degree even for Parliament, which had him imprisoned. Nedham, upon release, switched sides to support King Charles I with a new paper, *Marcus pragmaticus*. The pragmaticism would come in handy, even if this publication was short-lived. After another stint in prison following the king's execution, Nedham returned to republicanism under the rule of the Commonwealth (1649–53), only to serve as Oliver Cromwell's pet propagandist during the one-man rule of the Protectorate. His new publication was called, somewhat fittingly, *Marcus politicus*.

Cromwell brooked no dissent and distrusted the democratic culture through which the Commonwealth emerged from the grip of royal power. Though he eschewed monarchical pomp, in the end he ruled no better than a king and found himself adrift, despite Nedham's propaganda. The Restoration of a new king, Charles II, was accompanied by the Licensing Act of 1662, according to which press freedom contracted under an official Surveyor, the censor Roger L'Estrange, who had been a royalist pamphleteer at the beginning of the Civil War. Newspapers, he warned in *The Kingdom's Intelligencer*, "make the multitude too familiar with the actions and counsels of their superiors, too pragmatical and censorious, and gives them not only an itch but a kind of colourable right and license to be meddling with the government."[4] That was the idea, anyway. The English experiment in the public sphere thus collapsed and had to wait until the Glorious Revolution and the repeal of the Licensing Act toward the end of the century to enjoy the freedom of news-print once more.

We shouldn't blame the lost opportunity of this midcentury period on the Restoration, for limiting press freedom and the rights of citizens can be expected with monarchical power. We might expect more from a commonwealth, but John Milton foresaw problems in the Long Parliament's designs as far back as 1644, a year after the first Licensing Act sought to exert propagandist control. Addressing the deliberative body with a speech that was published as the *Areopagitica: For the Liberty of unlicenc'd Printing*, Milton delivers an impassioned defense of free expression. As the subtitle makes clear, freedom of speech also necessitates freedom of the press. While he doesn't invoke isegoria, the Greek concept of freedom and equality of speech, Milton admires the democratic scope of Athens and Rome at length in his plea. The *Areopagitica* failed to reverse the system of prior restraint, yet it remains notable for its surprisingly realistic account of how a culture of open communication works. Freedom of expression, that is, would not eliminate grievances, "but when complaints are freely heard, deeply consider'd and speedily reform'd, then is the utmost bound of civil liberty attain'd."[5] Milton admits that freedom involves not an escape from disputation but an unavoidable collision with it. Nothing can be decided in advance. Later, he notes that reason is but choosing, an exercise in preference or taste, reflecting the grapple of public sentiment. This liberty is predicated, he argues, on the free writing and free speaking that Parliament had engendered. Forget government itself as a system. First, Milton says he wants the liberty to know, to utter, and to argue above all else. To formalize licensing would restrict such freedom and undercut whatever gains the Commonwealth had made. Parliament chose power at the expense of liberty, however. It couldn't trust the freedom of expression.

The American colonists were willing to wager that they could. Starting in the 1720s, an irreverent secular press emerged in opposition to the creative jeremiads of religious oratory. These elements merged for the first time as James Franklin's *New England Courant* mocked the devout stylings of Increase Mather and his son, Cotton, amid a small-pox scare. Cotton had argued that the disease involved possession by the devil; Increase, as president of then Harvard College in the seventeenth century, had rationalized the dubious witch trials. The Mathers didn't spoil for a public fight, though. "Boston's religious leaders," it has been said of the time, "were not the sort to turn the other cheek."[6] The Mathers accused Franklin and his teenaged apprentice brother, Benjamin, of constituting a Hell-Fire Club. Increase took to the pages of the staider *Boston Gazette*, run by the postmaster, fondly recalling how governments in the past would have suppressed such a publication for criminal libel.

The elder Mather, then in his eighties, passed in 1723 but not before enjoying some small satisfaction in witnessing James Franklin imprisoned. To continue as a printer, he would have to obtain the clearance of prior review by running drafts of the publication past the provincial authorities. This would not stand, so the Franklins cleverly installed young Benjamin, who at that point had only published under the nom de plume Mrs. Silence Dogood, to serve as publisher. The *Courant* continued as other newspapers and pamphlets arose. "A pamphlet or broadside can bang the drum; a newspaper, reappearing weekly or biweekly, can roll the drum," notes the journalism historian Mitchell Stephens.[7] The first daily would not arrive until the 1790s—and journalism, as a formalized practice, much later still.

In the more immediate aftermath of the Zenger trial, news-print publicized the celebrity culture of the day, which revolved around religious rhetoric. The orators of the Great Awakening caused a sensation with their revivals as audiences swooned, literally passing out at the fevered pitch of a new evangelism. Jonathan Edwards breathed fire and brimstone, for certain, but he also managed to invoke the ideas of John Locke to distinguish between divine and civil authorities. His famous oration, *Sinners in the Hands of an Angry God*, was published as a pamphlet in 1741. George Whitefield, meanwhile, commanded the attention of thousands with his booming voice as he toured the colonies from Boston to Savannah. Benjamin Franklin's *Pennsylvania Gazette*, based in Philadelphia, was among the newspapers that shone a spotlight on Whitefield. It was reported that upwards of fifteen thousand people attended his funeral in 1770.

The spheres of religion and politics continued to merge with the growing relationship between Samuel Adams and Jonathan Mayhew, two Harvard classmates. Adams launched the *Independent Advertiser* in January 1748, with Mayhew, a Unitarian minister, a frequent contributor. They formed their partnership in response to an unpopular military impressment by a British naval commander, Charles Knowles, in 1747. When riots subsequently broke out in Boston, Governor William Shirley published a letter in the city's newspapers demanding an end to the chaos. In response, Adams published a pamphlet under the guise of Amicus Patrie, defending what he considered to be the natural right of protest against civil authority. The exercise of dissent was not just an expectation but grounded in law, to Adams's thinking. Then Mayhew's newspaper work caused a stir and landed his printer in jail. After the *Advertiser* folded, he published a pamphlet under his own name, *A Discourse Concerning Unlimited Submission and Non-Resistance to the Higher Powers*, reflecting on the centennial of Charles's execution. The free-expression mantle of Milton in print and speech was extended without qualification. If the Zenger trial formed the germ of the American Revolution, Mayhew's *Discourse* was, as John Adams later reflected, its "morning gun." Mayhew mixed a healthy distrust of arbitrary authority with a reverence for the divine *and* free expression. The technology of this medium, news-print, was facilitating the rights of citizenship entrusted to the free exercise of religion and speech and press and petition.

Before that capacity could be tested, the next decade brought a cooling of tensions between Britain and its colonies as they rallied together against the French in the Seven Years War. In 1754, before the war began, Ben Franklin's *Gazette* had published a political cartoon depicting a sliced-up snake representing the colonies with the inscription Join, or Die. The image was exhibited as a show of unity, a nifty bit of propaganda. The British went on to vanquish its longtime foe and enjoy a brief period of calm with its colonists. Yet pecuniary interests, like new media themselves, have a way of disintegrating social order. To improve the Crown's finances after a near decade of war, a stamp tax was applied to all manner of paper in 1765, including published news-print. The duty was considered a reasonable ask for two reasons. First, the colonists stood to benefit from the expenditures of the Seven Years War and now ought to contribute to the public coffers. Second, London newspapers had been subjected to the tax since 1712. At a penny per page—not excessively onerous—it did little to stall the thriving public sphere of talk in coffeehouses, where citizens pored over newspapers prepared by the likes of Jonathan Swift and Daniel Defoe.

Nevertheless, the colonists viewed the Stamp Act as a tax on knowledge, on politics, on business enterprise, and on the free exercise of citizenship. A key difference between England in 1712 and the colonies of the 1760s was that news-print was already pervasive in the latter, a bedrock of its culture. Papers were in the hands of a citizen populace whose literacy rate numbered over half of all adult males across the colonies. And the margins for these independent American publishers, who did not print books for an aristocratic elite, were thin. Thomas Green started the *Connecticut Courant* in 1764, its first page a ringing endorsement of the medium: "Of all the Arts which have been introduc'd amongst Mankind, for the civilizing of Human-Nature, and rendering Life agreeable and happy, none appear of greater Advantage than that of Printing."[8] Perhaps fittingly, the newspaper continues as the *Hartford Courant*, the longest-running newspaper in the Americas. The Stamp Act, which passed in March 1765 and was due to take effect that November, underestimated the extent to which colonial identity had been shaped by printing. The homes of the royal governor and the chief tax collector of Massachusetts were vandalized before the act went into effect. Samuel Adams contributed to the *Boston Gazette* and formed the Sons of Liberty, a clandestine group that burned tax collectors in effigy. They were based in Boston yet relied on a communication network hooked up to papers in New York. The publications supplied fresh outrage, Mayhew's sermons compared the legislation to slavery, and the Sons of Liberty effectively coordinated political acts of resistance.

Meanwhile, Patrick Henry stood in the Virginia House of Burgesses, famously declaring, "If this be treason, make the most of it." The condemnatory resolutions of that body were published from Charleston, South Carolina—where the *Gazette and Country Journal* was introduced specifically to oppose the Stamp Act—up through Franklin's *Gazette*, and farther north, to the papers of Boston. Colonial news-print primed their audiences, bellowing that they would have to shut down if the tax went into effect. In the weeks leading up to the legislation's enactment, the *Maryland Gazette* and the *Pennsylvania Journal* included the headline "Expiring: In Hopes of Resurrection to Life again," accompanied by an image of a skull and crossbones. The colonies, at the time a grab bag of different places, became linked. Ben Franklin, as the colonial postmaster since the 1750s, had facilitated this through spearheading improved roads and offering inexpensive, single-rate newspaper delivery.

The authorities were afraid to even distribute stamped paper, so Parliament relented, as the Stamp Act could never be reliably enforced. The repeal did little to stop the colonists' agitation, though, and the cycle repeated itself after the British Parliament passed the Townshend Acts in 1767. A lawyer from Philadelphia published a series of columns in the *Pennsylvania Chronicle* entitled "Letters from a Farmer," arguing that Parliament could not issue taxes without colonial representation. The "Letters," in an early example of syndication, were circulated as columns published in other newspapers, as was Samuel Adams's chronicling of the general perfidy of British soldiers in the *Journal of Occurrences*. A young Thomas Jefferson was instrumental in recruiting a patriot press editor to open a new publication in Virginia. John Adams wrote refutations in response to the Tory press, some of whose offices were smashed up. In 1770, the *Boston Gazette* reported that British soldiers exclaimed, "Yes, by G——D, root and branch," when asked whether their intentions were hostile in the moments leading up to the Boston Massacre. Paul Revere published one-sided drawings of the event. That notable act of resistance, the Boston Tea Party, was hatched in 1773 in the office of one of the *Gazette* publishers. "The Liberty of the Press is the Great Bulwark of the Liberty of the People," wrote the Massachusetts Assembly, when ordered to sanction the *Gazette*. "It is, therefore, the incumbent Duty of those who are constituted the Guardians of the People's Rights to defend and maintain it."[9]

The press was not only defended but expanded. Isaiah Thomas created the *Massachusetts Spy*, which called itself the "American Oracle of Liberty." He repurposed Franklin's "Join, or Die" image and pilloried the royal administration, comparing its tyranny to that of a festering polyp. In a replay of the Zenger trial, a grand jury refused to indict Thomas, against the prosecutor's wishes. Then the Coercive Acts outlawed group meetings, an infringement on the right to assemble. Boston's *Spy* evacuated, moving to Worcester. It covered the Battle of Lexington in 1775, and the clamor of its independent spirit radiated from New England. From Philadelphia in early 1776, Thomas Paine published *Common Sense*, a pamphlet running less than fifty pages. Its soaring rhetoric encouraged separation, as would the Declaration of Independence later that summer. Both should be celebrated in and of themselves as original and powerful discourses of freedom, yet the success of each communicative act relied heavily on the technological environment of news-print at the time. Within a few months, over one hundred thousand copies of *Common Sense* had been sold. Paine's style connected with the mass of colonists. Jefferson's Declaration of Independence, short as it was, also made for easy news copy: two lede paragraphs are followed by a series of readily digestible bullet points. The *Pennsylvania Evening Post* published it first, on July 6; over the next two weeks it appeared in Baltimore, New York City, and papers throughout New England. After the declaration reached New York City and was read aloud, a mob tore down a statute of King George III and melted it into ammunition. A newspaper in Williamsburg, then the capital of Virginia, published the declaration on July 20, and a copy of the document reached Charleston on August 2.

News of the declaration did not hit London until mid-August. By then the Massachusetts Assembly had already devised a new system of post offices to improve networked communication even more. British military forces posed a major threat, but the revolutionaries mobilized news-print to their advantage. Papers in New York City moved upstate; the *Connecticut Courant* started its own paper mill; and Thomas's *Spy* exhorted women to donate rags that could be converted into newsprint as an essential service to the community. In late 1776, the first of Paine's *Crisis* pieces appeared in the *Pennsylvania Journal* and spread from there. George Washington had Paine's works read aloud to motivate troops. The one colony that retained a strong semblance of Tory support was Georgia. While other organs of the royal press existed, and the British enjoyed naval supremacy and strong numbers, no effective means of mass communication could coordinate their propaganda efforts.

The news-print culture of open communication cleared a space for the rhetoric of democracy. For Jefferson, this meant that the basis of American government was public consent, facilitated through newspapers. How the ensuing government was structured is another matter. In *Common Sense*, Paine argued for a single legislative body with expansive voting rights. The US Constitution, drawn up in 1787, created a bicameral legislature along with executive and judiciary branches of government. *The Federalist Papers* were published in newspapers to secure their approval among the states. As with Rome, there is nothing inconsistent between a republican form of government and a democratic society. The United States decided to be both.

But we know that the United States has never fully trusted its democratic foundation. Its constitution counted a slave as three-fifths of a human being, and it continued its practice of slavery until the American Civil War. The nation abetted a genocide of American Indians, tore up treaties with them, and sequestered them to reservations; it denied women the right of public participation for far too long; and to this day it has waged and propagandized unnecessary, destructive wars. But the blunders are a reminder that democracy is a site of struggle. We can certainly argue that the American founding was an exercise in oligarchical maintenance—a way of consolidating power for a colonial gentry. And no doubt the colonial press, even in the North, helped perpetuate slavery by printing advertisements for runaway slaves. That that institution was supported is to the everlasting discredit of the printers. But democratic societies—and the open communication systems on which they depend—at least create the space for political contestation and change. And yet, precisely because democracy guarantees no outcome, it constantly frustrates our expectations. The hope, of course, is that each democracy "bends toward justice," to borrow Martin Luther King's famous dictum. What seems true in any case is that a more just society can potentially arise through the continual agitation of political commitments expressed in an open environment of communication, even if that environment can always be gamed and exploited.

The American Founders, to their credit, recognized this paradox—at least at first—and thought they had a solution to it. Some of the first acts of the new nation sought to support open communication. That meant designing a postal service for free networks of correspondence to thrive and granting copyright protections to authors for up to fourteen years. Knowledge of every kind was to be circulated through the new republic, and the 1792 Post Office Act subsidized local newspapers through the direct support of printing contracts while prohibiting the violation of the privacy of letters. A national newspaper, the *Gazette of the United States*, was published by a former patriot press editor, John Fenno, who enjoyed official patronage. And when the nation's capital moved from New York City to Philadelphia, so did the *Gazette*. States were encouraged to implement public education for new citizens. And with a respected statesman, George Washington, serving as the nation's first president, a certain calm was expected, one lacking factional disputes and rank partisanship.

But the paradox is always there. The Founders, bright as they were, succumbed to the pursuit of power. Democracy compelled them. The bond between James Madison and one of his coauthors of the Federalist Papers, Alexander Hamilton, dissipated as each assumed a primary role in establishing opposing political parties. A democracy, especially one with a constitutionally protected freedom of expression such as the United States, naturally produced a raucous, partisan culture, with media used as the crucial political weapon. The *Gazette* became a mouthpiece for the Washington administration; its purpose was to portray government actions in a favorable light, with Treasury Secretary Hamilton and Vice President John Adams as chief contributors. To combat this, Madison and Jefferson organized the *National Gazette*, published by Philip Freneau. The paper provided information about government activities but also criticized the handling of the economy. Hamilton discovered and publicized that Freneau had been hired by then secretary of state Jefferson. After first denying his role in subsidizing the paper, Jefferson wound up resigning, and the *National Gazette* folded upon its loss of official patronage. Jefferson, complaining to Madison about Hamilton's power of propaganda in private correspondence, urged him to "take up your pen, select the most striking heresies, and cut him to pieces in the face of the public."[10]

The era of the partisan press had begun. Open communication meant ferocious rhetoric between Federalists and Republicans and competing newspapers supported by the parties and politicians themselves. And no amount of popular education or public information could curtail the proliferation of personal attacks and rabble-rousing content. Even without the *National Gazette*, partisan rancor grew in the Republican press to counteract Federalist power. Benjamin Franklin Bache, as publisher of the *Aurora*, did not mince words, accusing President Washington of "political iniquity" and "legalized corruption." The attacks on John Adams, the second president, were worse. James Callender, a journalist who had fled England on sedition charges, called Adams a hermaphrodite and publicized an affair of Hamilton's. "It was the happy privilege of an American that he may prattle and print in what way he pleases," reflected Callender, who found a patron in Jefferson.[11]

Federalists responded by passing the Alien and Sedition Acts in 1798, a stunning rebuke to the First Amendment and a clear targeting of the Republican press. The sedition component sought to maintain unity during a period of hostility with France, criminalizing false criticism of the federal government. That the legislation was signed by Adams should have been a staggering embarrassment for the man who had protested the Stamp Act a few decades prior in the pages of the *Boston Gazette*. Matthew Lyon, a sitting congressman from Vermont, was the first person charged under the Sedition Act. After his conviction, he nevertheless won reelection from prison. The last person charged in the lead-up to the tumultuous election of 1800 was Callender. The defense attorneys marshaled together by Jefferson were no match against the Federalist prosecutor, Samuel Chase.

Thomas Jefferson won the presidency and let the Alien and Sedition Acts lapse, pardoning the journalists who remained in prison. Then it was his turn to face the paradox. In an 1801 letter to Elbridge Gerry, he complained that "the printers can never leave us in a state of perfect rest and union of opinion," and in an 1803 letter to Pennsylvania governor Thomas McKean he confided that "nothing in a newspaper is to be believed." He tells McKean he hopes a few choice libel prosecutions can restore integrity. At the time, a Federalist editor from New York, Harry Croswell, was standing trial for violating a state statute of criminal libel. Specifically, Croswell published that Jefferson had once paid Callender to defame Adams and Washington. The initial trial was presided over by the chief justice of the New York State Supreme Court, Morgan Lewis. At first, he denied Callender's right to appear as a witness, an appeal remedy rendered moot as Callender, inebriated, drowned soon after. Lewis then insisted that the truth standard adopted in *Zenger* was not permissible, leading to Croswell's conviction. In appealing before the New York State Supreme Court, Croswell retained Alexander Hamilton to represent him. It was only right, seeing as the publication in question, Croswell's the *Wasp*, merely repeated a charge first printed in another *Federalist Paper*, the *Evening Post*, which had been founded in part by Hamilton.

Hamilton revived the arguments of Zenger's lawyer, Andrew Hamilton (no relation), pleading that truthful statements are exculpatory. The conviction, nevertheless, was upheld. Both the Federalists and the Republicans seemed eager to weaponize the media of the time, along with the law, to pursue political victory. Perhaps that shouldn't surprise us, but such exploits did shock some members of the founding generation, who thought they could do away with the messiness of democratic politics. The crassness of the early republic and its partisan press also debunks the hagiography of the Founders. There was a unity forged in rebellion through news-print and in the agreement to a constitution, but that just set the terms of future contests.

Jefferson himself embodied the paradox and appeared ignorant of his own complicity. As president, he encouraged Republicans to impeach Supreme Court Justice Samuel Chase, who had prosecuted Callender years before. The vice president, Aaron Burr, presided over the trial in the Senate, which acquitted Chase. This was after Burr killed Alexander Hamilton in a duel following some suspect remarks the latter had made about the former in his *Evening Post*. Burr served only one term as vice president and was later arrested, not for the duel but for treason charges related to his designs on western territories and Mexico. Here, too, Jefferson's conduct revealed a man beset by contradiction: the architect of American democracy was brought low by an obsession with concentrating and wielding his own power. As president, he had publicized his zeal for a guilty verdict against his former vice president before the trial, issuing blanket pardons for those willing to testify against Burr and claiming executive privilege against receiving judicial subpoenas himself. Burr was acquitted, since John Marshall, chief justice of the United States, effectively instructed the jury that only actions, not ideas or speech, could constitute treason.

The early American republic was a chaotic public sphere dominated by "unfettered press practices," as Leonard Levy has written.[12] Yet the Founders tried to convince themselves that they were not creating a democracy, that they were not igniting party politics, and that they were above mere rhetoric. Their own communicative practices reveal otherwise, and we would have to imagine a United States of America without a Bill of Rights amended to the Constitution to imagine a republican system without democracy as such. The First Amendment ensured that democratic practices could flourish even and despite the hostilities it unleashed.

In France, the explosion of news-print on the scene offered a very different cautionary tale. Democracy had collapsed before the country's constitution could even be inaugurated. The revolutionaries, in the end, refused to tolerate the liberty they had initially espoused. Oaths demanded submission and commemoration rather than ongoing deliberation. Though a wild candor in news-print content accompanied the start of the French Revolution in 1789, this openness was ultimately rejected. "Paradoxically," wrote Jeremy Popkin, "the same newspaper press that provided the public dimension and the means of communication required by the Revolution's new style of politics was also one of the driving forces behind the divisions and conflicts of the revolutionary decade."[13] The Jacobins thought they had uncorked freedom, equality, and reason to defend the public against the arbitrary dictates of royal, noble, and religious power. Yet the result of mandating unity was spasms of violence that equaled if not surpassed the past cruelties of the monarchy and the church.

News-print was perhaps too novel for the French. Despite a brief burst of pamphleteering that flourished during the upheavals of the Fronde in the mid-seventeenth century, the country was subject to draconian print restrictions for many of the next hundred-plus years. The Declaration du Roi from 1757, for instance, threatened a death sentence for those caught writing, printing, or distributing tracts that promoted heresy or offended royal authority. While the weekly *Gazette de France* offered government propaganda, the nation's best source of news was often imported from the Netherlands, in the worldly *Gazette de Leyde*. Denis Diderot was hounded as he sought to bring his famed *Encyclopédie* to print. Enlightenment culture was both an elite and a subversive pursuit, nourished by the underground trade of books and *libelles* (slanderous political books or pamphlets) that formed a "basic diet of illegal literature," with vigorous discussions about these publications held in the salons of Paris.[14] Ideas in and of themselves did little to move the public absent a flourishing trade of news-print, but that changed in 1789 as a clergyman, Emmanuel Joseph Sieyès, published a pamphlet entitled *What Is the Third Estate?* In this call to democracy comparable to Thomas Paine's *Common Sense*, he encouraged the people's representatives to declare themselves a National Assembly.

The storming of the Bastille was ignored by the government-run *Gazette*, and it had taken weeks before the *Gazette de Leyde* informed its French readership of the news. No matter: the Parisian public was enjoying a newfound access to news-print, and what happened at the Bastille became a major media event, a mass inspiration. A firsthand account was composed that evening in what began as a one-off pamphlet, the *Révolutions de Paris*, that expanded into periodical publication. It was one of several newspapers that emerged in the second half of 1789. Some offered outrageously partisan opinion, others affected neutral reporting about public affairs. Camille Desmoulins began by publishing a fiery pamphlet, *La France libre*, that summer, and later oversaw other newspapers. Jean-Paul Marat, a physician who had engaged in press battles in England years before with a pamphlet, *The Chains of Slavery*, founded *L'ami du peuple*. Jacques Pierre Brissot, imprisoned in the past for pornographic *libelles*, assumed editorship of *Le patriote François*. The publisher Charles-Joseph Pancoucke, who oversaw a literary magazine and once produced an expanded version of the *Encyclopédie*, began *Le moniteur universel*. The Parisian correspondent for the *Gazette de Leyde*, Pascal Boyer, launched his own publications as well. Moreover, various newspapers spoke in the voice of a character from the French theater scene, Père Duchesne. He represented the sans-culottes by damning the elites, sprinkling *fuck* in his prose, and, in the various drawings in which his work would appear, smoking a pipe. In 1790, the editor and writer Jacques Hébert tried to consolidate the personage as his mouthpiece in his publication, *Le Père Duchesne*.

Journalists played an active political role in the new government, and newspapers facilitated the "real public space" of the French Revolution, as Popkin has noted.[15] Yet of the various newspapermen listed above, only Pancoucke would escape a politically motivated death. Marat, who had encouraged executions himself, was assassinated in his bathtub; the rest were guillotined. In total, one-sixth of Parisian journalists were executed. Thomas Paine, then living in France as an honorary citizen, was imprisoned. While Article XI of the 1789 Declaration of the Rights of Man included press freedom, it did carry a notable caveat: those enjoying freedom of speech and press shall be responsible for the abuses of such freedom, according to the law. Defining the law was—as always—a fluid affair, especially with Maximilien Robespierre, a former pressman himself, put in charge of the Committee on Public Safety in 1793 after the trial and execution of King Louis XVI. The Reign of Terror spoke to an inherent fear—not just of summary executions and political violence but also a deeper distrust of democracy itself. Robespierre helped draft a new constitution; it passed the National Assembly and was then voted on in a nationwide referendum, garnering over 99 percent of the vote. Yet it was never adopted, proving that the freedom of open communication can motivate a democratic revolution, but maintaining comity in a free society is an altogether different challenge.

To Edmund Burke and conservative thinkers ever since, the French Revolution portends the dangers of democracy. Burke, in his famous *Reflections on the Revolution in France*, derided the National Assembly as a "farce of deliberation with as little decency as liberty. They act like the comedians of a fair before a riotous audience."[16] Many of Burke's warnings were justified by subsequent events, and indeed he had been writing in 1790, well before the Terror materialized. The profane burlesque that ensued, from his vantage point, was the very creation of the National Assembly, the very launching of a culture of communication. France barreled ahead, he insisted, not by the force of great statesmen but rather by "spreaders of false news." Burke observed a paradox at work: the French Revolution was spawned and facilitated by newspapermen who, now activated in official politics, were themselves unqualified for the work of political reform. They could do little but foment excitement, he argued. The *Reflections* is, on the whole, a reasonable warning about the dangers of unleashing democratic forces without any moderating institutions in place.

But Burke's "Letter to a Member of the National Assembly," published the following year, reveals his reactionary nature. He instructs his readers that there is no peace or liberty without monarchy. He blames the revolution's inspiration entirely on Jean-Jacques Rousseau, as if the sans-culottes, led by Père Duchesne, were toying with the philosopher's ideas. Democracy is portrayed as a vice incapable of duty, reason, and virtue—overrun, in France's case, by sophistic usurpers. Burke then tells us how he really feels:

I can never be convinced that the scheme of placing the highest powers of the state in churchwardens and constables, and other such officers, guided by the prudence of litigious attorneys and Jew brokers, and set in action by shameless women of the lowest condition, by keepers of hotels, taverns, and brothels, by pert apprentices, by clerks, shopboys, hair-dressers, fiddlers, and dancers on the stage, (who, in such a commonwealth as yours, will overbear, as already they have overborne, the sober incapacity of dull uninstructed men, of useful but laborious occupations) can never be put into any shape, that must not be both disgraceful and destructive.[17]

Like Plato, Burke knows the paradox and fears it. Democracy, in his view, is an untamable beast. He hedges a little by concluding the "Letter" with the demand that people be prepared for civil liberty in proportion to their morality and propensity for justice and wisdom. Burke is hardly the first to make such a claim, and perhaps there is some truth in it. Yet he presupposes some natural order of which democracy is a violation. But the only alternative to a free society is an unfree society, and Burke seems to prefer the stability of the latter to the chaos of the former.

In fairness, democracy is disruptive. And communication among people, freely expressed, can lead to ruinous outcomes. Bad choices are only part of the problem, though; the larger concern, for our purposes, is how democracy can be gamed through media in the first place. Napoléon Bonaparte, whose reign ended the aspirations of the French Revolution in the guise of supporting its principles, weaponized this knowledge. His rise to power was secured not through military might but rather through propaganda efforts that glamorized such prowess and promised to curb external enemies. His Egyptian campaign bogged down in Syria, but not to worry: word reached France that it was a stunning success, and so the nation welcomed Napoléon back as a hero. The revolutionary parties practiced internecine warfare among themselves; Bonaparte simply used the press to blame England for the agitation. When newspapers questioned his growing stature and authoritarian designs, Napoléon appealed to the Directory government to tamp down on what he considered to be absurdities in the press. He then started his own publication, *Journal de Bonaparte et des hommes vertueux*. During the Italian campaign, he began another paper, one exclusively for the military. After he became emperor, press freedom contracted in a subordinate role to official bulletins, which were posted at churches and town squares, read aloud to soldiers, and dutifully reprinted by newspapers. Napoléon's visage, like Gutenberg's, was everywhere—emblazoned in publications as well as on home goods and currency. He insisted he was upholding the ideals of the revolution—a ridiculous claim reflecting the dangers of democratic dissimulation.

From the Reformation to the American and French Revolutions, the potential of news-print offered both a check on power and new opportunities for a diverse, heterodox set of voices. It wasn't that reason or truth had triumphed inasmuch as a public sphere had emerged flush with new opinions. A contest was set but not decided: monarchs and aristocrats and religious authorities would simply have to compete. While this new communications technology cleared democratic space, the expansion of such media was repeatedly offset by excess and exploitation. The American Revolution spawned a republic beset by partisan bickering; the French Revolution imploded in violence and was followed by a propaganda regime led by an emperor who feigned fidelity to democratic ideals. A key lesson for us is that the people who best understood the unwieldy nature of media and democratic culture were often the ones seeking to stifle inconvenient expression. Neither Jefferson nor any of his contemporaries could control the forces they unleashed, and their efforts to do so exposed them as hypocrites and exacerbated the paradox. As it turns out, the rise of news-print was just the beginning of a long, recurring cycle of media innovation creating democratic space followed by periods of political exploitation and instability.

4

THE RISE OF THE PUBLIC(S)

FROM A FULLER WORLD TO
MORSE'S MACROCOSM

She was a Sophist in the strictest sense of the term. She had designed a popular training series, "Conversations," whereby other women could pay her to teach them how best to communicate in society, just as the Greek speech teachers had done in the past. She also drafted a thorough rhetorical treatise to defend the role of women in public—not unlike Gorgias's *Encomium of Helen*. But it was never her intent to become a great chronicler and defender of democracy across two continents. She only came to New York City, like so many others, to become a star. Besides, she had witnessed the crude face of democracy up close and had found it wanting. She was shocked upon arriving in Rhode Island, where a protest movement turned revolutionary shadow government, the Dorr Rebellion, had to be put down through a declaration of martial law. She wrote that she found herself surrounded by "a city full of grown-up people as wild, as mischief-seeking, as full of prejudice, careless slander, and exaggeration, as a herd of boys in the play-ground of the worst boarding school."[1]

That was before. Two years later, in 1844, Margaret Fuller became a star. Literally. Her byline, in Horace Greeley's penny-press newspaper, the *New York Daily-Tribune*, was limited to an asterisk. As the former editor of Ralph Waldo Emerson's transcendentalist journal, the *Dial*, she might have stuck to reviews of high culture. Yet this Romanticist became an intrepid reporter covering the plight of asylums, prisons, and impoverished women. She became one of the world's first war correspondents. And she, Margaret Fuller—the doyenne of scholarly

respectability in New England who once bristled at the stuffy abolitionists, the dreamy-eyed utopians, and the chaotic Dorrites around
her—also became... *political.* She heralded the auspices of democracy
and free expression while excoriating the concentration of wealth and
power. "Wherever this impulse of social or political reform darts up its
rill through the crusts of selfishness," she wrote in December of 1844,
"scoff and dread arise and hang like a heavy mist above it."[2] Fuller had
concealed her gender before, publishing the book *Summer on the Lakes*
as S. M. Fuller. By 1845, when her *Dial* argument on gender, "The Great
Lawsuit," was updated as a book, *Woman in the Nineteenth Century,* her
authorship had been made clear. She then was one of the first to review
Frederick Douglass's autobiography, asserting in the *Tribune* that it
was "an excellent piece of writing, and on that score to be prized as a
specimen of the powers of the Black Race, which Prejudice persists in
disputing."[3] Her Fourth of July column a few weeks later railed against
the fraud and selfishness that abounded. The country was at least a
democracy, she allowed, which presented its citizens with temptations
to ill *as well as* inducements to good.

Fuller had touched on the paradox. The freedom of an open society
of communication could be simultaneously extolled and lamented,
praised for its virtues and scorned for its excesses. These insights
proved helpful as she worked as a foreign correspondent chronicling
the rise and fall of democracy in Europe during the Revolutions of
1848. She also managed to play an active role in helping the fledgling but ultimately doomed Roman Republic. Perhaps no other person from the nineteenth century connected the hopes and tragedies
of democracy in the modern world as she had. To be sure, Fuller's
efforts largely failed. The abolition of slavery would only be secured
by a war resulting in the death of several hundred thousand Americans. The European democratic Revolutions of 1848 faced reactionary backlashes, prompting restorations of autocratic power. Wom-
en's suffrage would not be actualized nationally until the twentieth
century.

Yet in Fuller's work we find that the nineteenth century offered the
start of something different, culturally and politically. New technologies brought global changes to communications and transportation

and the economy. New modes of thinking compelled reassessments of human life and society, from literature and philosophy to science and political ideology. It was the dawn of publics, various interest groups who could enjoy mass entertainments as well as collaborate to further social causes. New conduits of entertainment, information, and opinion emerged from new media—the penny press, photography, the telegraph, the yellow press, muckraking—as citizens absorbed new rhetorical styles. People could champion progressive change or identify with the reactionary passions of nationalism and racism. This impact meant that the world became more democratically open, even if enduring victories for democracy were resisted. By harnessing the new and speedy resources of communication, an emerging class of public figures could convince and coerce the public and various publics to their causes. This was also, therefore, the dawn of publicity. Some of these campaigns were morally righteous, others ghastly commercial. The aperture of the paradox continually opened and closed during the nineteenth century, culminating in the early twentieth century with World War I, the Bolshevik Revolution, and the American constitutional amendment guaranteeing women's suffrage.

Fuller's career marks a through line in these changes to media and politics. She saw and identified the contradictions that make democracy necessary and difficult. Having witnessed the quick glow and death of European liberty, the star of the *Tribune* returned home in 1850 with her Italian partner and their young child, only to drown off the shore of Long Island. Fuller almost made it back; the shipwreck was only a few hundred yards from a beach of onlookers. She spent hours stranded in the ship's forecastle until the mast broke and swept her away. Perhaps at some point in those hours of despair she recalled something prophetic, if tragic, she had written about democracy in a dispatch for the *Tribune* two years prior: "I have witnessed many a shipwreck, yet still beat noble hearts."[4]

Margaret Fuller was born in 1810. That same year a Berlin journalist, Heinrich von Kleist, published a novella, *Michael Kohlhaas*. It's a bloody story of a good and simple horse trader who was wronged by a corrupt nobleman. This strange book is important for two reasons. First, despite the grim toll of the plot, its prose is offered in the dry, matter-of-fact style of journalistic understatement. Second, it paints the pursuit of justice with a stark, elusive brush. Neither law nor politics can deliver us from arbitrary power. Kleist, a tragic figure who entered a murder-suicide pact with an acquaintance the next year, was amused by this. The book is darkly funny. Kohlhaas is described in the lead paragraph as both righteous and appalling. "The world would have blessed his memory, if he hadn't followed one of his virtues to excess," Kleist wrote.[5] Elsewhere, the author had written a treatise on rhetoric celebrating the imperfection of speech. We have no idea of the true meaning of what we're saying at any time, Kleist argued; communication is a wobbly wheel on the other end of an axle from thought.

We might regard *Michael Kohlhaas* as haunted by the figure of Napoléon Bonaparte. The book was published after he conquered Prussia, where Kleist had been arrested by the French for espionage. The French Revolution, as we know, terminated in terror and empire. War stretched across the European continent, and the Bourbon Restoration, beginning in 1814, would dampen the dreams of even Napoléon's pseudo-liberal tyranny. The Carlsbad Decrees of 1819 among the German states were erected specifically to eliminate freedoms of speech and press and the vision of independent nationalism. During the next century, the German states spectacularly failed at arresting liberalism and nationalism alike. A fair amount of blame for this has been directed at Johann Gottlieb Fichte, a philosopher whose *Addresses to the German Nation* of 1808 called for unifying a fatherland. Yet Fichte was a cosmopolitan thinker who supported the rights of free expression and a free press. He publicly supported the early years of the French Revolution and was forced out of an academic position in 1799 for a philosophy journal he edited. No great fan of the Napoleonic invasion, he concluded that German *Kultur*—which he said exercised all forces of liberty—could support a nation that might better defend itself. In the hands of nationalist figures like Otto von Bismarck and Adolf Hitler, such thinking would be abused. But Fichte's point was that Germany, as a central European nation linked by its culture, would have no reason to initiate imperial designs against others. His work can be accused of naïveté in this regard, but for at least the first half of the nineteenth century, liberalism and nationalism went hand in hand.

Such movements did not always lead to actualizing democratic ideals. On the other side of the globe, a decade-long slave revolt in the French Caribbean colony of Saint-Domingue created Haiti. Led by Toussaint Louverture, the Haitians had dispatched not just the French but also encroachments by the Spanish and the British. "We have dared to be free—let us continue free by ourselves, and for ourselves," proclaimed Jean-Jacques Dessalines, the governor-general who succeeded Louverture, in announcing Haitian independence. "Peace to our neighbors, but accursed be the French name—eternal hatred to France; such is our principles."[6] Within months, the Haitian declaration's hostile rhetoric prompted a massacre of the remaining French settlers, and Dessalines, who like Napoléon assumed the status of emperor, was assassinated two years later. Haiti might have benefited had the other democracy in the hemisphere, the United States of America, recognized its status. But Southern politicians in thrall to slavery, beginning with President Thomas Jefferson, were terrified by what the Haitian experience portended.

Similar hopes were dashed in Latin America when Simón Bolívar, who led a liberation from Spanish rule, ultimately blanched at the possibilities of democracy for the emerging republic of Gran Colombia. "All should not be left to chance and the outcome of elections," he told the Congress of Angostura in 1819. "No form of government is so weak as the democratic."[7] With a strong, centralized executive anticipating Caudillo politics, Gran Colombia expanded into new territories. It lasted only so long as Bolívar was in power, splitting apart within months of his resignation and death in 1830. The problem with mixing a president for life with a hereditary senate is that it offers no more guarantee of wise rule than a misguided democratic mob.

Not all Latin American revolutionaries agreed with Bolívar. Vicente Rocafuerte saw where Gran Colombia was headed and fled to Philadelphia, where he translated and published the foundational works of American independence in Spanish. His pocket-size book from 1821, *Essential Ideas for All Independent American Countries That Want to Be Free*, brought the ideas of Thomas Paine, the Declaration of Independence, and the US Constitution to Hispanic audiences throughout the Western Hemisphere. Later, Rocafuerte served as a Mexican diplomat to England and returned home to Ecuador, serving as that country's second president. He implemented a series of educational and commercial initiatives while ushering in a new, more liberal constitution. Then his successor, Juan José Flores, replaced that framework with what Rocafuerte called a Charter of Slavery.

By this time, the United States had recovered from the ugly gnashing of Federalist and Republican teeth, soon entering a period known as the Era of Good Feelings. John Quincy Adams, who had seen his father's presidency end at the hands of Jeffersonian celebrity, even came around to serve in the Republican administrations of James Madison and James Monroe. In this he departed from the antidemocratic screeds of former Massachusetts congressman Fisher Ames. A Federalist stalwart who nevertheless despised the emergence of party factions, Ames wrote before his death in 1808, "Of all governments, the worst is that which never fails to excite, but was never found to restrain those passions, that is, democracy. It is an illuminated hell, that in the midst of remorse, horror, and torture, rings with festivity."[8] But Americans had largely absorbed the passions of their public sphere. The exuberance of the press was now expected, and factional party disputes largely receded. Somehow, stability was forged from the chaos Ames had worried so much about.

This steadiness was partly attributable to the thriving American postal network that subsidized newspapers. Delivery was free in each county, and newspapers could be shipped for a flat rate of 1.5 cents anywhere else in the country. Although by 1820 the largest circulation for a newspaper had numbered only four thousand subscribers, print publications comprised half of all postal mail. Letters of private correspondence, typically less in weight, carried the burden of costs in order to facilitate the dissemination of public information. Stagecoaches and a network of roads helped ensure the delivery of newspapers, replicated later with mail boats on the Ohio and Mississippi Rivers. Technological advances fueled this cultural infrastructure as the Stanhope iron press came to America, increasing speed. Plentiful New England forests allowed for paper to be created from wood pulp instead of linen rags. The printing of literature benefited from stereotyping, which set and reduced the cost of book publishing; yet thanks to America's rather loose copyright laws, fiction continued to rely on the distribution of periodicals.

Such was the milieu in which the young Margaret Fuller was raised. Her father, Timothy, a Harvard-educated lawyer from Massachusetts, served as a Republican congressman while also insisting on a classical education for his daughter. Even in this time of general comity, he opposed the forcible removal of the Seminole Indians and the slavery-abetting Missouri Compromise. In 1824, he published a pamphlet in support of John Quincy Adams for president. Adams prevailed against Andrew Jackson despite not garnering the most popular votes. Without a victor in the Electoral College, the decision was left to the House of Representatives. Timothy Fuller left Congress that year, having succeeded in his task, but Jackson and those around him plotted revenge, decrying the "Corrupt Bargain" that had stymied the will of the people. To gain victory in 1828, Jackson's southern colleagues worked with a slick political operator from New York, Martin Van Buren, to create the Democratic Party. State headquarters were instructed on how to inundate newspaper editors with partisan communications. Substantive issues like slavery were ignored. The battle of personality was more important, and it was accompanied by the first glowing campaign biography—of Jackson. One Democratic newspaper suggested that Adams, as the ambassador to Russia, had procured an underage American virgin for the debauched taste of the tsar. A Cincinnati publication countered by suggesting Jackson's wife was an adulterer, his mother a common prostitute. The repolarized partisan press in 1828 was further facilitated by the increasing expansion of white male suffrage, and the new president rewarded fifty-nine newspaper editors with patronage positions in the government. "A so-called democratic style of electioneering had emerged," write Nancy Isenberg and Andrew Burstein of the election. "When it wasn't a name calling contest, it was a chaotic showcase of constructed personalities."[9] Thus, the fine-tuned rhetorician, Old Man Eloquent, lost out to Old Hickory as the projection of ethos triumphed over the careful argumentation of logos.

After Jackson's populist wave washed over American politics, John Quincy Adams became the only president to serve in Congress after his term in high office. He was a thorn in Jackson's side, for the most part, but joined his successor to ward off the nullification crisis of 1832–33 initiated by the man who served as vice president to both, John Calhoun of South Carolina. A constitutional breakdown was averted, but this conflict over a state's right to nullify federal law within its borders served as a prelude to the Civil War. Adams's stature grew as he successfully defended the rights of African passengers of the ship the *Amistad* before the US Supreme Court. Perhaps his greatest contribution to American democracy was reversing the congressional prohibition of discussions about abolition.

The renewed partisan press of 1828 delivered for Jackson, but soon it became just one layer among others in a bustling culture of expression and information. The number of newspapers in the United States doubled between 1828 and 1840 as access to printing materials and new technological efficiencies began to have an effect. New publications were geared toward not just elite partisan debates but also new publics. In 1827, the first African American newspaper, *Freedom's Journal*, began in New York City. The next year brought the rise of the *Cherokee Phoenix*, the first Native American newspaper, in Georgia. Frances Wright, an editor at the *New-Harmony Gazette* in Indiana, delivered the first female public oration in US history on July 4, 1828. At the time, Wright was pilloried as the Red Harlot of Infidelity, yet she persisted, courageously involving herself in public affairs. Her Independence Day speech warned how calls for change caused alarm in the world. It inspired a tradition, continued most famously by Frederick Douglass's oration from 1852, "What to the Slave Is the Fourth of July?," in offering a strenuous critique exposing the nation's own hypocrisies and shortcomings. As Wright also observed, the "clear sighted provision" of the US Constitution was that it allowed for "the frame of government [to] be moulded at will by the public voice, and so made to keep pace in progress with the public mind."[10] In Philadelphia in 1828, William Heighton created the *Mechanics' Free Press*, a publication geared toward urban laborers. A weekly offshoot of Heighton's newspaper started the next year in Utica, New York, vowing to report on "the cause of justice—the cause of right—and fearlessly to fling our gauntlet in the face of iniquity and wrong, under what roles soever they present themselves to our view."[11] Other types of periodicals began to emerge too. Sarah Joseph Hale started *Ladies' Magazine* in Boston in 1828. The publication was soon bought out and merged with *Godey's Lady's Book*. "Husbands may rest assured," Hale wrote in an early issue, "that nothing found in these pages shall cause [your wives] to be less assiduous in preparing for [your] reception or encourage to 'usurp station' or encroach upon the prerogatives of men."[12] Although Hale did not engage explicitly in political reporting and avoided the question of women's suffrage, her work consistently lobbied for women's equal access to education, fair wages, and safe working conditions.

A more overt form of political reporting began in 1831 as William Lloyd Garrison founded a Boston newspaper, the *Liberator*. Its main theme was opposition to slavery, and one of its top editors was Maria Stewart, an African American woman. Threatened and burned in effigy, Garrison fled to England for a time to escape hostile reactions to his publication. He also published the works of Sarah Grimké and Angelina Grimké Weld, sisters who, as South Carolinians, opposed slavery. Their own written works were banned and confiscated in their home state and throughout the South. The siblings collaborated with Angelina's husband, Theodore, a leading figure in Garrison's American Anti-Slavery Society, to publish *American Slavery as It Is*, a pamphlet constructed through the analysis of some twenty thousand newspaper clippings. It was, one scholar has summarized, "a gruesomely gothic documentary account of what exactly happens to a human body when subjected to the practice of chattel slavery."[13] Angelina was a fine orator in her own right; her Pennsylvania Hall address, delivered in Philadelphia in 1838, brought down the house. Advocating for abolition and accusing Northerners of complicity, she articulated the horrors of slavery and demanded a space for the right of petitioning against it. During her speech, a mob gathered outside, interrupting it by breaking the new building's windows. Before dawn, Pennsylvania Hall had burned to the ground. Another mob formed in the Midwest to oppose another abolitionist, Rev. Elijah Lovejoy. As editor of the *St. Louis Observer* in Missouri, a slave state, he issued denunciations of the institution. Consequently, the newspaper's premises were vandalized, its printing press destroyed. When in 1836 he sought to move across the river to Alton, Illinois, Lovejoy's new printing press was stolen and tossed into the water. In 1837, his *Alton Observer* offices were surrounded by a mob and set on fire. As he rushed outdoors to escape the flames, he was shot and killed.

In Europe, the Bourbon monarch Charles X overstepped by abolishing freedom of the press in France. The legislation was rebuked, leading to protests, votes of no confidence, and the July Revolution of 1830, which installed a more liberal constitutional monarchy. Reading of this event in French newspapers networked across the border, Belgians objected to their own lack of press freedom in an effort to gain independence from the Netherlands. In addition, the Swiss instituted press freedom among its cantons. That November, newspapers like *Gazeta Polska* and *Nowa Polska* fueled the Patriotic Society of Poland in its November Uprising against Russian rule. In 1831, the German state of Baden authorized press freedom; the next year a celebration, the Hambach Festival, was thrown by journalists demanding democratic rights and introducing the German tricolor flag. When a young journalist from Genoa, Giuseppe Mazzini, witnessed two of his newspapers being shut down by governmental authorities, he decamped to Marseille to found the Young Italy movement, clamoring for republican unification. England passed the Reform Act of 1832, which expanded representation. All these currents largely ended up as trial runs for the disappointments of the 1848 Revolutions, which Margaret Fuller observed firsthand. The French were still ruled by a monarchy, the Netherlands interfered with the sovereignty of Belgium, the Russians stamped out the Polish revolution, the German states reinstated the Carlsbad Decrees, Mazzini's revolts failed, and the British refused to fully repeal the stamp tax. The European spasms of 1830–32 are remembered as liberal agitations that failed, but they spawned a wave of democratic fervor. This would help an emerging pauper press in England, which circumvented taxes on knowledge and encouraged the Chartist movement demands for more representation. The backlash would also propel Germans, Poles, and other exiles, like Mazzini, circulating through Europe in an effort to galvanize their ideals.

One young Frenchman decided to go beyond Europe. A government lawyer who defied some members of his family by welcoming Charles's abdication, he requested the new Minister of the Interior to fund a trip to the United States so he could study its penitentiary systems. However, the prison report was a dodge for realizing a larger project: writing *Democracy in America*. Alexis de Tocqueville's ship arrived in 1831 to great fanfare in New York City newspapers. In the first publication he read upon his arrival, Tocqueville was surprised to note how President Jackson was openly called "a heartless despot whose sole concern is to cling to power."[14] The mayor gave him a tour of the prisons, and Tocqueville, returning to France a year later, indeed submitted a report on US penal institutions to his superiors. But it was his ability to get out of New York and explore the rest of the country that formed his impressions for the grander study. He dined with John Quincy Adams and sailed with Sam Houston. He witnessed the forcible removal of Choctaw Indians and traveled as far south as New Orleans before heading north to Washington, DC, where he met with President Jackson and observed debates in the US Congress.

For Tocqueville, the key to American democracy was its decentralized quality. Newspapers throughout the nation as well as local associations assured a dispersion of power, in contrast to the centralized nature of government. As for press freedom, Tocqueville was puckish yet fully committed: "I love it out of consideration for the evils that it prevents far more than for the good it does."[15] While he expressed some worries about tyrannical majorities, the rights of a free press and assembly allowed for cultural norms to flourish. These mores, as he called them, arose from the experiences, habits, and opinions of the people and provided a check on democratic excesses. Tocqueville also recognized a democratic counterweight in the law. In the American setting, this was evidenced at the time (and ever since) through the sheer preponderance of lawyers. Their ability to navigate federal, state, and local authorities and draft contractual agreements helped broker necessary relationships among citizens and corporations as well as between the public and the state. This helped mitigate those unruly passions of democracy. Still, Tocqueville admitted that the resources of democracy are imperfect. As a political system, he found it "often works against itself without intending to."[16]

A democracy can only learn through experience, drawing from its mistakes. Some nations, Tocqueville worried, might not practice such patience or learn such lessons. If he sounds ambivalent about the whole enterprise, that's kind of the point: the two volumes comprising *Democracy in America* are admirable for offering an honest, sobering assessment rather than a panegyric. The pratfalls of a free society are fierce and subject to the peculiarities of the culture in which it takes place. Every democracy, not just America's, is exceptional. When considering Tocqueville's legacy, it's rather strange to note that by the time *Democracy in America* was finally published—the first volume appeared in France in 1835, an American translation in 1838—it had become out of date. Tocqueville left in 1832, and American media would forever change in 1833.

A new form of journalism took over that year. The penny press began with Benjamin Day's *New York Sun*, its motto It Shines for All. The *Sun* offered a smaller paper at a cheaper rate than the sixpenny papers, such as the *Journal of Commerce*. The latter publications relied on a subscription model and were more than three feet tall, meant to be unfurled on a large table or writing desk. The sixpennies were also selective about advertising and relied on an elite readership. The penny press, on the other hand, was hawked by newsboys on the street, and it sold space to any business or individual to market their wares, including Help Wanted and Classified sections. The newspaper's size was tidy enough that it could be read on the go. Moreover, its content changed. As Michael Schudson has written, "In the 1830s the newspapers began to reflect, not the affairs of an elite in a small trading society, but the activities of an increasingly varied, urban, and middle-class society of trade, transportation, and manufacturing."[17] Specifically, this meant journalism covered what we know today as news—not limited to politics as such but capturing the entire panoply of social life, including crime reports and human-interest stories that featured the idiosyncrasies of the public. The advent of the steam press in 1835 increased the *Sun*'s publishing speed and output.

The penny papers' success was the first step in creating what we know of as mass culture. That's not to suggest, however, that the penny press was committed to informing the public ethically. In 1835, on the day Halley's Comet appeared, the *Sun* published the first in a series of articles that fabricated an astronomical discovery on the moon. To lend the "news" a patina of scientific credibility, the report attributed the findings to a supplement of the *Edinburgh Journal of Science*, courtesy of an esteemed Sir John Herschel, who was said to have built an observatory in South Africa. Winged humanoid creatures existed on the lunar surface, it was claimed, along with a host of other remarkable phenomena. The Great Moon Hoax caught on, with other newspapers rushing to confirm the discovery as it was established with so much scientific dross. The perpetrator, a *Sun* editor named Richard Adams Locke, intended the series as a satire, but he and Day welcomed the increased attention (and circulation). Eventually, another penny paper got wise to the fabrication: James Gordon Bennett, who had created the *New York Herald* that year, accused Locke of concocting the "news" out of whole cloth.

For Bennett, his *Herald* did not just expose the *Sun* but ultimately eclipsed it. If the *Sun* was silly and sensational, the *Herald* would mix that silliness with a tone of moral seriousness. "We shall support no party—be the organ of no faction or coterie, and care nothing for any election or candidate from the president on down," Bennett wrote in the first edition. "We shall endeavor to record facts, on every public and proper subject, stripped of verbiage and coloring, with comments when suitable, just, independent, fearless, and good tempered."[18] The passage is one of the first paeans to journalistic objectivity: independent facts reported on absent any political bias and divorced from values. Yet Bennett and his *Herald*, like journalists and news outlets ever since, often failed to live up to such a standard. This wasn't because all journalists intentionally sneak bias into reporting. All communication, like it or not, is rhetorical. The success of the *Herald* reflected Bennett's distinct style, not his factual reporting. On the one hand, it offered the mercantile class a Money Market column. On the other, it sensationally reported on wolf and kangaroo hunts, rapes and suicides, and political gossip. By the end of the *Herald*'s first year, it had begun running satirical columns whose author was pretending to be President Jackson.

The murder of a local prostitute and the resulting trial and acquittal of a wealthy patron caused a further sensation redounding to the *Herald*'s popularity. Bennett rushed to the scene and surveyed the contents of the woman's room in the brothel. No detail was too salacious to include, such as the description of her exquisite corpse. Coverage was nonstop. Before the trial, Bennett had pivoted to a larger discussion of the morals of society, speculating as to how a nice girl from a small town could get mixed up in such a terrible tragedy in the big city. He offered his readers an interview with the victim's madam and bemoaned the spirit of the age (despite being one of its chief progenitors). Bennett insisted on the defendant's innocence as part of a vast conspiracy involving the most powerful men of society, while the *Sun* gave a more straightforward assessment: a young man of privilege abused his station, and now, backed by a high-powered defense team, he was trying to get away with it. The papers bickered back and forth, each accusing the other of fabrication. "For all their invocations of journalistic principle, for all their proclamations of civic duty," one scholar has written of the competition, "these furious editors were making up their stories as they went along."[19]

Yet a free press was accepted, warts and all, as cheap penny papers flooded the northern and midwestern states. In 1842, a young lawyer by the name of Abraham Lincoln was challenged to a duel in Alton—where Reverend Lovejoy met his fate—for ridiculing the state auditor, James Shields. In an article written for a local paper in the voice of an old lady, Rebecca, Lincoln had called Shields a fool and a liar incapable of truth. When Shields discovered the perpetrator, satisfaction was demanded, and each man grabbed a sword. Honor was restored and a fight averted when Shields recognized the taller Lincoln's advantage. Illinois experienced other hostilities over a free press at the time: in 1844 Joseph Smith, the leader and prophet of the Church of Jesus Christ of Latter-Day Saints—as well as a presidential candidate that year—declared the *Nauvoo Expositor* a public nuisance. Before its press was destroyed, the *Expositor*'s one issue had exposed the faith's then secret practice of polygamy. Smith was arrested, but as various regional newspapers decried his actions a mob descended on the jail and murdered him before he could stand trial. America's free press was not to be messed with.

It's no great surprise that the penny press would eventually turn *political*. Bennett had already established something of a sensational conservatism, but from the other side came Horace Greeley, who created the *New York Daily-Tribune* in 1841. Having edited *The Log Cabin*, a Whig periodical for the 1840 election promoting the party's successful campaign slogan, Tippecanoe and Tyler Too, Greeley sought to create a cheap sheet that would add a blend of politics and high culture to combat the baser instincts of the penny press. He actively lobbied for labor rights and abolition while also designing a network of correspondents, like Jane Grey Swisshelm, who reported from Washington, DC. In the *New York Sun*, Edgar Allan Poe would publish "The Balloon-Hoax," as it was later known, his "account" of crossing the Atlantic Ocean, but more serious work, like his famous poem "The Raven," appeared in the *Tribune*. The publication's offices, moreover, were just down the block from P. T. Barnum's American Museum. Barnum, the fabulist entertainer, had edited a Connecticut newspaper between 1831 and 1834, but gave it up after the third time he was accused of libel. (He wouldn't be the last journalist to pivot to a public relations career.)

Greeley admired Margaret Fuller's book *Summer on the Lakes*, and after her essay "The Great Lawsuit" was published in the *Dial*, he persuaded her to move to New York. When she became a foreign correspondent, Fuller's first stop was the United Kingdom, where she interviewed the Romantic writer William Wordsworth about the Corn Laws and chronicled meetings with the Scottish historian and essayist Thomas Carlyle and the exiled Italian revolutionary Giuseppe Mazzini. She found Carlyle as exhaustingly arrogant as he was brilliant, and she admired Mazzini as a beacon of liberty. One novel approach to Fuller's European dispatches was her translation and inclusion of contemporary newspaper accounts and public statements accompanied by further commentary. Before the Revolutions of 1848 that rocked Europe, she had spent the year anticipating political change in her writings. Fuller identified the rot in the Austrian Empire as its censure of the press and prohibition of the rights of association. She spent time in Paris befriending the novelist George Sand as well as the exiled Polish revolutionary-poet Adam Mickiewicz—each of whom agitated for democracy. In a dispatch published on New Year's Day 1848, she reports communicating to her European friends the following: "I take pride here that I may really say the Liberty of the Press works well, and that checks and balances naturally evolve from it which suffice to its government."[20] Fuller qualified such patriotism by suggesting the United States gave rise to darker political ambitions than elsewhere. Specifically, she criticized the continuance of slavery and the ongoing Mexican-American War as reflecting how democracy cannot cure our human desires to oppress, rob, and imprison others.

The Revolutions of 1848 began, in fact, in late 1847 as a brief civil war broke out in Switzerland. As the country had ensured press freedom in 1830, this revolution featured conservative Swiss cantons trying to break away. The secession was stopped and a new constitution, resembling the framework of the United States, passed the next year. Fuller was closer to the start of the action in Rome when in January 1848 there was an uprising in Sicily against the Neapolitan king. From the Eternal City, she chronicled how Pope Pius IX offered hope with some liberal concessions but then absconded as the tumult for democratic independence proceeded. Mazzini reentered the Italian scene and, with other revolutionaries like Giuseppe Garibaldi, founded the Republic of Rome. Surveying the Continent, from France to Hungary, Fuller shared her excitement: "The struggle is now fairly, thoroughly commenced between the principle of Democracy and the old powers, no longer legitimate."[21]

Although England escaped the specter of revolution during 1848, Marx and Engels's *Communist Manifesto* was first published in London that February. It was not widely read. The city's top paper, the *Times*, provided skeptical reports from throughout Europe about the democratic revolutions. This raised the ire of Fuller, who wrote that the publication couldn't be trusted. But if the United Kingdom's mixed regime of a constitutional monarchy was spared the torrents of change, the same couldn't be said of France. Its royal government decided to crack down on banquets, as these large repasts had been a ploy to circumvent laws against political assembly. At one such affair in 1847, a beloved national poet and representative in the Chamber of Deputies, Alphonse de Lamartine, famously called for a revolution of contempt. By February 1848, the royal government had had enough and prevented a banquet in Paris. Protesters marched in defiance, and the National Guard fired on and killed some fifty citizens. A funeral wagon dragged the corpses all over the city that night, and barricades were erected by the morning. With spasms of violence breaking out, Émile de Girardin, the publisher of *La presse*, one of France's first penny papers dating to the 1830s, confronted King Louis-Philippe in person, demanding he resign. The king complied, and a provisional government, destined to be a republic, was formed. It was headed at first by Lamartine, the poet-politician, and Alexandre Ledru-Rollin and Louis Blanc, each of whom had founded newspapers.

Close to five hundred new newspapers began in 1848 alone, but the Second Republic was almost immediately caught between calls for elections and social demands. This tension was aggravated by radicals like Louis Auguste Blanqui, a political prisoner who had just been released, and Pierre-Joseph Proudhon, an anarchist with a major newspaper following who sought to delay elections until structural reforms were in place. The government tried to split the difference, pressing forward with elections in April while initiating National Workshops that aimed to secure full employment. Sand, the novelist, became the new democracy's chief publicist, issuing "Bulletins of the Republic" out of the Ministry of the Interior. "The elections, if they do not lead to the triumph of social truth," she wrote, "will be [the republic's] damnation."[22] Electoral returns suggested that the Parisian Left didn't have much national support. As Jonathan Israel writes, "Paradoxically, the birth of French democracy and comprehensive adoption of adult male suffrage had resulted in empowering the Catholic vote with the ironic consequence that there were many more nobles, landowners, and especially clergy in the new legislature than in any of Louis-Philippe's assemblies."[23] The Left revolted that June in an attempted coup that further alienated the public.

France then planned a presidential election for December. Louis-Napoléon Bonaparte, trading on the celebrity of his name, was a top contender. He had lived most of his life in exile, attempted two coups, and served as a London constable putting down a Chartist demonstration. His 1839 book, *The Napoleonic Idea*, sold half a million copies by declaring a vague love for nationalist liberty and an aversion to political factions. He declined to run in the April elections, having surmised that the people were too intoxicated with joy and hope. "All these illusions must perish before a 'man of order' can make himself heard," he said.[24] Bonaparte's sense of timing was impeccable. In returning to throw his hat into the presidential race, he, the nephew of Napoléon I, promised to restore order. That word became the slogan of his campaign, splashed across posters that could be found all over the country. He garnered three-quarters of the vote in a runaway victory. Ledru-Rollin, the candidate representing the social-democratic Montagnard Party—which had spurred the republic to begin with—only mustered 5 percent.

Such is democracy. It's a means of allowing open communication to influence others, not a system designed to ensure specific policies. Less than a year into office, the new president decided, in a blatant disregard for French law, to send an expedition to Rome to restore the pope as a sop to his religious base of voters. A siege ensued. Democracy was crushed, and similar disappointments played out across the German states and in Hungary and Poland. In Rome, Fuller left her newborn son with a nurse in the countryside and supervised a hospital for wounded soldiers while continuing to write dispatches about the bombardment. She excoriated Pope Pius IX, who issued an Allocution disavowing his previous liberal sympathies. Her denunciations would anticipate his hostility to any reforms until his death in 1878, save for declaring papal infallibility. The Roman Republic fell, and Mazzini and Garibaldi were forced into exile. In Fuller's last dispatch for the *Tribune*, published in January 1850 right before she made her fateful trip home, she lamented that all the worst men were in power.

Margaret Fuller was a legend, a pioneering democrat and journalist. Her contributions to feminism and literary criticism were enormous. And she would have likely returned home a hero, as so many noteworthy things had happened while she was away. Motivated in part by *Woman in the Nineteenth Century*, Lucretia Mott and Elizabeth Cady Stanton organized the 1848 Seneca Falls Convention on Women's Rights in Upstate New York. Frederick Douglass, who had founded a newspaper the year before in nearby Rochester, attended and encouraged the gathering to pass a Declaration of Sentiments demanding equality and the franchise. It reads as an indictment, much like the prosecutorial style of Fuller's "Lawsuit," and acknowledges the blowback of "misconception, misrepresentation, and ridicule" likely to appear. Sure enough, Bennett's *Herald* dismissed the gathering as a "Woman's Wrong Convention." He was committed, moving forward, to championing the exclusion of both Black persons and women in public life. Stanton was happy that the Declaration was at least published alongside the vitriol. However, she couldn't help but reflect later on how "all the journals from Maine to Texas seemed to strive with each other to see which could make our movement appear the most ridiculous."[25]

Before Seneca Falls, Douglass had been a hundred miles west, in Buffalo, for the Free-Soil convention. It catered to a subset of abolitionist Democrats who called themselves the Barnburners, a reference to farmers willing to burn down their shelters so as to eliminate rats. Also in attendance was a young journalist named Walt Whitman, who had been fired by a Brooklyn newspaper for his political opinions. The convention resulted in the nomination of former president Martin Van Buren, who was joined on the ticket by Charles Adams, John Quincy's son. Van Buren was likely the man most responsible for Andrew Jackson prevailing over Charles's father in 1828. Now here he was, decades later, representing an abolitionist party. The ploy didn't pay off, as Van Buren might have guessed: carrying the day for the Whig Party would be another Southern general, Zachary Taylor. Oddly enough, the Whigs had largely opposed the war. Taylor was simply an empty vessel of ethos who could be marketed as "Old Rough and Ready." Van Buren garnered just 10 percent of the vote, but it was enough, as a third-party candidate, to help swing the election in Taylor's favor.

American politics may have remained stagnant, mired continually in compromises to protect slaveholder interests, but the culture of the United States was changing. Fuller would have returned to a country that had expanded and eagerly embraced new media such as photography and the telegraph. Both communication technologies were introduced to America by an art professor at New York University, Samuel F. B. Morse. Born to a Federalist preacher from New England, Morse wound up embracing democracy—sort of. He had famously been commissioned to draw a portrait of the Marquis de Lafayette during one of his American tours in the 1820s, but in the 1830s he turned nativist. Amid the swirl of anti-Catholic fervor, he wrote articles for the *New York Observer* under the pen name Brutus, attacking those whose very presence would despoil the United States. He failed to win a New York City mayoral election under the nativist banner, but his articles formed the basis of an 1835 book, *Foreign Conspiracy against the Liberties of the United States*. In it, Morse charged, "That a vigorous and unexampled effort is making by the despotic governments of Europe to cause Popery to overspread this country is a fact too palpable to be contradicted."[26] As with most reactionary political figures, he attacked the secular press for willfully ignoring a major threat. Morse was a rabid conspiracy theorist and an early example of what Richard Hofstadter would later term the paranoid style of American politics. But he also joined a league of American supporters for Polish democracy later that decade while in Paris. It was there, in 1839, that he met Louis Daguerre and learned the intricacies of his daguerreotype, bringing the process and tools back with him to America.

Photography took off in the United States, capturing reality by inscribing an image or impression in time. At first, the medium was limited to portraitures that took up to half an hour per exposure. Photography snatches a fleeting moment, yet the daguerreotype was grounded in an artificial contrivance. Bodies were disciplined to sit still to meet the demands of the technology. Books and newspapers were media that had made this demand before, but now the public could actively collaborate as participants in making media themselves—about themselves. A photograph distills reality, thereby mediating our knowledge of what is real. Print news accomplished this through imparting a record that presumed to tell us what was true. Photography furnished us with an image that could show us what was, or had been, real. Both media aspired to reveal reality but were attenuated by the pressures of time and space that inherently distanced us from the material events themselves.

Morse's development of the electromagnetic telegraph—along with his co-invention of a novel linguistic code—sought to collapse that distancing. It arrested the spatial calculus that had kept us separate. Even with recent innovations like canals, railroads, and steamboats, a chasm still prevented an immediacy of knowledge. The telegraph changed that, capturing reality by erasing time *and* space altogether.

Whereas photography reproduced and objectified bodies and space, the telegraph disembodied communication from space. In 1844, Morse demonstrated the telegraph for the first time between Baltimore and Washington, DC, by messaging WHAT HATH GOD WROUGHT? This rhetorical question was offered with humility, perhaps a bit of self-loathing, for Morse knew what he had done, not in spite of but because of his religious heritage. He had not declared "God is dead," as Friedrich Nietzsche would later in the century, but he may as well have. Morse probably recognized that telegraphic communication displaced God with connectivity, rendering the power of God less awesome. Nietzsche's follow-up line to his infamous provocation was, "And we have killed him." To attribute God to the telegraph reflected Morse's confession. God had been clear with us about the Tower of Babel, smiting our attempt to construct a universal language of perfect communication. It was a warning Morse knew he had failed to heed. A little less than a century later, Sigmund Freud wrote that humanity had become something of a "prosthetic God" because of its media technologies, which had assumed the status of "auxiliary organs." That power may be strong, but all these communicative enhancements were likely to still give humanity "much trouble at times."[27]

Freud was right. We've been dealing with the consequences ever since. To this day, we inhabit Morse's Macrocosm. His fascination with images, nativism, nationalism, democracy, and the connectivity and speed of communications still drives our world. It has only been intensified. The velocity with which communicative change has occurred since the telegraph has been incredible. Whereas the gifts of speech and the phonetic alphabet and the printing press had been spaced out over thousands of years, in under two centuries we have experienced multiple revolutions in connection through image, text, and sound. The goal promised human clarity; the results were endless levels of combustion and fascination. As Daniel Walker Howe sharply observes in his history about the period, "Better communication did not necessarily foster harmony."[28]

It was also obvious, within days of Morse's first message, that the telegraph wasn't some idle curiosity reserved for theological abstraction. He quickly began to facilitate a different kind of speculation. The

DC line had terminated at the Capitol, but since party conventions were held in Baltimore that presidential year, Morse was able to cable back political news of the gatherings. The time to relay information between the two cities via horseback had been six hours. Now information was instantaneous. This is how James Polk came to be the first dark-horse candidate, surprising those in Washington who learned of his nomination. Just as quickly, news traveled that Silas Wright had rejected an offer to stand as vice president. And so "the news" became a horse race in which journalists chronicled the jockeying of political fortunes. Economic speculation emerged too as a response to the telegraph. Political revolutions rocked Europe in 1848, but in America the telegraph would wire Chicago and New Orleans that year with trade information from commodities exchanges. Time could be organized into distinct regional zones as information flowed across space.

Also in 1848, several New York newspapers, including the *Sun* and the *Herald*, joined forces to create what would become the Associated Press. By centralizing information, the telegraph, according to James Carey, "snapped the tradition of partisan journalism by forcing the wire services to generate 'objective' news, news that could be used by papers of any political stripe."[29] Because space along the wire was limited and cost money, telegraphic reporting required short, declarative sentences full of information—a language, Carey added, "of strict denotation."[30] As a sign of this shift, one of Horace Greeley's former correspondents at the *Tribune*, Henry J. Raymond, established the *New York Times* in 1851. Offered at just a penny, its first editorial declared a preference for dispassionate information, promising to be "temperate and measured in all our language."[31] The American version of the *Times* would be joined in this noble effort the next year by its English cousin, the *Times* of London. As its editor John Delane wrote, "The first duty of the press is to obtain the earliest and most correct intelligence of the events of the time, and instantly by disclosing them to make them the common property of the nation."[32] The publication Margaret Fuller so deeply distrusted was now against Louis Bonaparte's autocratic desires and faced official criticism from British leaders for its attacks. "We are bound," Delane clarified, "to tell the truth as we find it without fear of consequences—to lend no convenient shelter to acts of injustice and oppression, but to consign them to the judgment of the world."[33] Within a few years, one of his reporters, William Howard Russell, gained notoriety as the world's first war correspondent for his coverage of the Crimean War. It's a distinction that ignores Fuller's work from Rome, but Russell's contribution was that he publicized the role of courageous common soldiers and not their aristocratic superiors. The charge of the Light Cavalry Brigade swept proudly past, doomed to its efforts but ennobling the spirit of Britain, nonetheless. Such purple prose inspired Florence Nightingale and other members of the public to support the war effort. Interestingly, although Russell's reporting could appear in the *Times* more quickly because of the telegraph, he was simultaneously writing private letters back to Delane about his deep concerns regarding British military leadership. Delane then discreetly shared these complaints with government officials, inducing changes in command.

Proclamations of neutrality and the desires for dispassionate copy connoted something else, beyond journalism. They augured a separate but increasingly interrelated variable of the modern struggle for democracy: liberalism. It functions as both an idea and a set of social practices that inspire confidence in managing the unruly passions of the public. In democracies as much as autocracies, liberalism has occupied a middle ground between the demands of the Left and the reactions of the Right. The great problem of this philosophy is that it has continually sought to have its democratic cake and eat it too. Liberalism assumes that the world is knowable and that progress is inevitable so long as the market is free and rational thought is allowed to flourish. Both *Times* newspapers were joined in this endeavor by new magazines emerging during this period, such as the *Economist* in England and the *Atlantic* in the United States. All four of these publications continue to exist, almost two centuries later.

Democracy and liberalism are often conflated, and their distinctions can be confusing to spot. We often associate free speech and the ability to check arbitrary power with liberalism, yet those were clearly the foundations of Athenian democracy. We tend to locate democracy with an expansion of the voting franchise and government's ability to reflect public opinion, but these were actually liberal inventions from the nineteenth century. A liberal democracy may signal, for historical purposes, voting as well as individual freedoms and civil liberties, along with those of and for the press in addition to freedom of speech. Such a society requires persuasion, but persuasion is thought to be best regulated by an elite cadre of interlocutors armed with factual knowledge and engaging in good-faith argumentation. Universal education, the rule of law, a free press, and established norms for public discourse further help guide society. Through this process the public can be steered, with various consensus points reasonably achieved. As one liberal, John Stuart Mill, confidently assured readers in his 1859 tract, *On Liberty*, "It is not too much to require that the wisest of mankind ... should be submitted to by that miscellaneous collection of a few wise and many foolish individuals, called the public."[34] In fairness to Mill, he also recognized that the will of the people might be controlled by simply the most numerous or passionate among its participants, leading to oppression. Thus, precautions would be needed. Liberal democracy is precisely this wager: we can have our freedom and manage it well. By valuing compromise, norms, and the rule of law, democracy can be contained.

An idealist conservatism running from Plato through Victorian writers such as Thomas Carlyle and John Ruskin rejected this view. Responding to Mill a year after the publication of *On Liberty*, Ruskin published a series of articles in *Cornhill Magazine* excoriating the delusions of liberalism. Chief among them was the utilitarian pretense of a liberal political economy, which he called the dismal science. The works provoked such an outcry that the editor of *Cornhill*, William Thackeray, canceled Ruskin's series. Later published in book form as *Unto This Last*, Ruskin advanced an aristocratic socialism that nonetheless insisted on universal education. "By my measure," he wrote elsewhere, "one man of parts and rank would outweigh in voting a whole shoal of the mob."[35] As an art critic, he resisted and resented all forms of empiricism—no easy task considering that *On Liberty* was released the same year as Charles Darwin's *On the Origin of Species*. Victorian England provides a challenging test case for us in general, as it was not wholly a democracy. Yet its public sphere had consistently widened with the reduction and then outright repeal of the stamp tax, and reform legislation that increased representation was continually introduced, if slowly. Beyond Queen Victoria, women were largely excluded from that sphere, but England hosted spaces for liberals like Mill, scientists like Darwin, artists in prose and paint from Dickens to Turner, conservative socialists like Ruskin, a Catholic theologian like John Henry Newman, a radical like Engels, and even a Jewish prime minister, Benjamin Disraeli. Of course, the cultural freedoms of the public sphere benefited from an imperialist framework spanning multiple continents that subjected people against their will. Jamaicans and the Irish, no less than Kenyans and the denizens of India—to say nothing of laborers toiling in the dank factories of Manchester processing imported cotton from slave labor in the American South—might have considered the diversity of English public opinion rather quaint.

In any case, London provided a good vantage point from which to observe both the hypocrisies and the potential of all these nineteenth-century currents of public life. Soon after Louis Bonaparte assumed emperor status as Napoléon III, a London-based writer published some thoughts about the short-lived Second Republic as a series in a New York magazine, *Die Revolution*. "Seldom was an event trumpeted ahead with more certainty and longer beforehand than the 'inevitable victory of democracy,'" this man wrote, adding, somewhat acidly, "No party exaggerates to itself the means at its disposal more than the democratic, none deceives itself with greater heedlessness on the situation."[36] In light of the events following 1848, the point was strict but fair. The series would not be published as a book in Europe for over a decade, and by then the author, a German named Karl Marx, had been kicked out of multiple European states for his journalistic work. "The free press is the omnipresent open eye of the spirit of the people," he remarked in a Dresden publication in response to a censorship decree.[37] In 1848, just before moving to London, he had been arrested for editing a Cologne newspaper whose subtitle promoted it as the "Organ of Democracy." Marx's work caught the attention of Greeley, who hired him as a decade-long correspondent for the *New York Tribune*. Marx replaced Fuller, that is, and his articles resembled her dispatches in that they aggregated news and supplemented it with commentary. He offered more structural, ideological analysis than Fuller, tracing the economic flows underscoring events from around the world so that readers in New York could learn about the geopolitical travails of China, India, and Turkey. During the American Civil War, Marx refuted British support for the South in the pages of the *Tribune*. He assailed how the war was sold in England as a mere conflict over tariffs. He also quoted from, and lambasted, pro-Confederate coverage in the *Economist* and the *Times* of London, the latter having removed Russell as their war correspondent for not reflecting its editorial priorities vigorously enough.

Marx wasn't the only influential German in American journalism. A slew of European immigrants arrived in the aftermath of 1848, among them Karl Peter Heinzen. Though he had been kicked out of Bonn University for sedition and Marx dismissed him as bourgeois, Heinzen, who was mostly destitute throughout his life, founded one of the more influential German-language newspapers in the United States. His *Der Pioneer* began in Kentucky in 1850, and he helped establish the Louisville Platform of 1854, a statement of principles which stood for labor reforms, women's suffrage, and the abolition of slavery. Heinzen and other immigrants had to contend with George D. Prentice, the influential editor of the *Louisville Journal* and an intellectual firebrand of the Know-Nothings, an anti-immigrant movement turned political party. Prentice's reactionary prose led to riots in Louisville that killed German and Irish immigrants in 1855. Heinzen moved north, where he remained for the rest of his life publishing German-language newspapers. The Know-Nothings had been founded out of a clandestine society, the Order of the Star-Spangled Banner, that propounded nativist ideas. Thomas Whitney, one of its leaders, summed up its philosophy in the tradition of Morse with the publication of his 1856 tract, *A Defence of the American Policy, as opposed to the encroachments of foreign influence, and especially to the interference of the papacy in the political interests and affairs of the United States.* "What is equality," Whitney asked, "but stagnation?"[38] The Know-Nothings netted one hundred congressmen over the course of its short existence, and its presidential candidate, former Whig president Millard Filmore, received over 20 percent of the vote in 1856.

Against this expanding secret public seeking to constrain democracy was a broader mass culture open to change. Harriet Beecher

Stowe's novel *Uncle Tom's Cabin* was released in installments by an abolitionist weekly paper, the *National Era*, beginning in 1851. When transformed into a book, sales reached several hundred thousand copies in its first year of publication. Lajos Kossuth, a Hungarian journalist and exiled leader of his country's short-lived independence in 1849, toured the United States, even addressing Congress. "The spirit of our age is Democracy," he declared to the Ohio state legislature in an 1852 speech. He added, in a turn of phrase anticipating President Lincoln's famous utterance, "All for the people, and all by the people."[39] And though Fuller's friends and colleagues like Ralph Waldo Emerson and Henry David Thoreau had once shied away from her public-political phase, they, too, became involved in promoting abolitionist and anti-imperialist causes. America could no longer retreat from the question of slavery, hiding behind political compromises and secret oaths to ignore the issue. Public confrontations, from Stowe's book to the actions of John Brown, made that clear. Emerson and Thoreau had met Brown in Concord, New Hampshire, and voiced their support for his actions in the violent chaos of the Kansas free-state drive as well as his later raid on Harpers Ferry, Virginia, for which he was tried and convicted of treason. The Republican Party had been created in 1856 in the wake of the dissolution of the Whigs. Members weren't, as a whole, anti-slavery so much as against its continued spread. For their first presidential candidate, Republicans nominated a celebrity explorer of the American West, John C. Frémont. He would lose, as would a certain Republican senatorial candidate from Illinois two years later.

Candidate Abraham Lincoln's seven debates with the incumbent, Senator Stephen Douglas, as they toured the state have been celebrated for their formal reasoning and respectable exchanges. People gathered and listened for hours, carefully parsing the logical back-and-forth. But what made the Lincoln-Douglas debates such a national sensation was that newly trained stenographers could dispatch the arguments, via telegraph, to the press. As Lincoln discovered, formal logic doesn't always translate into what's morally right or persuasive. For it was Douglas, not Lincoln—the future savior of the American project— who best appropriated liberal-democratic rhetoric. "Nothing is more honorable to any large mass of people assembled for the purpose of a fair discussion than that kind and respectful attention that is yielded, not only to your political friends, but to those who are opposed to you in politics," one of his replies began.[40] Yet Douglas's platitudes were placed in the service of the expansion of one of the cruelest, most inhumane social systems in human history. This wasn't simply a matter of archaic morals and outdated racist views; Douglas specifically invoked democracy as its shield. "It is no answer to this argument to say that slavery is an evil, and hence should not be tolerated. You must allow the people to decide for themselves whether it is a good or an evil," he said. "Whenever you put a limitation upon the right of any people to decide what laws they want, you have destroyed the fundamental principle of self-government."[41]

Rhetorically, Lincoln was trapped. Neither he nor the Republican Party stood for outright abolition. Yet to oppose the expansion of slavery, they had to argue that the practice was anathema. Yet if Douglas won the battle, Lincoln, in more than one way, won the war: the press notoriety he gained from these debates gave him a national platform, one that served him well as a compromise candidate within the Republican Party in 1860. Soon enough after his electoral victory, however, he was beset by calls for secession from the Union. To preserve Southern institutions, "the time for action has come—now or never," declared an editorial from the *Charleston Mercury*. The next month, South Carolina seceded, followed quickly by six other Southern states. Lincoln demurred. His first inaugural address, from March 1861, sought to preserve the Union, arguing that it was inviolable. Henry J. Raymond's *Times* and Horace Greeley's *Tribune* criticized the president, demanding a plan. Then shots were fired at Fort Sumter.

The war did not go well for the Union. There were lost battles, obstinate generals, a chaotic atmosphere of public information, and rampant corruption in the War Office. The first defeat at Bull Run was misreported in the North, and editors like Wilbur Storey of the *Chicago Times* instructed his reporters as follows: "Telegraph fully all news you can get and when there is no news send rumours."[42] This environment of loose information was reined in when Edwin Stanton took over as secretary of war. He not only assumed control of telegraphic communications but penned a War Diary column for newspapers. To

Stanton's discredit, he devised a secret police force and wasn't opposed to outright censorship, having arrested journalists who had published a phony letter about a compulsory draft that led to riots in New York City. But with Stanton's help, Lincoln had the first-ever war room installed in the White House, an office that could deploy the telegraph for communicating directly, in real time, with his generals in the field. The president was obsessed with the thing, staying glued to it for updates and sending off missives to his commanders.

When General Robert E. Lee of the Confederacy headed north to Pennsylvania, his Union opposition, General Joseph Hooker, excitedly informed the president that Richmond, Virginia, the Southern capital, was left undefended. Hooker thought he could take it. Lincoln said no. The symbolism of the South claiming a victory in Union territory was too great a risk. The president knew that the public was already weary of the war effort, and with some Northern newspapers souring, he couldn't afford more negativity. But Hooker, in increasingly fraught messages, insisted on Richmond, and when the president refused again, the general resigned. Lincoln quickly appointed George Meade acting general. He followed directions by hastening Union forces to Gettysburg, securing the high ground. Despite taking on heavy casualties, the Union held and won the battle. The war would go on, but momentum had shifted. To celebrate this victory, a dedication ceremony was held at Gettysburg a few months later. Some fifteen thousand people attended, and the keynote speaker, the nation's top orator, had planned a speech that in his mind would reverberate through human history. Standing beneath the serene sky, the eloquent voice of the mighty rhetorician broke the silence of God and nature. His epic oration, some two hours long, situated the battle and the war for all posterity.

Then the president of the United States spoke for two minutes.

Lincoln's pithy remarks defined the character of the nation itself. Many of us know it well: equality and liberty, a new birth of freedom, a government of, for, and by the people. In less than three hundred words, Lincoln managed to combine these themes along with a solemn remembrance of the brave men who struggled and died on that hallowed ground. The keynote speaker, now long forgotten, was Edward Everett—a former US senator and secretary of state famous for giving public lectures across the country. Orations like his didn't play well on the telegraph, though. Everett had arranged beforehand for his speech to be printed in a gilded book by his publisher. Yet the Associated Press reporter covering the event rushed the stage and asked for Lincoln's script. The news agency needed copy to be brief and to the point in order to disseminate it. Lincoln supplied that need with his brevity, and within forty-eight hours the president's speech would be printed on front pages of newspapers as far away as California. The telegraph made his address both readily available to the public and easy to digest. Surely Lincoln was being too modest when he declared, "The world will little note nor long remember what we say here." For within a few days, it was clear that his speech was *the* speech at Gettysburg.

In one of the odder twists of fate, Stanton, a man of authority hostile to the free press, can be credited with devising the inverted pyramid style of presenting facts, from most important to least important, in journalism. Mere hours after Lincoln's assassination, Stanton assumed control of the government and dashed off a report that would be printed in the *New York Herald* the next morning. The lede perfectly encapsulates the questions *who, what, when, where,* and *how* in an opening paragraph worthy of emulation by cub reporters and journalism students to this day: "This evening, at about 9:30 P.M., at Ford's Theatre, the President, while sitting in his private box with Mrs. Lincoln, Mrs. Harris and Major Rathbone, was shot by an assassin, who suddenly entered the box and approached behind the President."[43] Lincoln's legacy, even in death, contributed to the modern era of mass communications.

The tools of media had changed the public environment but not the scope of democracy. "It ought never to be forgotten that a republic without a press is an impossibility, almost a contradiction in terms," declared the Irish American journalist E. L. Godkin in a new publication from 1865, the *Nation*, an offshoot of William Lloyd Garrison's *Liberator*. "The modern newspaper is the equivalent of the Greek agora, the only means possessed by the citizens of interchanging thought and concerting action."[44] These freedoms and tools rewarded a certain set of skills, however. In the case of Lincoln, this wasn't a bad thing. But Lincoln was a rare politician, as rhetorically gifted as he was morally grounded. Democracy, as we know, does not prohibit demagogues from employing those very same tools. Lincoln's successor, the Southerner Andrew Johnson, represented a case study in democratic bad faith. The war had ended and emancipation had been declared, but Johnson was not above asserting, "This is a country for white men and, by God, as long as I am president it shall be a government for white men."[45] Like Stephen Douglas, he invoked democratic rhetoric to suggest that Southern states submit Black voting rights to statewide referendums. His trail of invective was accompanied by riots in Memphis and New Orleans. As declared in the latter's *Crescent* newspaper in 1867, "It is our general belief, fixed and unalterable, that this country was discovered by white men, peopled by white men, defended by white men, and owned by white men, and it is our settled purpose that none but white men shall participate in its government."[46] Not that every media outlet agreed. *Harper's New Monthly Magazine* cartoonist Thomas Nast ridiculed Johnson as "King Andy," a *Chicago Tribune* headline trumpeted "The Ravings of a Besotted and Debauched Demagogue," and the *Atlantic* labeled him a dictator. Jane Grey Swisshelm, Greeley's former correspondent, started her own newspaper, the *Reconstructionist*, in Washington, DC, though her attacks on Johnson led to the destruction of her printing press in an act of arson.

After Johnson left office, progress was squandered despite the opportunities for expanding democratic rights and African American representation in the South. This was because of another in a long line of tragic compromises in American politics fueled by partisan media organs. On the night of the presidential election in 1876, returns indicated that Samuel Tilden, a Democrat from New York, would comfortably win. It would have been the party's first taste of electoral victory in two decades. (In the 1872 election, the lifelong Whig and Republican, Horace Greeley, lost decisively as a Democrat while Susan B. Anthony was arrested for voting.) Republicans, while nominally overseeing Reconstruction, had increasingly lapsed into corruption, giving Democrats—and, by extension, white Southerners—an opening. Tilden's popular vote margin approached three hundred thousand votes, so he went to bed that night thinking he would become the next president of the United States. As he slept, Daniel Sickels, a

Republican partisan for whom Stanton and Lincoln secured an acquittal by pleading the insanity defense in his 1859 homicide trial, got busy firing off telegraph messages. Republican politicians in Florida, South Carolina, Louisiana, and Oregon were instructed not to concede. While most newspapers printed news of a Tilden victory, the staunchly pro-Republican *New York Times* reported that the outcome was still in doubt. Its editors collaborated with party headquarters to disseminate news of a potential path for Rutherford B. Hayes. To secure this path, negotiations in Congress had to take place, and the result was that Hayes could be president if federal troops were removed from the South. That agreement led to the abject terrorization and subjection of Black people in the South for almost a century. Among the various humiliations of this period, we might briefly mention the first and only successful coup in US history, which took place after the 1898 election. A massacre of an untold number of Black citizens coerced the entire city government of Wilmington, North Carolina, into resigning. That summer, a Black newspaper in the city, the *Daily Record*, had published an editorial refuting charges that Black men posed a threat to white women. Burning down its offices that fateful November day was the first action of the mob, a prelude to more widespread, wanton violence in the coming hours and days.

The *Daily Record* was not the only Black publication to be torched in the 1890s. In Memphis, the offices of Ida B. Wells's publication, *Free Speech*, fell to arson after the *Memphis Daily Appeal* suggested as much, hoping to stamp out a voice it called "the black wretch." An African American born into slavery, Wells had also published the pamphlets *Southern Horrors: Lynch Law in All Its Phases* and *The Red Record*. She debunked myths concerning Black people through investigative journalism and helped inspire muckraking, a tradition that explored social ills to effect reformative change. It would reach its peak of influence over the next decade as Jacob Riis pioneered long-form reporting and photojournalism in covering the plight of the urban poor for *Scribner's*; *McClure's* published Ida Tarbell's takedown of Standard Oil's monopolistic practices; *Collier's* and *Ladies' Home Journal* exposed fraudulent medical claims; and *Cosmopolitan* documented corruption in the United States Senate. Muckraking gained opprobrium from

President Theodore Roosevelt's criticisms of scandalmongering, but he ultimately agreed to social and political reforms based on the ensuing coverage. Though Wells's work struggled to create structural changes to liberate African Americans, her example cleared a path for other Black voices in American media, including that of W. E. B. Du Bois. Portions of the sociologist's famous work, *The Souls of Black Folk*, originally appeared in the *Atlantic*, and he would go on to found and edit the *Crisis*, a magazine published by the National Association for the Advancement of Colored People (popularly known as the NAACP).

That's not to suggest that American journalism was always interested in advancing social causes. Distinguishing between the serious and the silly became a challenge in the mainstream press. Joseph Pulitzer, a Hungarian Jewish immigrant, juggled these poles in a career that evolved from dogged reporter to legislator to media mogul. He began his journalism work in St. Louis, writing for a German-language newspaper and eventually moving into ownership. He also wrote dispatches for the *New York Sun*. Pulitzer's success was owed to his understanding of the business of news. He purchased the *St. Louis Dispatch* and immediately merged it with the *St. Louis Post*, creating the *St. Louis Post-Dispatch*. In particular, he foresaw how evening papers afforded more up-to-date information, thanks to the telegraph, along with more time to be read, thanks to the emergence of the electric light. Pulitzer's first editorial promised that the newspaper would "serve no party but the people" as "the organ of truth," following "no caucuses but its own convictions," and would "oppose all frauds and shams wherever and whatever they are," advocating for "principles and ideas rather than prejudices and partisanship."[47] He crusaded for the public good and found it so lucrative that he was able to purchase the *New York World* in 1883.

Pulitzer offered his brother Albert, then publisher of the competing (and more popular) *New York Journal*, a chance to consolidate the news outlets for better market share. When Albert refused, Joseph hired away the *Journal*'s managing editor. The *World* achieved popular success by its fusion of entertainment and information known as yellow journalism, a concept partly stemming from Pulitzer running a color comics section, led by the strip *The Yellow Kid*. While the term *yellow journalism* implies sensationalism, its style of reporting should also be remembered as changing the look of the modern newspapers, organized with separate sections for news, opinion, lifestyle, and sport. It structured the various aspects of mass culture we know today, and Pulitzer benefited from the recent introductions of newsprint and linotype presses. Newspapers were now easier for readers to handle, and cheaper and more efficient for publishers to produce. In the last three decades of the nineteenth century, the number of American dailies rose from just under six hundred to well over two thousand.

Given the cultural and technological changes to America, Pulitzer's insight was to expand the typical readership of mass-market newspapers, catering to women and immigrants as much as to businessmen and laborers. As a result, the *World* increased its readership fifteen times over. Its hybridized style of reporting could be seen in the career of one of Pulitzer's most legendary reporters, Elizabeth Cochrane, who wrote as Nellie Bly. She had started at the *Pittsburgh Dispatch* writing investigative series about the role of women in society as well as political corruption in Mexico. After coming to the *World*, she went undercover at the Women's Lunatic Asylum in New York City and exposed systematic mistreatment of its patients. The series prompted political reform to address the issues Bly highlighted. The next year, she attempted a publicity stunt on behalf of the *World* with the goal of circumnavigating the globe in eighty days, to achieve the journey described in a popular Jules Verne novel. She accomplished the feat, sending back dispatches for publication in the *World*. The serious and the silly had now fully merged.

Another enterprising young Pulitzer reporter was a Harvard dropout named William Randolph Hearst. The son of a US senator and mining baron who owned the *San Francisco Examiner*, the young man soon left New York to run his father's paper. Unlike Pulitzer, who maximized his profit by publishing one newspaper at a time, Hearst envisioned a networked newspaper chain. He expanded his reach in 1895 by acquiring the seldom-read *New York Journal*, which had been discarded by Pulitzer's brother. Hearst exacted Albert's revenge by scooping up some of the *World*'s top writers in addition to *The Yellow Kid* comic. The paper also sold for a penny, boasting the motto "You can't get more news; you can't pay less than one cent." In a departure from the politically singular editorial voices of most newspapers, the *Journal* offered an op-ed page featuring different columnists with a variety of perspectives. Then in 1897, a circulation war between Hearst and Pulitzer heated up as the *World* and the *Journal* jockeyed for coverage of the mysterious appearance of a headless torso in New York City. Each offered competing rewards to the public for information, using new photographic illustrations to show gruesome details of the dismembered corpse. Hearst even rode his bicycle to a suspect's apartment and leased it out so his reporters could investigate.[48]

The *New York Times* had undergone a management change by then. Its new owner, Adolph S. Ochs, conceived a motto, All the News That's Fit to Print, and published an editorial outlining the direction of the paper. It would "give the news impartially, without fear or favor, regardless of party, sect, or interests involved," and offer editorial columns as "a forum for the consideration of all questions of public importance, and to that end to invite intelligent discussion from all shades of opinion."[49] Ochs's liberal spirit is upended, as if on cue, by the next paragraph of his column, which assures readers of his intentions to maintain the *Times* "as a non-partisan newspaper—unless it be, if possible, to intensify its devotion to the cause of sound money and tariff reform." Once again, we find the noble precepts of liberalism extolling its own virtues above the partisan fray while blind to its own political commitments. Not that political commitments are misguided: it's just that the pretensions of liberal discourse can't often, or for long, conceal their own political commitments. And liberal discourse can be a political commitment of its own. As an example, the *Times* skewered the *World* and the *Journal* for their coverage of the headless torso: "The freak journals, those startling and irrepressible caterers to the gross and savage side of human nature are having a particularly fine time with their new 'murder mystery.'"[50]

The Hearst-Pulitzer rivalry over the missing torso was but a prelude to the next year, 1898, when the papers drummed up the march to war with Spain after the explosion of the USS *Maine* battleship off the coast of Cuba. The ship's destruction resulted in the deaths of over 250 American servicemen and was likely an accident, but the *World* and the *Journal* asserted it was a Spanish plot. A front-page graphic illustration in Hearst's paper revealed cables from a mine rigged to execute the blast. "The entire country," the journalism historian Rodger Streitmatter has written, "seemed to be seething under the daily onslaught of misinformation and sensationalism."[51] President William McKinley was at first reluctant to attribute the damage to the Spanish, but he relented and opted for war. Both newspapers sent a phalanx of reporters to cover the hostilities, and Hearst himself traded in his New York City bicycle for a horse to report on battles firsthand. Telegraph dispatches sent from Key West supplied enough news for the *Journal* to publish up to forty daily editions, and by the end of the Spanish-American War both publications had doubled their readership to over a million per day. In supplanting Spanish holdings not just in Cuba but also the Philippines, the United States started to exert its own force as a geopolitical power. As a democracy, the nation featured not the clairvoyance of perfect communication but a chaotic atmosphere of competing, contradictory rhetorical forms.

Morse's Macrocosm was beginning to draw the world closer, but not always in the most helpful ways. Incidentally, this fact contributed to the end of Napoléon III's empire and the rise of a new democratic endeavor, the Third Republic. Though over 80 percent of French voters approved a May 1870 plebiscite reiterating their support for the emperor (and some slight reforms), he would be captured by Prussian forces by early September. How did this come to be? It started innocently enough. King William I of Prussia met with the French ambassador, Vincent Benedetti, at a spa in Ems to hash out a plan for peace in Europe. A Hohenzollern relative of William's had been offered the vacant Spanish throne, a prospect the French found intolerable. "Public opinion has burst into flames, is being brought to white heat, and is going to overwhelm us," France's foreign minister cabled Benedetti in Ems.[52] King William and Benedetti were able to reach an agreement, however, and the relative withdrew his claim. The French, egged on by Parisian newspapers and military leaders clamoring for war, then instructed Benedetti to press for a declaration from the king that no Hohenzollern would ever deign to sit on the Spanish throne. The king politely refused, thinking the matter over, and warmly shook Benedetti's hand at the train station before the ambassador took leave.

A member of the Prussian foreign office telegraphed news of the agreement and the second demand made of the king to the Prussian chancellor, Otto von Bismarck, back in Berlin. He happened to be dining that night with Field Marshal Helmuth von Moltke, who wasn't opposed to a conflict with France. The two doctored the telegram slightly and disseminated a version of the encounter that suggested outright hostility between the Prussian king and Benedetti. Ultimately, the edits to the Ems Dispatch were nugatory; the fever for war would not have been arrested on either side had the original telegram been disseminated verbatim. The French were the first to declare war, besides. Complained one French politician, "Certain papers, instead of reporting what happened, are resorting to guesses and assumptions, deviating from objectivity, and placing themselves in contradiction to the facts."[53]

What Bismarck did do was use the impending Franco-Prussian War as a way to bring the southern Germanic states together with the north. Germany as a nation-state was formed in early 1871 at the zenith of its triumph in the war. The new country acquired the Alsace-Lorraine region of France as part of the terms of victory. With Paris under siege by Prussian forces, the makeshift new French government fled. By the time it attempted to return, following the truce, a Paris Commune had been formed. The National Guard retained all the ammunition to protect the city from the siege. The rest of the military obeyed the new republican government. Newspapers were suppressed, proscribing views found disagreeable. It took a bloody week of civil war to end hostilities and put down the Commune, which, for the few months it existed, had been heralded as the dictatorship of the proletariat. As in 1848, French republicans and the socialists couldn't get along. The Right hated them both: it had been deprived of an emperor, the military had been repulsed, and the loss of Alsace-Lorraine shamed national pride. While the French Right assumed a hurt irredentism, Germans, now united under King William and led by Bismarck, resented French resentment.

This toxic stew simmered, but hostilities throughout Europe subsided in the aftermath of the Franco-Prussian War. The great powers liberalized with more parliamentary representation, freer expression, and universal education. This put conservatives in a tough spot politically. How was one to protect the old order of privileges associated with aristocracy in an open public sphere? How could publics react favorably to concentrated power in societies that assumed more democratic formations? Nationalism, that's how. A great rhetorical switch took place after 1870 in Europe and the United States alike. Before then, independence and democracy had been expressed as nationalist ideals. Think of the Hambach Festival of journalists that first waved the German flag. In America, Margaret Fuller and the abolitionists, along with Lincoln, had hoped to liberalize and preserve the Union. To establish Italy, it took the continual agitations of Mazzini and Garibaldi. Now that these societies featured more representation in their congresses and parliaments to go along with more openly communicative publics, it was necessary to find some prism through which a more radical politics could be kept at bay. Vague but glorifying appeals to the character and honor of the nation-state did the trick. Such a rhetoric could justify anything as long as it was shrouded in cultural identity. Any substantive debate could be short-circuited in this fashion. Truncated arguments could be supported by nationalist newspapers slinging images, slogans, and headlines that wrapped themselves in the glory of the flag.

To pull all this off, the rhetoric of nationalism had to be more than just a frame. It needed to give people a chance to cheer as well as distract them from actualizing the liberal ideal of deliberative debate. To make the discourse of nationalism whole, it was consummated with imperialism. We see this in the fomenting of war in Cuba by the likes of Hearst and Pulitzer. But even before then, Americans had been all too comfortable with imperialist expansion across the West and in the South Pacific, which required taking land from indigenous peoples. The term *Manifest Destiny* had been introduced by John L. O'Sullivan, a magazine editor, in 1845 during the lead-up to the Mexican-American War. While some wanted to annex all of Mexico, this gambit was struck down, as it would have expanded slavery even more. Texas, at the time, was enough. As American government and politics after the Civil War became a host of maladministration, imperialism offered a gesture sure to please the public.

Europe wasn't much better. Nationalism there meant pursuing imperial strategies in the Scramble for Africa. The sheer number of people and resources that could be exploited stretched across the Continent and brought back untold material wealth. Citizens, meanwhile, could read about military achievements, the spread of Christianity, and the peregrinations of figures like the journalist Henry Stanley Morgan. A Brit by birth who happened to serve both the Confederate and the Union militaries during the American Civil War, Morgan made a name for himself locating Dr. David Livingstone, a missionary. That trip to Africa was funded by the *New York Herald*, and his future jaunts were supported by London newspapers. Morgan later became an agent for King Leopold II of Belgium in erecting the Congo Free State, a handy moniker disguising the atrocious pillage of that land. Looking back on this period from 1915, a year into World War I, W. E. B. Du Bois wrote in the *Atlantic* that what the world had was a new theory of democratic despotism. It had relied on empowering the wealth of ordinary white European citizens, not just the princes, at the expense of colonized peoples of color. That such brutal practices occurred during a period of purported democratization created what Du Bois suggested was an easily explained paradox. Yet the increased wealth of average European citizens, he concluded, had the deleterious effect of increasing personal as well as national jealousies in Europe. Du Bois saw through this nationalist-imperialist schema with clear eyes: "Democracy is a method of doing the impossible," he wrote, with "but one adequate method of salvation—the giving of democratic weapons of self-defense to the defenseless."[54]

Occasionally, though, nationalism is just ... nationalism. Enter fin de siècle France 1894, some two decades into the Third Republic. Its culture of open communication sparked impressionist art, naturalist fiction, and, soon enough, cinema. The political Right, lacking the Crown and still humiliated from ceding land to Germany, expressed itself through the church and the military. These two variables translated in public into a nationalism that relied on anti-Semitic tropes. Édouard Drumont's 1886 book of hate, *Jewish France*, sold over one hundred thousand copies in a year. When a custodial worker discovered in the rubbish of the German embassy a torn document revealing the existence of a French spy, Alfred Dreyfus, a Jewish artillery officer who just so happened to have been born in Alsace, became the top suspect. The handwriting on this *bordereau* didn't match Dreyfus's at all, but an anthropometric expert from the police—Alphonse Bertillon, the man credited with inventing the mug shot—was cowed into reporting that the Jewish captain may have been carefully skilled in auto-forgery. The anti-Semitic Drumont, now the editor of a nationalist newspaper, *La libre parole*—which translates as "Free Speech"—broke the news. He worked himself up into a lather: the Germans are spying on us, he reported, and the perfidy, as he had long warned, owes to the Jewish menace. Dreyfus, he alleged falsely, had confessed his guilt. Justice is demanded, and military intelligence, with the case out in the public, could not pull back. At the court-martial, a secret dossier was produced for the judges unbeknownst to the defense. Found guilty of treason, Dreyfus was ordered to lifetime imprisonment on Devil's Island, off the coast of a French holding in South America.

Before being cast away, Dreyfus had endured a degradation at the École militaire. Twenty thousand people surrounded the spectacle, screaming "Death to the Jews," as Dreyfus, in full regalia, had his insignia and buttons ripped off, his sword broken in two. The man shouted, insisting that the whole of France knows him innocent, yet the captain assigned to escort him from the ceremony told the press afterward that he had whispered an admission of guilt. Maurice Barrès, a nationalist author who attended, found the degradation "a more exciting spectacle than the guillotine."[55] Barrès, with Drumont, led the anti-Dreyfusards who publicly championed his guilt. They opposed what they termed the Syndicate, composed of Jews and "public intellectuals"—where this term originates—who defended the traitor and dishonored France. Two polarized publics emerged: a conservative nationalist-religious camp and a cosmopolitan liberal-leftist consortium. They waged a war in ink.

In 1896, more evidence from the German embassy arrived on the desk of the Statistical Bureau. Among the collection was a *petit bleu*, a messaging paper used in pneumatic tubes that connected the offices

of Paris at the time. It was addressed to another French officer, a lout-
ish gambler named Esterhazy. The investigator, Lieutenant Colonel
Georges Picquart, obtained a sample of Esterhazy's handwriting and
matched it with the initial *bordereau*. Exact. No matter: Picquart was
shipped off for duty in Tunis and then imprisoned. Yet a facsimile of
the *bordereau* was then made public, reprinted in a newspaper, and
even Esterhazy's stockbroker recognized his hand. Major Hubert-
Joseph Henry, who had testified against Dreyfus twice at the 1894
court-martial, next forged a document from that year to prove his guilt.
Outraged, the vice president of the Senate, Auguste Scheurer-Kestner,
published an open letter in *Le temps* and spoke on the parliamentary
floor as to Dreyfus's innocence. He was swiftly removed from office.
Esterhazy was acquitted.

This all became too much for Émile Zola, the celebrated novelist
who had typically stayed out of political disputes in public life. In early
1898, he addressed the president of the republic with "J'Accuse," an
article published in *L'aurore*. The editor who ran the piece was Georges
Clemenceau, a journalist who had covered the American Civil War and
would twice go on to serve as prime minister of France. The country
had witnessed an infamous spectacle of injustice, Zola wrote. Hundreds of thousands of copies of *L'aurore* were sold as his piece drove
conversation. "Women are happy to salute, in this time of weakness
and of cowardice, an act of moral courage," wrote a journalist in *La
fronde*, a women's newspaper started by Marguerite Durand the month
before.[56] Despite this support and loyalty from elsewhere, Zola soon
was convicted of libel and fled to England.

Later in 1898, Henry's forgery was discovered, and he was imprisoned. He died by suicide. The matter should have been over. But
no. Henry did not bring shame on himself by concocting evidence.
According to the anti-Dreyfusards, this was a man who so loved the
nation and his God that he could not but help sacrificing himself. He
did it to honor France and eliminate Jews from the army. It was actually
the hatred of the Dreyfusards that caused his ruin. This was the take
given by Drumont's *La libre parole*, which launched a fund-raising
campaign for Henry's widow. In addition, the publication shamed
La fronde for its refusal to support a single mother. Durand, herself a

single mother at the time, had no truck with the anti-Semitism of the anti-Dreyfusards. "In all things," she wrote, "one must have the courage of one's own opinions, and not demand respect from a world whose prejudices one wittingly goes against."[57]

In 1899, Dreyfus was brought back for a second court-martial in the small, conservative town of Rennes. Totally removed from modern communications while imprisoned on Devil's Island, he knew nothing of the affair being carried out in his name. He had become a shell of a man by this time, shackled as he had been for years in a small hut. The second court-martial caused another sensation. Dreyfus's lawyer was shot and wounded in broad daylight, but the trial was not delayed. The would-be assassin got away, the moment crystallized in a front-page graphic by Le petit illustration, which enjoyed a million weekly readers. The defense team was a mess, struggling not to offend the military. Dreyfus could barely stand in court, nor could he articulate the moral indignation the Dreyfusard crowd expected of him. The judges knew of Esterhazy, they knew of the rigged evidence at the first trial—and yet found Dreyfus guilty once more.

Dreyfus soon received a presidential pardon, but he wasn't restored to his rightful place in the military. Some Dreyfusards took exception that after five years' imprisonment for the injustice, he dared not continue pressing his case for acquittal. Dreyfus himself was but a symbol, his justice a victory to be won for the public. Only in 1906 was his innocence fully declared by the highest court in the land. Two years later, when Dreyfus attended a ceremony for the late Zola at the Panthéon, he was shot. He survived, but the would-be assassin was easily acquitted. Then from the ashes of anti-Dreyfusardism a new political movement rose in 1908 with its own daily newspaper, L'action Française. It was devoted to the blood-and-soil ideology of nationalism and anti-Semitism but, in itching for war in 1914, privileged a broad militarism for all Frenchmen to join in and recover Alsace-Lorraine. In a few short years, the newspaper returned to anti-Semitic rhetoric with renewed vigor. Dreyfus, for his part, reentered the military during World War I and served his country with distinction—as he had intended all along.

The drama and spectacle of the Dreyfus affair anticipated the destruction of Europe and the paradox of democracy in the first half of the twentieth century. What was supposed to have been a cool, reasonable age of liberalism and scientific enlightenment grew continually unstable due to a chaotic democratic public sphere of new media. We noted above the great conservative switch to nationalism that justified itself in the guise of imperialism. But the Dreyfus affair demonstrates the degree to which the grandeur of nationalist rhetoric also relies on ethnic identity, which can be religiously and/or racially bound. France, obviously, produced both, and had a strong democratic public sphere and republican political tradition to counter such currents. Russia was different, structurally speaking. Since the early nineteenth century, it had enjoyed something of a lively literary culture carried out by "thick journals" exclusive to intellectuals and tolerated, at least in part, by autocratic tsardom. What few Russian newspapers existed were subject to pre-clearance, and earlier revolutionary efforts may have failed because of a lack of mediated coordination. After the Crimean War, newspapers were given wider latitude, but within a few years Tsar Alexander II was complaining about the "intolerable debauchery" of the press.[58] Even so, reforms in 1861 allowed for the emancipation of serfdom, the establishment of local governments, and the conducting of trials by jury. A mild allowance for press freedom was instituted in 1865. A boulevard press arose in which citizens in Moscow and Saint Petersburg could peruse and purchase a variety of newspapers sold at kiosks. Some, like *Golos* (The voice), exercised their editorial independence to critique the government, and others, like the *Moscow Herald*, championed slogans such as Orthodoxy, Autocracy, Nationality.[59]

In 1869, a little-known scientifically minded bureaucrat named Nikolai Danilevsky decided to publish a series of articles in the magazine *Zariia*. When the series was published as a book, *Russia and Europe*, a few years later, Danilevsky attracted attention for outlining a pan-Slavic movement bringing together Russia and other eastern European countries. Their historical, linguistic, and Eastern Orthodox religious ties, he argued, would inspire a noble commitment to progress and combat the Roman and German influences from the rest of the Continent. "All these streams must run together into one broad basin on the wide plains of Slavdom," he concluded.[60] To effect this, Russia would have to raise a pan-Slavic consciousness and help liberate its racial brothers.

sheets also emerged, including a troublesome little publication named *Pravda*, which previously could only be published abroad. Among its early editors was a Georgian Marxist who had changed his name from Dzhugashvili to Stalin, meaning "steel"—a masterstroke of celebrity branding. Stalin had also published a pamphlet addressing how communism intersected with nationalist culture. This editor could be rather ruthless, a punctilious micromanager who dared even reject submissions by Bolshevik leaders such as Vladimir Lenin.

By 1914, tsarist officialdom had found public opinion out of control, both ideologically revolutionary and recklessly sensational. About the only hope Nicholas had in keeping things together was reusing the old playbook of pan-Slavic unity. Conveniently, he would have a chance to prove himself after the dull, unlovable heir to the Austro-Hungarian throne, Archduke Franz Ferdinand, was felled by members of a Serbian terrorist group in Sarajevo. Despite clear warning signs and a heads-up from the Serbian government about the plot against him, Ferdinand had paraded about the streets with lax security and was assassinated. In the aftermath, according to the historian Christopher Clark, "with incredible speed by the print media, most of the familiar narrative was in place."[61] Viennese newspapers, never quite fans of Ferdinand during his life, emblazoned their front pages with mourning stripes of black, decrying the loss of their heir. What is to be done?, they asked. *Schickalsschlag*, a stroke of destiny to be realized, answered Vienna's influential *Neue freie Presse*. Now was the chance for the Austro-Hungarian foreign minister, Count Berchtold, to teach the Serbs a lesson. He had helped annex Bosnia and Herzegovina back in 1908 during the First Balkan Crisis but was seen as a bit too soft on Serbia and Russian influence after the Balkan Wars of 1912 and 1913. In between, Austria had been embarrassed when over fifty Serbs were arrested for treason and acquitted on appeal. The *Neue freie Presse* greeted this initial charade of sorrow by publishing treason accusations against Austrian politicians who, it claimed, were being bribed by the Serbian kingdom. The charge was based on phony documents and retracted in the face of libel claims.

Berchtold's grand plan was to issue ten demands of the Serbs. They could either unconditionally accept the ultimatum within forty-eight hours, or else face war. Yet Berchtold had to hold off on this scheme for over a week, for just then the president of the French Republic was visiting Russia. This situation required a delicate balance, as Berchtold explained in a cable to the Austro-Hungarian ambassador in Berlin: "We are obliged to prevent public opinion in the Monarchy, which favours our policy, from cooling in its enthusiasm, and yet we cannot allow the press to get up too much steam, so that other powers might think of mediation."[62] Serbian government officials, no strangers to criticisms of intense nationalist sentiment, were under immense pressure once they received the ultimatum. For the Serbian press after Sarajevo, writes one historian, "widely transgressed the limits not only of minimum decorum but of elementary prudence."[63] Yet the kingdom of Serbia relented, agreeing in part or whole to all the demands, save for one. It was a remarkably conciliatory document it passed back to the Austro-Hungarian ambassador. Kaiser Wilhelm II of Germany breathed a sigh of relief, figuring that this could all be negotiated away. At most, maybe a brief little occupation of Belgrade was in order since Austrian territory began on the other side of the Danube from the Serbian capital. No big deal, right?

Not exactly. Berchtold had instructed his ambassador to cut off all diplomatic relations if the Serbs did not unconditionally accept every aspect of the ultimatum. Austria-Hungary was now in a state of war, even though it would require a couple more weeks to fully mobilize. "Vienna burst into a frenzy of delight, vast crowds parading the streets and singing patriotic songs till the small hours of the morning," the British ambassador reported that day to Sir Edward Grey, the foreign secretary. "Now the floodgates are open, and the entire people and press clamoured impatiently for immediate and condign punishment of the hated Serbian race."[64] The next few days offered one final chance to avoid bloodshed across the Continent. Unfortunately, whatever hopes existed for peace in Europe were entrusted to a pair of royal cousins whose powers of miscommunication were legendary. World War I finished both of their reigns (and one of their lives), but the ham-fisted Willy-Nicky telegrams reveal leaders in a political system simply incapable of navigating modern forms of media. "An ignoble war has been declared on a weak country," wrote Tsar Nicholas. "The indignation in Russia, shared fully by me, is enormous. I foresee that very soon I shall be overwhelmed by the pressure brought upon me, and be forced to take extreme measures which will lead to war."[65] Notice his use of the passive voice: if only this monarch could rid himself of this meddlesome nationalist fervor for Pan-Slavism. Kaiser Wilhelm appreciated his cousin's predicament, responding, "I fully understand how difficult it is for you and your government to face the drift of your public opinion."[66] Wilhelm had blamed his own subordinates for getting him into such a fine mess. Nicholas was a mess himself, confusing Wilhelm's first telegram as a response to his second missive. He had just approved mobilization but now rescinded the call, much to the chagrin of Russia's top military brass. The tsar was not going to be responsible for a monstrous slaughter. But then he confided to Wilhelm a bit too casually how a premobilization of troops had been in place five days earlier, which set off German plans for premobilization. Wilhelm had other problems. His chancellor ignored his requests for mediation and accidentally gave away plans for invading Belgium to the British while simultaneously requesting their neutrality. To distract the public from the killing of Irish protesters in Dublin, leaders in London were quite eager to bolster their nationalist legacy as the protector of a state like Belgium.

The guns of August were then drawn across the board. The conflict soon gave way to trench warfare, stalemate, and mustard gas. By the end, the Kaiser had fled, thus ending the German Empire. Austria-Hungary and the Ottoman Empire were finished. Russia experienced the paradox in 1917 when a liberal-democratic revolution that did not last the year terminated with the Bolsheviks in power and *Pravda* as the only permissible news outlet. (That fellow Lenin had proved to be for freedom of the press before he was against it.) We need not mourn the loss of autocratic states, but we should understand how these expanding publics got caught up in a world war.

Karl Kraus knew. The Viennese journalist operated his own magazine, *Die Fackel* (The torch), for several decades. Like an Austrian version of H. L. Mencken, his biting social commentary lampooned and lambasted the idiocies of public opinion—with the stylings of the *Neue freie Presse* and Freudian psychoanalysis serving as particularly rich targets. But Kraus's humor took everything seriously. To him, advertisements, newspapers, and posters were the defining attributes of such a society, not an afterthought. This new world of media furnished opinions free of intellect and divorced entertainment from art. He dared others to find him guilty of overestimating the press. In late 1914, he delivered a speech, "In These Great Times," which was also published in his magazine. Newspapers, Kraus suggested, were to blame for the war. This conflict was but a trifle, he found, "as compared to the intellectual self-mutilation of mankind by means of its press."[67] The truth was that news items didn't provide statements chronicling the contents of life but were, in fact, the contents themselves. Media are reality—a new reality, for sure, only different. The press wasn't a messenger of an event, Kraus said, but *the event itself*, just as the power of speech doesn't reflect reality but forms it.

The American philosopher William James had a sense of this back in 1904, addressing the World's Peace Congress with a reality check it likely didn't appreciate. "The plain truth is that people *want* war," he told those assembled.[68] Who among us, James asked, does not open a newspaper and check for news of violent conflicts? His idea was to "cheat the foe" by leaving the possibility of war alive but preventing hostilities. What he offered was an ethical framework for dealing with democratic mass publics and nationalism. To accomplish this, one would have to confront the naïveté of liberal thinking. "Reason assumes to settle things by weighing them against one another without prejudice, partiality, or excitement," James noted. "But what affairs in the concrete are settled by is and always will be just prejudices, partialities, cupidities, and excitements."[69] The cynicism of the quote is only matched by its accuracy. James wouldn't live to see the events of the War to End All Wars, but he might have been amused to discover how President Woodrow Wilson brought the Americans to the fight. Though he campaigned for reelection in 1916 on staying out of hostilities, Wilson was given a media pretext for making the world "safe for democracy" once British intelligence intercepted, decoded, and shared a telegram from the German foreign minister, Arthur Zimmermann. The communique not only admitted that Germany was about to embark on a submarine campaign against American ships but promised Mexico its long-lost territory stretching from Texas to Arizona if it helped keep the Yanks in check. The news caused a furor, especially as Zimmermann did not deny its authenticity. In the end, over one hundred thousand American troops lost their lives, and the Wilson administration used a campaign of propaganda and negating civil liberties to sustain the military effort.

The scope of Morse's Macrocosm was now global. His own nativist-nationalist sentiments trumped the peaceful potential of his godlike communications technology. "I trust that one of the effects [of the telegraph] will be to bind man to his fellow-man in such bonds of amity as to put an end to war," Morse once predicted.[70] Margaret Fuller wouldn't have shared such confidence. She got to see the precarious transformations of democracy up close and personal, and she knew how hard it was to maintain. Victories are possible, though. A year before World War I concluded, Carrie Chapman Catt, a peace activist and suffragist, had composed an open letter to Congress declaring that women's suffrage was inevitable. She delivered it as a speech across the country. In it, she turned Wilson's hypocritical language against itself, appropriating his definition of democracy as her declaration that "those who submit to authority have a voice in their own govern-ment."[71] What begins with expression ends with the franchise, and Catt deftly employed not only the words of Wilson but those of Jefferson and Lincoln to make her case. She continued, "However stupidly our country may have evaded the logical application at times, it has never swerved from its devotion to the theory of democracy as expressed by those axioms." The tone rings of Fuller. The Nineteenth Amendment to the US Constitution was introduced in 1919 and became law in 1920. Democracy was on the march.

Yet the paradox reminds us over and over: the world is never truly safe for democracy—not for long anyway.

5

THIS IS FASCISM

The first inklings of fascism could be seen at the White House on February 18, 1915, when President Woodrow Wilson hosted a screening of the D. W. Griffith film *The Birth of a Nation*. Cinema's first blockbuster, the movie is an epic portrayal of a culture's mass suffering under tyranny until a band of freedom fighters gathers to liberate the people. Those freedom fighters are members of the Ku Klux Klan (KKK), and the tyranny is democracy itself, composed of Black Americans who, following the Civil War and emancipation, participated in Southern local and state governments during Reconstruction. "It's like writing history with lightning," President Wilson was reported to have said after the screening on the White House lawn. "My only regret is that it is all so terribly true." The next evening, the National Press Club showed the film to more than three dozen US senators and the chief justice of the United States, Edward White—himself a former member of the KKK.

A movie wouldn't normally have opened in the nation's capital before it had in New York City, but Griffith, fearing objections from the NAACP, sought to "blunt [the] protest" during a time when municipalities could censor the exhibition of films.[1] The immediate goal was favorable publicity to prime national audiences and exhibition sites for what was unquestionably an inflammatory, racist film that decried the opening of American democracy during Reconstruction. By premiering the film in Washington, Griffith stamped *The Birth of a Nation* with the imprimatur of the US government. The movie itself featured title

cards that selectively quoted from Wilson's previous works as a historian. The famous "lightning" quotation from Wilson is apocryphal,
though—another part of Griffith's publicity campaign for the film. "I
was gratified when a man we all revere, or ought to, said it teaches
history by lightning," the director told a New York newspaper shortly
after *Birth's* premiere.[2] Similar language appeared in an advertisement
for the film in the *Atlanta Constitution* later that year, but the full quote
attributed to Wilson wouldn't be printed for another two decades.

This is not to absolve President Wilson, a champion of racism and
Jim Crow. Nor is it to take at face value his decision to "make the world
safe for democracy" as his rationale for entering World War I, given
his promotion of the Espionage and Sedition Acts and the formation
of the Committee on Public Information to propagandize America's
involvement in the conflict. But Wilson wasn't a fascist. He had neither
the charisma nor the energy. Neither did the two newspaper owners
from Ohio who vied to succeed him in the 1920 presidential election:
Democrat James Cox and Republican Warren Harding, the eventual
winner. In the case of *The Birth of a Nation*, Wilson proved to be an
unwitting pawn. Griffith could exploit the man and his status because
the film's source material was *The Clansman*, a novel and play written
by Thomas Dixon Jr., an old classmate of Wilson's. At one point, the
White House had to issue a statement clarifying that the president
did not approve of the film and exhibited it only as a courtesy for an
old friend.

The novel, which inspired lynchings upon its release, is melodra-
matic and ridiculous. It suggests that American democracy became
unhinged *after* the assassination of Abraham Lincoln. "The masses
were swept away from their moorings, and reason destroyed," Dixon
wrote.[3] Reconstruction is then depicted as an imposition on the South,
carried out by crafty legislators modeled on real-life abolitionists like
Congressman Thaddeus Stevens. "We are a conquered race. The iron
hand of Fate is on us," laments one character, a white Southerner.[4] At
the nadir of cultural dissolution, the Grand Dragon of the KKK is able
to rally the high-minded: "Men of the South, the time for words has
passed, the hour for action has struck."[5] The big idea here is to effect
an extrajudicial killing of a Black man for sexually assaulting a white

woman—a long-running trope of American racism—then fling the body on the lawn of the Black lieutenant governor's home. The discovery of the body winds up sending "a thrill of terror to the triumphant leagues," so much so that "a gale of chivalrous passion and high action, contagious and intoxicating, swept the white race" into a "triumph ... of incredible grandeur."[6] Dixon's book cherishes one of the most singularly tragic sequences of events in American history, and its contents are glorified onscreen with *The Birth of a Nation*.

The *Clansman*, as a novel and play, and *The Birth of a Nation*, as a film, aren't fascist because they're racist. Though racism would emerge as a feature of the Nazi Party through its anti-Semitism, racism isn't a necessary ingredient of fascism. Benito Mussolini's rise demonstrated that racism isn't indispensable to fascism, as Italy did not turn to racist imperialism and anti-Semitism until a decade after he gained power. In fascism, different media are deployed strategically as part of a broader antidemocratic push. Indeed, fascism can only emerge from, and within, democracy itself. "Crucial to the whole process," the historian Richard J. Evans has written, "was the very way in which democracy's enemies exploited the democratic constitution and democratic political culture for their own ends."[7]

In much of the Western world, fascism leveraged the paradox to wage a battle against open society, combining various media in propaganda efforts to engineer spectacles—momentous experiences that overwhelmed public cultures of democracy. The time was ripe, both politically and culturally. The United States had begun to open more democratically, with progressive initiatives such as women's suffrage, the personal income tax, increased regulation on commerce, and direct elections for senators. The Europe that had surfaced from World War I featured constitutional republics possessing more democratic features. Accompanying this shift was the rise of new communication technologies, such as cinema and radio, which blended with more established cultural offerings such as tabloid newspapers, graphic posters, and book publishing. These media delivered not just technological transformations but new opportunities for social exchange, most notably evinced through the creative techniques of advertising and public relations. The result was a truly mass society and mass culture, blending entertainment and politics in novel ways. The wall between high and low culture, elite and popular art, private and public politics began to collapse.

But this wasn't a boon for popular rule. On the contrary, people were being manipulated in more sophisticated ways. New media and propaganda techniques helped prime the population for passive consumption. To Edward Bernays, the father of public relations and a nephew of Sigmund Freud's, propaganda organized the chaos of social life by engineering consent. Whereas universal literacy was supposed to liberate citizens to think for themselves, in what Bernays mocked as "the democratic doctrine," ideas and entertainment were merely purchased wholesale by the mass—with rubber stamps. "Modern propaganda," he wrote in 1928, "is a consistent, enduring effort to create or shape events to influence the relations of the public to an enterprise, idea or group."[8] The people, in this thinking, deserved to be influenced, needed to be influenced. For Bernays, propaganda was a public service. The only way the masses could make any sense of the world was to have it reduced to slogans and clichés. American culture was treated to commercialized advertising and entertainment meant to foster obsessions with celebrities and brands.

The Birth of a Nation featured another specific type of fascist content, expressed in mythic form. One scholar of fascism, Roger Griffin, refers to this as palingenesis, a framing device to emphasize cultural and national renewal.[9] The mythic core of palingenesis transcends time and space, flowing from some imagined past through a present that can be funneled into some spectacular future. For Dixon and Griffith, this meant facilitating the Lost Cause myth that the South was a noble culture threatened by Northern aggression and the empowerment of Black persons. The Invisible Empire of the KKK and its violent tactics are glamorized to the extent that they serve this Lost Cause myth, preserving the past by battling in the present to restore a future greatness. Fascism also promulgates the myth of sinister internal enemies that are simultaneously weak and devious. There is little coincidence, then, that in the fall of 1915, accompanying the release of *The Birth of a Nation*, the KKK regrouped. Taking advantage of the publicity for the film, which would premiere in nearby Atlanta two weeks later, William James Sim-

oply of American democracy, the Klan cloaked itself in white robes, masks, and high pointed hats as a pseudo-secret paramilitary organization. No true leader emerged, and a charismatic demagogue is needed to activate the full power of fascism. American life was nevertheless filled with domineering and sensational characters, people who flirted with fascism by exploiting media resources. William Randolph Hearst employed the slogan America First across his network of newspapers to oppose President Franklin Delano Roosevelt and his New Deal plan to combat the Great Depression. FDR was not above propaganda himself, initiating press conferences at the White House and delivering Fireside Chats on the radio. He also flirted with packing the Supreme Court and ran for president in four consecutive elections, exceeding the customary two that was later mandated as a constitutional amendment. Elsewhere, the governor-turned-senator from Louisiana, Huey Long, commanded attention with radio addresses promoting the formation of Share Our Wealth societies across the country. Before his assassination, Long also had presided over a tax on knowledge against large-circulation newspapers in the state in response to critical coverage; it was later overturned by the US Supreme Court. Perhaps the closest America came to experiencing the true face of fascism was Father Charles Coughlin, a radio personality who dominated the airwaves first on CBS and later on his own network, buoyed by his own magazine, *Social Justice*. Coughlin was anti-Semitic to the core, blaming Jewish conspiracies for the Great Depression and supporting Nazi Germany. He doctored telegrams and read them aloud on the air to suggest that American Jews were somehow responsible for the Bolshevik Revolution. Coughlin also flirted with the German-American Bund, which held a pro-Nazi rally for over twenty thousand people in New York City's Madison Square Garden, and then he championed the America First Committee, which opposed any European intervention. He was joined on the committee by the famed pilot Charles Lindbergh, who earned celebrity status for making the first solo transatlantic flight. Despite speculation that Lindbergh would challenge FDR for president, the aviator limited himself to delivering speeches opposing American's entry into World War II because of the German superiority in arms.

Against the backdrop of these fascist flirtations, an important shift

the *Nation* reporting from Tulsa "found it means that Negroes were uncompromisingly denouncing 'Jim-Crow' cars, lynching, peonage; in short, were asking that the Federal constitutional guarantees of 'life, liberty, and the pursuit of happiness' be given regardless of color."[14] Holmes would dissent again in the 1925 decision of *Gitlow v. New York*, which punished another socialist and upheld the state's Criminal Anarchy Law. Despite this setback, the majority acknowledged that the Fourteenth Amendment to the Constitution extended to the states and affirmed that free speech and free press were liberties of citizens in American democracy. In 1927, Brandeis wrote a concurring opinion for *Whitney v. California* which, joined by Holmes, declared that "deliberative forces should prevail over the arbitrary."[15] We might call this the essence of democracy. Deliberative forces require open communication, and while such forces may lead to exploitation, they nevertheless can serve as a check on arbitrary exercises of power.

All this served as a prelude to 1931 when a new chief justice of the United States, Charles Evans Hughes, authored the majority opinion in *Near v. Minnesota*. The 5–4 decision, which Holmes and Brandeis signed on to, upheld the rights of an anti-Semitic newspaper in the face of a Minnesota state law against public nuisances. Prior restraint was held unconstitutional by a slim margin, but in the words of Fred Friendly, the future radio and television producer, *Near* "infuse[d] with life and spirit an amendment which for 150 years had existed only as a basic skeleton."[16] The attorney representing Minnesota thought he had the case in the bag, suggesting that the law was purifying the press and that criticism of government was protected only if it was truthful. No, exclaimed the Jewish Brandeis in response. The whole point was to carve out space for power to be checked, regardless of truth. When the attorney then appealed to Holmes's previous decisions, the elderly justice sighed, admitting that he now possessed a different view. What *Near v. Minnesota* accomplished for a free press *Stromberg v. California* that same year would cement for free speech more generally. A state law banning the display of red flags as a symbol for opposing government was overturned 7–2, with Hughes again writing the majority opinion. The purpose of the First Amendment, he declared, was the "maintenance of the opportunity for free political discussion."[17] At a time when

in a fuguelike state of the mythopoetic imaginary. We saw this happen with Thomas Dixon and D. W. Griffith in America. Perhaps not coincidentally, European fascism also was initiated by a man of aesthetic talents. F. T. Marinetti, an Italian artist, led the futurism movement, which exalted speed, mixed media, and technology. Marinetti's first manifesto, from 1909, was disseminated widely, featured in newspapers all over Italy as well as in *Le Figaro* in Paris. His preface recounts the thrill of driving an automobile wildly. Tearing around bends in the road at breakneck speed, he approached a pair of cyclists, who frantically motioned him to drive past them. Their pleading, described as stupid and ridiculous, caused Marinetti to career into a ditch. As he emerged from the wreck, covered in grime, inspiration struck. Marinetti then dictated the principles of futurism, emphasizing "energy and recklessness" and "glorify[ing] aggressive action."[19] Time and space were dead, he declared. The automobile and the airplane inaugurated a new human perspective, and the velocity of modern life had to be harnessed as a force that could transcend reality. That could be accomplished with the blazing poetic form he created, known as words-in-freedom, but also with war, the great cleanser of the world, as he was fond of saying. To actualize this, futurism would need a political program whose sole purpose would be based on national pride, Marinetti later wrote.

A new aesthetic had thus been charted. The trite values of liberal democracy were dismissed as silly. Energy and aggression and violence were the lodestars of a vibrant new culture. Language was elastic and fungible, like glitter splattered across canvas. Parliament was a plodding sham, something to be overcome. Marinetti wasn't the most disciplined of figures, though, and certainly incapable of leading a mass movement. Fascism would not come to fruition until he collided with another enterprising media figure, Benito Mussolini, who possessed the necessary leadership principles. Both men became part of the nationalist, interventionist Left in Italy during World War I. Marinetti needed no convincing, but Mussolini, who had critiqued previous Italian imperial efforts, broke with the neutral popular socialist newspaper he edited, *Avanti!*, and began another, the Milan-based *Il Popolo d'Italia*, that championed the war effort. In mythical fashion, his columns insisted that Italy had a destiny of imperial greatness stretching back to the

Roman Empire. *Popolo d'Italia* encouraged protests against a liberal parliament seen as weak and eventually prodded the government to enter the war. It was the first time, but not the last, that democracy would buckle in the face of fascist encroachments. Both Marinetti and Mussolini volunteered to serve in the Allied forces and were wounded.

One might have expected the nationalist impulse to have been sated with the Italian victory at Vittorio Veneto, which resulted in the gains of Trieste and other places, but this only whetted the appetite for more Italian greatness. The port city of Fiume had been gifted to what would become the kingdom of Yugoslavia, a betrayal by Italy's erstwhile allies in concluding the war. Mussolini then called forth a *fasci di combattimento* in his newspaper, arguing that a political revolution ought to be galvanized. "It may or may not take a dramatic, sensational course. It may proceed on a faster tempo," he wrote on March 18, 1919. "As to the means? We have no formal principles. We accept whatever means may become necessary, the legal and the so-called illegal. A period is opening in history which might be defined as that of mass politics or of democratic hypertrophy."[20] When the new political party Fasci di combattimento met five days later, Marinetti was present. He reported reading a great destiny in Mussolini's face. The political platform issued from this initial meeting was surprisingly democratic in scope, calling for labor reforms and women's suffrage as well as standing firm on the need for freedom of conscience, the press, and political organization. It was also firmly against dictatorship. By the next month, however, members of this new party of "Fighting Leagues" burned down the offices of *Avanti!*, Mussolini's old paper, killing four people.

Fascism represents the zenith of the paradox, emerging from within democratic cultures to dominate and discard the enterprise. It demands democratic legitimacy and employs the free resources of open communication, but it rejects the very possibility of deliberation or debate. From the Latin *fasces*, bundled sticks with a protruding axe blade that symbolized a magistrate's authority in ancient Rome, the word *fascism* serves as a warning: we'll engage you in politicking, it says, but only with the symbolism and specter of violence ever possible and easily rationalized. Ahead of any totalitarian power grab, fascism arouses not just its own fervor but a chilling effect for others. It is animated by a desire to win public opinion on its own terms and at all costs. And yet the ostensible democratic nature of fascism is undercut by its own antidemocratic drives. This is partly why electoral success was something of a challenge for fascism, even at the height of its political power. While it could be seen as an explosion of populist energy, it struggled to secure a majority on its own and organically establish a government. Fascism relied on the abdication of democracy, which was, in the end, the whole point. Its great innovation was to initiate a pattern of fanaticism: use all the tools of communication at one's disposal to attain power, then close the loop with totalitarianism. Marinetti, for his part, may have figured this out. After a disastrous showing at the polls in the fall of 1919—the party garnered only a few thousand votes despite both men serving as candidates—he parted ways with Mussolini, calling him a megalomaniac.

That insight would be borne out, but not before Mussolini drew inspiration from the talents of another nationalist aesthete. In September of 1919, Gabriele D'Annunzio, the poet-playwright-soldier, worked with *arditi* shock-troop veterans to march on Fiume. It was an easy take. The goal was Italian annexation, but the government in Rome was reluctant to embrace such irredentism in the face of international pressure. D'Annunzio ran the city-state, declaring himself Comandante and the first Il Duce (The Leader). He established music as the state's central purpose. Some days he dressed as field marshal; others, as a Renaissance-era prince. One time he pretended to be Vladimir Lenin. The performances were fantastic, replete with daily parades saluting the *arditi*. D'Annunzio developed other political forms of pageantry that fascism would perfect: delivering speeches from balconies, developing catchy slogans, and having supporters wear black shirts. "We don't give a damn," chanted his famished backers, who were resorting to piracy to sustain themselves. From Milan, Mussolini served as his envoy to Italy, writing columns identifying Fiume, not Rome, as the true capital of Italy, and purporting to raise money for their brothers-in-arms. While he admired, even envied, the action, energy, and aggressiveness of D'Annunzio, Mussolini and his minions were also pocketing contributions meant for Fiume to subsidize their disastrous fall election campaign. Charges were filed, but Mussolini cut a deal to withdraw support for the Comandante in exchange for a free hand at funding his own paramilitary outfit, the *squadristi*.

The Italian military attacked Fiume on Christmas Eve 1920, to the notable silence of *Popolo d'Italia*. Mussolini obtained what he had coveted, some semblance of government recognition. He also may have observed that Marinetti and D'Annunzio lacked the ability to develop party hierarchy, strategic politicking, and totalizing propaganda. Mussolini's ability to adapt and control became a key to his success. Futurism offered a splendid imaginary, but it needed a practical side to its mythos. To this Mussolini offered a future that would recapture the glory of Romanita, an archaeological movement driven by the symbols of the ancient empire. His elasticity did not stop there. From the republican principles of the first fascist platform, the line now was strife as the origin of all things. Here Mussolini was assisted by not just the violent *squadre* but a system of fanatical local bosses called the *ras*, featuring the likes of Roberto Farinacci and Cesare Rossi, who edited another propaganda publication, the weekly *Il fascio*. Both would become central figures in Mussolini's later concentration of power. This more organized political structure netted the fascists thirty-five parliamentary seats in the elections held in May of 1921.

Clearly, Mussolini was no longer just some flagrant journalist or the political leader of a band of rabble-rousers. Despite notching less than 10 percent of the vote, he and the fascists now sat as members of the Chamber of Deputies. Later that year, a name change was in order: Mussolini was now in charge of the National Fascist Party. The next eighteen months were chaotic for Italian democracy, as the old guard struggled to rule as a majority and a banking collapse threatened the national economy. Violent altercations broke out between fascists and socialists. Mussolini initially agreed to a pacification pact to halt these acrimonious exchanges, suggesting that the Bolshevik threat had passed. Subsequently considered a turncoat by his followers, he quickly reneged and encouraged more battles in the streets. The militaristic rhetoric morphed into a dark reality. Too bad, Mussolini exclaimed, if some participants on either side died or were wounded. Fascists would bludgeon their opponents, and if one of their own should happen to fall, they'd throw a celebratory funeral that served to redouble the commitment of the followers.

Fascism relies on intransigence. Mussolini refused to engage or compromise. He turned down a cabinet post and an opportunity to contribute to a governing coalition. All along, his true target, as with all fascists, was democracy itself. To his mind, democracy had grown drunk on compromise and found itself paralyzed by "words, words, and more words—parliamentary and journalistic sham battles."[21] But to achieve what it wants, fascism also requires spectacle. It needs to establish, and continue, momentous occasions of political awe for a mass culture to experience. As Robert O. Paxton indicates, fascism is full of "exciting political spectacle and clever publicity techniques" as well as "the propagandistic manipulation of public opinion [to] replace debate about complicated issues."[22] With Mussolini, all this culminated in publicity for the March on Rome, to be held in late October of 1922, that would treat him as a great Roman general flanked by Blackshirts. The program was simple enough, Mussolini had admitted to the thousands gathered in Naples at the Fascist Congress shortly before the event. Fascists wanted to be in charge, to rule. "Our myth is the greatness of the nation," he continued. "And to this myth, this greatness, which we want to translate into a total reality, we subordinate everything else."[23] Blackshirts then seized municipal government offices in northern Italy and occupied railroad and telegraph stations. This new world valued the control of information and movement, as Marinetti imagined, and Mussolini figured out how to capture it. The official fascist announcement heralding the march promised it was not against the military, the people, or public order but limited to confronting the imbeciles and delinquents in charge of politics. Some fifty thousand fascist supporters gathered outside the Eternal City. That was enough. The mere threat of this impending spectacle of a mass demonstration coerced the sitting prime minister to resign and led King Victor Emmanuel III to have a proxy cable Mussolini, still in Milan, that he was welcome to form a new government—even though the various Italian fascist parties had never marshaled a majority, let alone a plurality, of votes. Democracy folded, as the fascists might have suspected. Mussolini took the reins of government, allowed his people to have a more subdued victory parade a couple days later, and then instructed them to clear out. In his first speech to the Chamber of Deputies, he taunted the legislators by calling them zealots of constitutionalism. He added that while he could have precipitated a massacre, he exercised restraint ... for now.

That time would come soon enough. Fascists, inspired by their Duce's rise to power, almost immediately burned down the offices of the *Avanti!* in Milan, again. Within a year, Mussolini ordered the beating and arrest of Raffaele Rossetti, the famous war hero, who dared utter, "Down with fascism." As the Duce would claim in speeches, "In internal politics, there is nothing to discuss; what is happening is happening by my precise and direct will and under my orders."[24] A royal decree was issued tamping down on freedom of the press, and Mussolini personally cabled the police chief of Turin to make life difficult for one journalist in particular, Piero Gobetti. A secret Cheka, based on the Soviet secret police, was formed, headed in part by Cesare Rossi, who took orders directly from Mussolini. The Acerbo Law was passed in 1923 as well. Sensing the continued inability of the National Fascist Party to win a majority or form a coalition, the new law handed the top party a two-thirds majority in parliament. The government created its own magazine, *Hierarchy*, in which Mussolini declared that liberalism was fine for the nineteenth century. Men were tired of liberty, he suggested, comparing its emphasis of consent to the shifting sands of a seashore. How could it truly exist or be entirely supplied? "No government," admitted the head of Italian government, "has ever existed which has managed to make everybody it governed happy."[25]

It is perhaps a fair point, and it hints at what the political theorist Richard Wollheim articulated as the paradox of democracy. This paradox is about consent, not communication. It is related to the paradox we're describing but more theoretical. Wollheim, who wasn't drawing from Mussolini but reached the same conclusion, articulates how democratic citizens continually face a fundamental contradiction. Your right to support or oppose a candidate or policy is assured, but if another candidate is elected, or an alternative policy is passed, you'll find yourself against someone or something while in fact supporting it, as a democratic citizen. Mussolini positioned fascism to solve this paradox of consent, specifically to justify the use of force at the service of the state. Fascist violence only ever occurred in self-defense, he claimed. Such thinking is ridiculous but not illogical. Total consent is impossible, so totalizing the political sphere is seen as a reasonable countermeasure. This helps fascists, as they abide neither criticism nor competition. They want legitimacy, but fascism can only deliver illusion, which is why film became such an important medium. The spectacle of reality could be transcended as a political instrument. D. W. Griffith proved this well enough in his imagining of the end of Reconstruction. For Mussolini, film provided an opportunity to have his March on Rome. Keep in mind, however, that the event never actually took place. The anticlimax did result in his achievement of power, but thanks to an American film produced by Samuel Goldwyn in 1923, *The Eternal City* featured Mussolini and King Victor Emmanuel witnessing the march from a balcony.

Even with the Acerbo Law in effect to tip the scales, the elections in the spring of 1924 were marked by fascist intimidation at the polls. Mussolini's party would "win" a plurality, but before the new government was seated, charges of political fraud had been leveled in parliament by the democratic-socialist opposition leader, Giacomo Matteotti. Earlier that year, he had published a book outlining the corruption and antidemocratic tendencies of the first year of fascist rule and was hard at work on a second. He was a funny, studious man. When at the end of May Mussolini hissed at him in the Chamber of Deputies to be brief and conclude his remarks, Matteotti said he would limit himself to crude facts. He then proceeded to read aloud newspaper accounts of fascist violence and ballot stuffing. After the fascist backbenchers called him a liar for reporting that a Genovese politician had been hospitalized for a blackjack attack, Matteotti suggested that maybe the man was devoted to Saint Francis and had flagellated himself. Mussolini seethed with rage. As Matteotti took his leave of a wrathful Duce, he remarked, "And now, my colleagues, you may prepare my funeral oration for the Chamber."[26] He knew well: the day before, a disappointed fascist legislator, Alfredo Misuri, had delivered a public rebuke to Mussolini and was promptly beaten and expelled from the party. Days later, Mussolini would anonymously author an editorial for *Popolo d'Italia* encouraging violence against Matteotti's person. Charges of electoral fraud were one thing. But Matteotti, as enterprising an investigative journalist as he was a vigorous opposition leader, had also discovered a secret deal with the American company Sinclair Oil—mired at the time in the Teapot Dome scandal—which stood to enrich government insiders and Mussolini's brother. Moreover, the kickbacks were also intended to subsidize fascist propaganda. Matteotti was slated to deliver a speech on June 11 outlining the corruption as well as publish a piece laying it out in a British magazine later that summer.

The article would be published posthumously. The anticipated speech was never delivered. Matteotti was abducted in broad daylight on June 10. The discovery of his body in August caused a sensation that threatened to implicate Mussolini himself as it exposed the Cheka. Though Mussolini protested otherwise and the *New York Times*, of all publications, provided him with cover, he was absolutely complicit.[27] In December of 1924, Rossi, the propagandist who led the Cheka, felt somewhat abandoned in jail—as did the other perpetrators. He was eventually released, but not before publishing a memo in *Il mondo* taking responsibility for arranging other beatings but not Matteotti's murder. Mussolini was, if nothing else, candid in response: the violence was his responsibility, he told parliament in January 1925, for he was in complete charge of the propaganda campaign. From there, new laws against press freedom were issued. A legal amnesty was declared for political violence in service to the state, and the few who were convicted of Matteotti's murder, defended by Roberto Farinacci in court, spent less than a year in prison. Rewarded for his fanaticism, Farinacci was appointed head of the party and led a purge of members. He extolled the virtues of force and maintained that politically, fascism ought to render its internal enemies innocuous.

One such enemy was the editor of *Il mondo*, Giovanni Amendola, who had been assaulted five times. The sixth time proved fatal. In 1925, he was tracked down by a fascist mob who clubbed him so severely that he succumbed to his injuries the next year in France. Shortly before he died, Amendola had cabled a friend: "The Fascisti have abolished parliament, and so I have lost my liberty of speech. They have abolished the liberty of the press and so I no longer write. They have assassinated me and so I have lost the liberty to live. All this is nothing. The evil is that they will end by assassinating Italy."[28] Another journalist, the satirist Piero Gobetti, was similarly clubbed to death. The politician and historian Luigi Albertini, who edited Italy's most circulated newspaper, *Corriera della sera*, was forced to resign. Despite all this, Mussolini insisted that Italy enjoyed the freest press in the world, liberated from the burden of reporting on political squabbles and sensational crimes. The militant, muscular journalism he so desperately craved, and forced, was encapsulated by a phrase coined by the right-wing journalist Leo Longanesi: "Mussolini is always right."

The scholarly consensus is that Fascist Italy never achieved a full totalitarian state, defined as complete bureaucratic control by a central party over every aspect of society—as in, say, the Soviet Union and Nazi Germany. This may owe to the designs of a corporate state or the general disorganization and geographic diversity of Italian society. Or the frantic reversals of policy directions that Mussolini oversaw. Whatever the quibble, there is no doubt Fascist Italy was most certainly *politically* totalitarian. The term itself can be traced to the murdered journalist Amendola, who used it to warn of what was to come. It was then reappropriated by the fascist scholar Giovanni Gentile, who served as Mussolini's minister of education and was tasked in 1925 with overseeing constitutional reforms. To Gentile, totalitarianism marked the possession of a certain ethical substance that afforded a total conception of life. The official new constitution of the National Fascist Party, completed in 1926, began by proclaiming its aim to realize the greatness of the Italian people, a greatness that would birth a pure Italian consciousness. This is all fairly vague stuff, but it evinces the maximum flexibility fascism offers: it consists of whatever can be enveloped in the mythos of a greatness destiny and the personality cult of a nationalist leader. Policies don't matter so long as a democracy of free expression, from speech to press to political organizing, is snuffed out. Fascism, in other words, uses communications propaganda to disrupt a civil society. Upon obtaining power, propaganda is then weaponized as spectacle to serve the myth of the state and its leader. This is the fascist move, as discovered by Antonio Gramsci, a communist member of parliament who was arrested in late 1926. From prison, where he would spend the rest of his life before dying of a series of maladies in 1937, he wrote a series of notebooks that were smuggled out and later published. The public under fascism, he observed, "is kept happy by means of moralizing sermons, emotional stimuli, and messianic myths of an awaited golden age, in which all present contradictions and miseries will be automatically solved and made well."[29]

The propaganda effort continued with a convergence of media forms in the late 1920s and the 1930s. Crowds gathered in town squares to listen to Mussolini's speeches on loudspeakers, which broadcast his radio addresses promoting the Ethiopian and Albanian invasion campaigns. Strikingly, he seemed able to command the attention if not the assistance of Americans in his desire to generate propaganda. The US ambassador who prepared the Duce's 1928 autobiography—which was serialized in the *Saturday Evening Post*—noted in the preface that not an insincere line could be found in what followed. The politics of fascism under Mussolini were such a joyful game, he wrote. Indeed. Fascism, at a very deep level, is a fantastic show that corrupts the high-minded and lower orders alike. Mussolini was featured in glowing terms through the various newsreels put out by the Hearst syndicate, and in 1933, at the height of his international fame, Columbia Pictures produced a documentary, *Mussolini Speaks*. Its promotional poster promised a look into a man who was making history. The film was narrated by a prominent radio newsman, Lowell Thomas. "No matter his politics," Thomas instructed in voice-over. "What matters is his personal magnetism." In the end, that was all that was left—the sad, pathetic egoism of a megalomaniacal dictator. Maybe that's all there ever was. Fascism, having done away with democracy, emptied itself of any direction other than the stylings and whims of Ducismo. Mussolini discarded trusted advisors and sought imperial adventures to overcome internal sclerosis. While the Italian fascists at first looked askance at the anti-Semitism of the Nazi regime, they wound up as followers by passing their own racial laws and contributing to the Holocaust. The Duce's big break came back in 1914 when he egged Italy on to dissolve an alliance with the Germans; his downfall, ultimately, was throwing in with them. By the end, he had been in charge of only a small redoubt in northern Italy thanks to his German pals, and then gruesomely executed by partisans before he could flee to Switzerland.

The legacy of Italian fascism is its smashing up of democracy from within, using myth, propaganda, and charismatic leadership as catalysts. What ought to concern us about the Italian experience is that fascism is predicated on the tools of democracy itself. There is a reason fascism does not rise in established authoritarian countries, despite its own designs on dictatorship. It is, fundamentally, a challenge to democracy relying on an aesthetic sensibility to debase the exchange of political discourse. Fascism wasn't limited to Italy either, for its rise to power became an inspiration for an Austrian veteran of the German army in World War I. Toward the end of that conflict, Adolf Hitler took civic training courses on public morale with the military, and his first appointment in the National Socialist German Workers' (Nazi) Party was in 1920 as the head of propaganda planning. But long before that, before his move to Germany, he had been a failed artist living in Vienna. As with Mussolini and other fascists, this aesthetic sensibility proved useful. Hitler also possessed the necessary ingredients of fascism writ large: mythical delusions of nationalist grandeur, a belief in his own superior leadership, and a burning hatred of democracy. In this man there was no grand philosophy of the *Übermensch* that he inherited from the likes of Nietzsche. More likely, the young Hitler admired the straightforward anti-Semitic politics of Vienna's mayor, Karl Lueger, and, in coming to Germany before the war, the racist work of the journalist and politician Theodor Fritsch, one of the first Europeans to appropriate the swastika symbol.

Like other young veterans, Hitler felt betrayed by the November Revolution of 1918 that led to the abdication of the monarchy, the loss of World War I, and the beginnings of the Weimar Republic. Whereas the Italian fascists were unhappy with the terms of success following their victory in the Great War, for many Germans the terms of surrender, both internally and externally, were shattering. Democracy, many believed, sprang from the *Dolchstoss im Rücken* (stab in the back) myth, according to which Germany was sabotaged by socialist political leaders, Jews, and an unruly press. These feelings were particularly pronounced in Bavaria, where the Jewish socialist Kurt Eisner had declared a People's State. During the war, Eisner, a journalist, had published unflattering evidence of Germany's instigation of the hostilities, and was arrested on treason charges. He was assassinated in early 1919 by a disgruntled nationalist from Austria who had served in the German military. It was not in fact Hitler but someone else with a similar biography. All the same, an example had been set.

The early years of the Weimar Republic were politically combustible. There were communist insurrections to put down and onerous financial terms from the Treaty of Versailles to meet, causing inflation and a lack of available capital. But 1919 marked the start of something new. Representation was fair, and women could vote. Article 118 of the constitution guaranteed Germans free expression and prohibited censorship. While newspaper publishing tended to be low circulation and highly partisan, radio, under the aegis of the post office, had been introduced right before the 1919 elections. Its rise was complemented by a spike in new magazines and the formation of German expressionist filmmaking. The man elected president, Friedrich Ebert, was a former journalist who served until his death in 1925. Ebert exercised Article 48 of the constitution, which granted him emergency powers to suspend civil rights, over one hundred times, and he continually filed libel suits against critical newspapers. Though he didn't win a single one of these claims, the repeated assaults on the press weren't a good sign. Nor was the increasing media consolidation of Alfred Hugenberg, who served in the Reichstag from 1920 onward and became a leader of the German National People's Party. His Hugenberg Trust controlled a features syndicate and an advertising agency that matted out premade copy for newspapers around the country. It also controlled the nation's commercial telegraph infrastructure as well as a film company.[30] Ebert and Hugenberg should not be blamed for the carnage that followed, but their illiberal machinations show how fascism spins out of a democratic culture. There is always the temptation to abandon democracy when it becomes inconvenient or in times of crisis. Indeed, democracy itself becomes the crisis along with all the institutions that prop it up — such as a free press. In many ways, fascists are the most attuned to the paradox; they recognize that democracy can unspool. Its openness becomes a means to power.

Hitler was impressed by Mussolini's March on Rome in 1922. A year later, he sought to create the conditions of a similar spectacle in Germany in the hopes that it would lead to an overthrow of the government. The Italian fascists had their Blackshirts, and the Nazis had their Storm Division of Brownshirts along with the Kampfbund, or Combat League. Mussolini gave rousing speeches and drew from his daily newspaper; Hitler equaled if not surpassed his Italian counterpart in dynamic oratory and made use of the Nazi daily print organ, the *Volkischer Beobachter*, along with the weekly *Der Stürmer*. The latter was published by Julius Streicher, whose avowed anti-Semitism surpassed even that of the young Führer. Hitler also oversaw the creation of placards and leaflets with abandon. It was early information warfare, which Germans were familiar with from World War I. In that conflict's late stages, the British propaganda office, headed by the media mogul Lord Northcliffe and staffed by such figures as H. G. Wells, orchestrated a campaign to flood the German population with four million leaflets promising the virtues of democracy. The grand idea behind the Beer Hall Putsch of 1923 was to overwhelm democracy by first controlling Bavaria. This would be done by holding the state's legal and political representatives hostage and coercing them to surrender the powers of government. Elsewhere, municipal and military holdings were to be seized and official communications controlled. Then the real march, to Berlin, could commence. Hitler hoped to make use of Erich Ludendorff, a World War I hero, as cover. At the Burgerbräukeller on the evening of November 8, shots were fired, hostages were taken, and free beer was passed out. Hitler's bodyguard unit, the Stosstrupp—an early forerunner to the SS—proceeded soon after to smash up the presses at the *Münchener Post*, and a press conference was held instructing other newspapers to publish good tidings about the new state. Unfortunately for the Nazis, they could not, like their Italian brethren, usurp telephone and telegraph offices. Military units had been alerted and sent to end the putsch, and the police force did not flip as expected. By the next morning, the insurrectionists were surrounded. Unable to mount an actual civil war, Hitler and the gang decided to concoct a Nazi parade through Munich.

There are some doubts as to who shot first, but over a dozen individuals died in the ensuing skirmish, including four police officers. Fallen Nazis were memorialized as martyrs, both in the immediate aftermath and through later party propaganda. "Through them," wrote Harold Gordon Jr., "ignominious failure was made into glorious defiance of tyranny."[31] Hitler bruised his shoulder but made an escape. Discovered a few days later, he was charged with treason. The resulting trial did not go to waste. This was an even greater platform of spectacle than the putsch itself. With a sympathetic judge whose sole goal, it appears, was to ensure Ludendorff was acquitted, Hitler was given leeway to address the court and, by extension, the nation at large. He caused a sensation that rationalized the entire fiasco and laid the groundwork for more fascist myth. On the first day, he deemed the November Revolution a terrible catastrophe; its perpetrators were the real traitors, he insisted, and the ensuing republic ought never to have been recognized as legal. In such a task as nationalizing the will of the German people, it would have been too easy and cheap to run for parliament. Hitler then managed, as all fascists do, to cast himself as the embodiment of the state, fulfilling its destiny. Newspapers throughout the country seized on the story. Hitler's monologues were a big hit. Although he was convicted of treason and sentenced to a five-year prison term, the court concluded that the perpetrators had acted out of a patriotic spirit.

Hitler had served less than a year before the Nazi Party agitated to set him free, albeit under parole orders to avoid politicking for a time. Hitler's time in prison didn't go to waste either, as he spent his sentence comfortably dictating his autobiography, *Mein Kampf*, a work of apocalyptic fantasy. It was here his anti-Semitism developed into a rabid obsession. The book is also preoccupied with space—specifically, the right of Germans to settle land to the east. The text is largely unhinged and often muddled, but it contains a deeply thought-out section on propaganda. You can see Hitler's post-prison plans taking shape: "The first task of propaganda is to win people for subsequent organization; the first task of organization is to win men for the continuation of propaganda."[32] The second task of propaganda, he added, is "the disruption of the existing state of affairs." The putsch had been disorganized and something of a pipe dream. Hitler now recognized that he needed more than mere specters of paramilitary violence; he needed to amass support throughout the whole of Germany and work from within the system, since the system itself provided the means to its own demise. To that end, he recruited a failed novelist and literary PhD, Joseph Goebbels.

The two shared, according to one scholar of Nazi propaganda, "a fervid nationalism, a craving for power, [and] contempt for the masses coupled with a belief in their manipulation."[33] Their passion coincided with a deep hatred of democracy, whose basis of equality, Goebbels felt, was suited to blockheads. Though he started out more a socialist than a nationalist and was initially skeptical of Hitler, Goebbels admired his rhetorical gifts. He even noted in his journal that Hitler, with a little coaching, could conquer the world. Hitler appointed Goebbels to the position of Berlin Gauleiter (party leader of a regional branch) in 1926, and the Nazis began to cast a wider net. Goebbels's great contribution to Nazism was his keen understanding of mass media. In particular, he believed that singular rhetorical acts were ultimately less important than sustained saturation. Public opinion wasn't some precise thing to be courted or measured; politics were about manufacturing a mood. Propaganda, he felt, must continually establish and perpetuate power, and that required deploying all the media tools available. And it was important not merely to flood the masses with a uniform message but to overwhelm their sensations with spectacular content. Naturally, Goebbels began by taking over the Berlin-based newspaper, *Der Angriff* (The attack), whose motto was For the Suppressed against the Exploiters! Posters promoting the publication abounded, and the paper featured columns signed off by Dr. G. and anti-Semitic political cartoons by Hans Schweitzer, whose pen name was The Hammer. At first, proceeds from party carnivals had to subsidize the paper; within a couple of years, *Der Angriff* generated so much advertising revenue that it was backing Nazi campaign activities all over Germany. The events themselves were no longer harangues hounding citizens into submission. The focus, Nicholas O'Shaughnessy writes, "was also on entertainment as well as organized outrage, and the numerous party-devised rallies and speaker meetings were not presented as grim duties for the faithful but as exciting events."[34]

After garnering less than 3 percent of the vote in the 1928 elections, Goebbels and Hitler recalibrated. Their anti-Semitism was toned down or at least made more selective—so much so that Ludendorff called the Führer a traitor to the cause. Solidarity was stressed. This period revealed the Nazis at their most fascistic: not because their rhetoric was devoid of dangerous themes, but because it stressed the myth of German greatness as a destiny that could transcend the crises of the Weimar Republic. Hitler insisted that democracy could be overcome. The economic crash of 1929 certainly helped their cause; it really did seem that the structure of government was incapable of meeting the challenges of the day. In 1930, the Nazis reached 18 percent of the vote and Goebbels was named the party's propaganda director. As the economy continued to decay and parliamentary governing coalitions failed to form, 1932 would provide three election opportunities. A year of spectacle ensued. Hitler flew around the country in zeppelins to deliver speeches while loudspeakers bellowed at open-air rallies. The cinema and radio offered new ways to communicate, and there were still newspapers, leaflets, and posters. The Nazis lost the presidency in a runoff, as the aging Paul von Hindenburg was reelected, but they managed a plurality of votes in the Reichstag in each of the other elections.

Conventional wisdom holds that fascist propaganda is grounded in the repetition of racism, violence, and lies. Fascism facilitated this tactic, but only at the level of content. More important, for propaganda at least, is structure—specifically, the structuring of reality that only forms of communication can shape. At the level of interpersonal communication, whether spoken or printed, persuasion is largely transactional. It needs to be convincing. A mass media environment combining reproduced images, sound, and text is different. It's absorbing, sensual. Goebbels and Hitler discovered how this communicative world could be influenced by an omnipresence or comprehensiveness of forms. They twisted the kaleidoscope through which people experience reality and rendered it flush with marches and parades, speeches and radio sound, leaflets and pamphlets, banners and posters, newspapers and newsreels. Oratory and print mattered just as much as electronic media. The implications of each medium and the rhetorical bits of propaganda were less important than their overall synergy. Fascism relies on spreading the field, a totalizing effect pertaining to what people know and how they are moved. Here is where the Nazis excelled, and it only accelerated as they assumed power.

Hindenburg and the old guard thought they could control Hitler in January 1933, when they appointed him chancellor. Nazis would be outnumbered in the cabinet, and Franz von Papen would serve as vice chancellor. Another round of elections was scheduled for that March. Maybe, the conservatives wagered, the fascist moment would be short-lived. The night of Hitler's ascension, a Nazi torch-lit parade was held in Berlin, the marchers circling the streets to make the crowd seem larger than it was. Goebbels provided play-by-play coverage on a live radio broadcast: it was a great awakening of the people, he exclaimed, and a frenzy of excitement. In late February, the Reichstag, which housed Germany's parliament, burned down. A communist was suspected and arrested. And so there was another act of capitulation—though not the last—as Hindenburg agreed to invoke the emergency decree powers of Article 48. Civil liberties were discarded and newspapers shut down. Political parties and the right of assembly were attenuated. State governments could be overridden, thereby calling for police action to be dictated from the federal level. The entire networked system of postal mail, telephones, and telegraph lines was seized, and Goebbels helped himself to total control of the radio airwaves. Such an environment allowed the Nazis to eclipse 40 percent of the vote, though a majority would elude them.

It didn't matter. Within a few weeks, Goebbels headed the Reich Ministry of Public Enlightenment and Propaganda; Heinrich Himmler led the SS, announcing plans for a concentration camp in Dachau where political prisoners would be remanded; and the Enabling Act passed on March 23, 1933. For the latter, the new German parliament agreed to render itself obsolete, and Hindenburg, in one last abdication of democracy before he died, signed on. On that day, Hitler signaled the government's intention to wage a systematic campaign to restore the eternal values of the German people. The entire cultural media apparatus, from the press and theater to film and broadcasting, would be harnessed to make this so, he declared. Which made sense. As Hannah Arendt, the German Jewish philosopher, pointed out in her landmark work, *The Origins of Totalitarianism*, mass leaders start out lying in order to create a reality marked by the hidden forces of history. Their contempt for facts is a necessity. Then, after they seize power, the time then comes "to make their predictions come true."[35] This they would accomplish not only through media propaganda but by capturing the entire edifice of culture. It was fitting, then, that the Reich Chamber of Culture was added to Goebbels's portfolio of responsibility. The Nazis began disrupting live performances in opera houses, symphony halls, and theaters. The age of Jewish intellectualism, Goebbels declared, was over. Art criticism was prohibited, a thousand magazines were shuttered, and book-burning spectacles were organized as the institutions of higher learning had to be brought in line.

The Nazi Party had willing accomplices in academe such as the esteemed philosopher Martin Heidegger, a party member who served as rector at the University of Freiburg. It mattered little to Heidegger that his Jewish mentor, Edmund Husserl, had been barred from campus activities or that his former student and lover, Arendt, had been arrested. When a plebiscite on whether to approve the Nazis and withdraw from the League of Nations was scheduled for that November, he captured the enthusiasm of the fascist project in a speech to students. "The national socialist revolution is bringing about the total transformation of our German existence," he had told them shortly before the vote, adding, "The Fuhrer alone is the present and future German reality and law."[36] Showing such support would help students do away with pesky propositions and mere ideas. Apparently, National Socialism provided the distinct opportunity for discovering Being on its own terms.

Heidegger wasn't the only prominent intellectual to dream of clearing a political space beyond democracy. During the Weimar days of the 1920s, Carl Schmitt developed a theoretical critique first of democracy and then liberalism, teasing them out as distinct problematic ventures. He was perceptive, if nothing else, in articulating how liberalism seeks to depoliticize the public. It's helpful to distinguish democracy from liberalism in this regard. But by 1932, with the publication of *The Con-*

cept of The Political, Schmitt had laid his cards on the table: "The specific political distinction to which political actions and motives can be
reduced is that between friend and enemy."[37] Here was the root of the
thing. Not politics, mind you, but the political itself. Wipe away the
former and the essence of political life stands revealed: there is "us" and
"them." The idea at the core of this thinking is that we can dispense with
the vulgarity of democratic politics and get down to the real business
of the political. Fascism thus promised a telos of unity that could stand
above the frustrations of democratic life.

And when the time finally came for the Nazis to consolidate their
power, they were ready. Schmitt had an opportunity to put his theory
of the political into action as a jurist. When Alfred Hugenberg, the conservative cabinet member and media mogul, finally sensed where the
Nazi game was headed, he threatened to step down and thereby end the
viability of the Enabling Act. Not so, argued Schmitt; the Enabling Act
itself actualized a different form of government, dictatorship, which
rendered democracy a moot option. The Weimar Republic was officially over, no matter who served in the cabinet. Hugenberg was too
late, his media power superseded.

To amass support in 1934 after their sham elections, their purges like
the Night of the Long Knives, and their general harassment of Jews, the
Nazis constructed their Nuremberg Rally for the big screen. The rally
had been held annually since the 1920s, but this time the filmmaker
Leni Riefenstahl stage-managed everything for her propaganda film
Triumph of the Will. That meant planning sets custom made for what
the camera could capture. The architect Albert Speer helped by constructing a Cathedral of Light to overpower the visual senses. The 1934
rally was one of the world's first pseudo-events, in the sense that it was
constructed for screening purposes only. When footage was ruined,
speeches were filmed weeks later and then spliced in with the rest.
The juxtaposition of shots of Hitler with those of the gathered crowds
exhibit an erotic dominance. Hitler had wooed the masses, and they,
for their part, couldn't help but swoon. Riefenstahl's works, as Susan
Sontag wrote, "are epics of achieved community in which everyday
reality is transcended through ecstatic self-control and submission;
they are about the triumph of power."[38] This created meaning contin-

ued with *Olympia*, Riefenstahl's 1936 portrayal of the Berlin Olympics. The film is obsessed with beauty, particularly bodies that encapsulated the Aryan ideal. Swooping camera angles focus in on the athletic grace of smooth speed and sinewy muscle while in the background perfect clouds rest just so. These athletes weren't jocks engaged in competition; they were gods to be exalted. The filmmaking, technically speaking, was as innovative as Griffith's *Birth of a Nation*, its central ideology equally as noxious.

Yet the astounding individual acts of fascist propaganda paled in comparison to the Nazi command of communications more generally. Once more, Joseph Goebbels understood the need for constant attention and overwhelming symbolic force. He and his various offices made innovative forays into broadcast television as people gathered to watch live transmissions, such as the opening ceremonies of the 1936 Olympic Games. Whereas feature-length films consume a great deal of time, newsreels could be quickly dashed off and shown in movie theaters. And the radio was particularly useful; Goebbels's weekly addresses framed newspaper coverage for the coming week, highlighting the supposed menace of Jewish citizens. He did know how to sensationalize an event, as when he whipped himself into a frenzy in his radio responses to the murder of a German diplomat in France in late 1938. That fever pitch triggered Kristallnacht, or the Night of Broken Glass, which destroyed Jewish homes, businesses, and synagogues. Importantly, this marked the first instance of Jews being rounded up and sent to concentration camps for no other reason than their religious affiliation. Thirty thousand in all were transported to the camps after this event—just the start of what would grow to millions in a systematic campaign of extermination, joined by an all-out war that ravaged the Continent.

One reason fascism succeeded (to the extent it did) in Italy and Germany, as opposed to other parts of Europe, is that the movements in these two countries dominated the public sphere across various media through the deployment of overwhelming propaganda. Only through creative and structural propaganda can fascism breathe life into its core myth, and only in the petri dish of democracy can it germinate. But it was hardly a sure thing politically. Many fascists throughout Europe had failed to gain traction. In western Europe, Georges Valois, who created the first French fascist party, le Faisceau, in 1925, imagined the Left and Right coming together for "national solidarity and *grandeur*."[39] The party didn't last beyond 1927. Fascist sympathizers would be rewarded, however, as a Jewish prime minister, Leon Blum, was hounded out of office in the 1930s in the run-up to the German invasion and the Vichy government. The British Union of Fascists (BUF) arose in 1932 behind Oswald Mosley, who imagined a "Greater Britain" in a book of the same name. Mosley oversaw the creation of two newspapers, the *Blackshirt* and *Action*. As support did not translate to parliamentary success, its propaganda director, William Joyce, increasingly moved BUF into a more explicitly anti-Semitic direction that led to violent confrontations. This did not attract BUF a large following, though Joyce went on to infamy as Lord Haw-Haw, providing Nazi propaganda over the radio airwaves during World War II.

In Eastern Europe, Gyula Gömbös rose to popularity with his visions of Greater Hungary and anti-Semitism. Though he vowed to eschew the latter—and did—upon being appointed to power by Regent Miklós Horthy, in the wake of Gömbös's death another fascist party, the Arrow Cross, emerged. It defined itself as Hungarist, and while failing electorally in the late 1930s, its leader, Ferenc Szálasi, gained prominence in his appointment to lead the violent, Nazi-backed regime during the last year of World War II. The Ustashe, led by Ante Pavelić, sought a similar goal in its designs for a Greater Croatia, whose destiny, he alleged, had been spoiled by integrating centuries before with Bosniak Muslims and Serbian Orthodox Christians. Whereas the Ustashe struggled to generate popularity in Yugoslavia, it was installed into power with the backing of Fascist Italy and Nazi Germany in 1941. Romanian fascism, meanwhile, offered its own brand of national destiny after the charismatic C. Z. Codreanu founded the Legion of the Archangel Michael in 1927. The Legionaries, who were also referred to as the Iron Guard, wore green shirts, as Codreanu developed not so much a political platform as a transcendental fervor for "national salvation."[40] They, like the Arrow Cross from Hungary, failed to garner so much as 20 percent of the vote in national elections.

In Spain, fascism began with Juntas de Ofensiva Nacional-Sindicalista (JONS) as the dictatorship of General Miguel Primo de Rivera faltered in 1930. JONS found little to no success until Primo de Rivera's son, José Antonio, spearheaded a more respectable brand of fascism, with mainstream conservative backing, in the Falange Española Party late in 1933. The parties merged in 1934, but the younger Primo de Rivera did not possess the necessary enthusiasm (or shame) to facilitate a fascist spectacle of myth. Within a couple of years, he was referring to members of his own party as fascist windbags. Such mixed messages perhaps had an effect, as Falange amassed only 0.7 percent of the vote in the 1936 elections that served as a prelude to the Spanish Civil War. The confusion about fascism's relationship to Spain from the 1930s owes to the fact that right-wing forces in that conflict were referred to as fascist, and Generalissimo Francisco Franco's forty-year dictatorship of Spain was presided over by a one-party state, whose name was Falange Española Tradicionalista de la JONS. This "traditionalist" aspect of Spanish dictatorship featured very little myth or spectacle, as the masses were mostly dulled into compliance. Franco and his supporters were by no means committed antifascists, but the conservative right-wing dictatorship that followed Spain's initial fascist movement should not be confused with fascism as such. Though Hitler and Mussolini provided material support to Franco's forces during the Spanish Civil War, the Generalissimo wouldn't return the favor.

A tour through the early history of European fascism reminds us that fascist movements can take many forms and spring up in many different contexts. The specific contours of fascism will vary from place to place and rely on imagining distinct cultural forms of greatness. Historians and political theorists have argued about fascism ever since World War II. Much of the literature tries to define fascist ideology or map out what's often called a "fascist minimum." But fascism is best understood less as a coherent ideology or set of societal conditions and more as a nascent movement propelled by mediated propaganda. Its hatred of democracy necessarily calls for its engagement, and trag-ically, democracy allows for this. In every case, fascism undermines democracy by turning free expression against it. As the philosopher and literary critic Walter Benjamin wrote, fascism "see[s] its salvation in giving these masses" their expression for them.[41] His key insight was to see fascism as a political aesthetic cultivated by and through

PLAYING CHECKERS

AN UNEASY TRIUMPH FOR
LIBERAL DEMOCRACY

The man was accused of wrongdoing after newspaper reporters unearthed evidence of a secret political fund. His allies started to abandon
him as one editorial page after another called for him to step down.
A once promising political career—having quickly proceeded from
congressman to senator to vice presidential candidate—now hung in
the balance, but there was time for one last play, a Hail Mary. So the
man did the only sensible thing: he turned to the new mass medium
of television and gave a speech about his ... dog.

By flying to Hollywood and broadcasting the speech from a sound-
stage, the man, Richard Milhous Nixon, created a moment and solidified a persona that reversed his reputation as a surly curmudgeon. He
admitted he may have illegally accepted political funds, but he asked
the public whether it felt that this was morally wrong, since, after all,
one of those "gifts" was an adorable cocker spaniel named Checkers.
This whole thing could be chalked up to just an honest misunderstand-
ing. Nixon had a story to tell, a story about his life that channeled the
intimacy of a television screen. He was born to modest circumstances,
and he and his brothers worked in the family store to make a go of
it. The war entitled him to a few medals, he supposed, and afterward
he and his wife struggled to make ends meet. She came from tough
Irish stock, and they didn't ask for much; they didn't take much either
besides that pooch.

This was not a real trial with a real jury but a case tried in the court
of public opinion. When Nixon said he didn't want to jeopardize can-

didate Dwight Eisenhower's chances for president by being his running mate, he left it up to Americans to contact the Republican National Committee and let it know whether he should remain on the ticket. Nixon promised to abide by whatever decision the public rendered, and he vowed in any case to campaign against the crooks and communists who had taken over Washington. The stunt worked: supportive letters, telephone calls, and telegrams overwhelmed the RNC. Eisenhower was happy to keep Nixon on, observing how the latter had been vindicated. Nixon had played Checkers on television and won through the image of his ethos. It was just enough to distract from the credible evidence marshaled against him.

So began the game of liberal democracy in the age of television. The rules of play were kept and enforced by a retinue of gatekeeping institutions, like network news and legacy newspapers. We had what you might call a monoculture—people got their information from the same places, and robust boundaries were in place for public discourse. Television flattened culture and elevated optics over substance in the political world, but the system worked as designed. Politicians could use that system to manipulate public opinion, while members of the press, as official minders of the sport, profited as referees. But in the predigital world, the barriers to entry were sufficiently high that only a handful of voices truly mattered. The mainstream press drove the narrative and framed the public conversation, which meant that politicians could be held to account when they crossed a line. Globally, it was an age of decolonization kicked off in the late 1940s as India became the world's largest democracy and the United Nations passed the Universal Declaration of Human Rights. But the rapid march of democracy obscured the precariousness of the structures propping it up. While there was suddenly a network of institutions and norms that were largely adhered to, there was also an undercurrent of cynicism and frivolity just beneath the surface. And the nature of the new communication medium of television privileged personalities over deliberation, entertainment over education.

Nixon's career embodied the virtues and limitations of this communicative environment. He skirted the rules and had been assessed a brief penalty, but he recovered by winning over the crowd. His captain,

Eisenhower, was considered a no-nonsense type. This was the general who had stamped out fascism on the beaches of Normandy. But he was ill suited for the televisual age. An ad agency exec brought into the campaign considered him an inept speaker, terrible for the new medium. A lack of oratorical prowess would not be a problem, though, for what mattered was burnishing an image—a carefully crafted brand—in front of the electorate. I Like Ike became the catchy slogan, and rather than purchase hours of programming to actually talk to the public, as politicians had first employed television, the campaign would put out commercial spots in thirty- and sixty-second increments. Eisenhower was promptly transformed into "the Man from Abilene" emanating from a small house in Kansas in the American heartland. With television, moments as well as personas could be manufactured to construct a sense of authenticity. One only needed to strike a folksy, trustworthy visage—certainly not too serious, and definitely not too ironic. The presidential campaigns of 1952 and 1956 had a perfect foil in the Democratic nominee in both campaigns, Adlai Stevenson. A curious, thoughtful man who had written for his family paper before going on to a distinguished career in government, he didn't stand a chance. In his 1952 Democratic National Convention speech, Stevenson asked the public to consider not just personalities but legislative objectives. The man was clearly out of touch. Success in this new communications environment required a confident artifice of entertainment facilitated through shameless self-promotion.

Nixon forgot this lesson as he campaigned to succeed Eisenhower in 1960, the election year that featured the first televised debates. Forgetting the illusion of modesty that once saved his career, on black-and-white television Nixon looked washed out in his gray suit. He hadn't availed himself of the CBS make-up professional, sat awkwardly in his chair, and tried to impress the audience with long-winded answers that demonstrated his mastery of policy. Contrast this with Nixon's opponent, the dashing US Senator John F. Kennedy, who wore a crisp black suit and sported a fine Palm Beach tan, sat comfortably with his legs crossed, and spoke in short, quick bursts. This new speaking style was perfect for sound bites that television news shows could replay. Public discourse had been truncated from the oratorical constructions of careful argument to snappy ten-second lines and thirty-second ads. Persuasion was not a matter of plotting out a convincing proof but combining the coolness of an image with the sharpness of the sound bite. During the debate, Kennedy even cocked his head slightly to project warmth through the television cameras. Polls showed that those who had watched the debate on television preferred Kennedy by a wide margin, even though Nixon commanded a lead among those who had listened in by radio. Kennedy played the game well. His staff included some television executives and the speechwriter Ted Sorensen, who had ghostwritten Kennedy's Pulitzer Prize–winning 1956 book, *Profiles in Courage*. Nixon lost the 1960 presidential election, and President Kennedy went on to deliver one of the most famous of inaugural addresses. "Ask not what your country can do for you," he intoned. "Ask what you can do for your country."

Nixon went on to lose the 1962 gubernatorial race in California and seemed done with politics. After a few years of lucrative work on Wall Street, he happened upon a young television producer named Roger Ailes. Ailes convinced him that television was much more than a gimmick. Nixon would reenter the game for the 1968 presidential election, his campaign led in part by an advertising executive, Harry Treleaven, and bolstered by a speechwriter, Raymond K. Price, who used to work on the editorial page of the *New York Herald Tribune*. Both were singularly focused on cultivating a likable image for Nixon. Joe McGinniss, who had access to the inner workings of the campaign for a book-length chronicle, *The Selling of the President 1968*, wrote of the pair: "It was as if they were building not a President but an Astrodome, where the wind would never blow, the temperature never rise or fall, and the ball never bounce erratically on the artificial grass."[1] Campaign memos were distributed among staffers with the apposite quotations from Marshall McLuhan in an effort to help Nixon play Checkers once more. He appeared on *Laugh-In*, the television variety show. "Sock it to me" was all he said, somewhat awkwardly, in his brief cameo. But it was enough to make Nixon endearing again. His acceptance speech at the Republican National Convention extolled America as a great nation composed of great people; it just needed to recapture its greatness, which he, Nixon, could deliver. He wouldn't barricade himself inside a television studio for an antiseptic campaign, he said soon after the nomination, yet that's exactly what he did. Nixon's campaign organized a series of televised shows for each region of the country, replete with a studio audience that cheered his answers. That young television producer, Ailes, was put in charge. He bristled that higher-ups in the campaign insisted on a diversity of audience members, including Black persons, Jews, and farmers: "Fine," he grumbled. "They all get their lousy little groups represented but we wind up with a horseshit show."[2] He did get his way on prohibiting reporters from attending. It would be a couple decades before Ailes's love of television could be combined with his hatred of diversity and the mainstream political press, but his vision was already fully formed.

To protect the "new" Nixon from himself, his 1968 campaign refused to participate in televised debates. Television advertisements highlighted a series of still photographs rather than have him talk directly into the camera. Nixon also campaigned on a secret plan to end the Vietnam War, a savvy move, since television coverage had turned critical for the first time in 1968 with the Tet Offensive. That trustworthy persona Walter Cronkite, who anchored the *CBS Evening News* and closed each broadcast by assuring the public, "And that's the way it is," openly feared that the conflict would end in a stalemate. In response, President Lyndon Baines Johnson supposedly said, "If I've lost Cronkite, I've lost Middle America." The quote is likely apocryphal, but in any event Johnson, who was reelected by historic margins in 1964, decided against running for another term in office. Of course, the assessment of whether the Viet Cong actually succeeded with Tet is a different matter. When an NBC producer pitched demonstrating how the attacks largely failed to achieve the objectives of the North Vietnamese, he was told by network executives, "Tet was already established in the public's mind as a defeat, and therefore it was an American defeat."[3] The secret plan mattered little to Nixon. He doubled down on prosecuting the Vietnam War in his first year of office, asking for support from the great silent majority of his fellow Americans. This term presumably referred to those citizens who neither participated in protests nor were taken in by critical media coverage. Nixon was joined in this endeavor by his vice president, Spiro Agnew, who denounced press critics in various contexts as "an effete corps of impudent snobs," "nattering nabobs of negativism," and "hopeless, hysterical hypochondriacs of history."[4]

Such rhetorical flourishes weren't even necessary in 1972, as Nixon faced a mild-mannered liberal opponent in George McGovern, whose acceptance speech at the Democratic National Convention was not delivered until after midnight. With no debates to present himself effectively to the larger public, McGovern, a gunner during World War II, was easily tarred as the radical Triple-A candidate, standing for amnesty, abortion, and acid. The election-year burglary of the Democratic National Committee headquarters at the Watergate Hotel in Washington, DC, was dismissed as third-rate and failed to garner much attention. When the scandal blew open in his second term, however, Nixon's paranoia got the best of him and he repeatedly obstructed justice. But that didn't necessarily seal his fate. Nixon made a crucial error when he inverted his televisual strategy from 1952. In the black-and-white Checkers speech, Nixon affected an unpretentious demeanor and talked about his dog. Against the backdrop of misconduct allegations in 1973, he angrily insisted, "Well, I'm not a crook." Another moment had been created, another persona solidified. With television, people must show, not tell, the audience who they are and what they are about. It requires performance, not honesty. Richard Nixon could play Checkers and win, but Tricky Dick betrayed himself by failing to harness the medium to his advantage.

Rather than face an impeachment trial, the president resigned. The press had finally got him, and Congress appeared to reach consensus on his guilt—not for the secret bombing campaign of Cambodia, not for the Watergate break-in itself, but for abusing his authority to obstruct justice. What Nixon needed now was a national television network or a newspaper chain with publications in every city. Unfortunately for him, that young producer who pulled him aside and schooled him on the importance of the medium of television wouldn't create and run a partisan cable news network for another two decades. His timing was also poor in that the cultural infrastructure necessary to his defense was just being theorized. In 1971, the same year Nixon appointed Lewis Powell to the US Supreme Court, the latter had composed a memo for the US Chamber of Commerce. In that document, he not only repeats the charges of a liberal bias among journalists and intellectuals; he also laments the emotional power of television. He wrote, "One of the bewildering paradoxes of our time is the extent to which the enterprise system tolerates, if not participates in, its own destruction."[5] In essence, Powell drafted an architectural blueprint for conservatives to fight back. It required creating a national network of partisan media organizations, public relations professionals, and think tanks to convince the public and politicians alike of the necessity for sustaining power. Powell knew exactly what he was talking about too. As a corporate attorney for tobacco companies, he saw firsthand what a persistent campaign of propaganda could accomplish in swaying public opinion. The Powell Memo remains one of the most ingenious and influential plans for political communication ever drafted in American history, and it was executed to near perfection in the coming decades.

Nixon, who rewarded Powell with a seat on America's highest court, would not benefit from the justice's vision, however. He would have to settle for one last indelible television moment as president: flashing his trademark V sign with both hands before boarding a helicopter on the White House lawn. Pardoned by his successor, Gerald Ford, Nixon stewed for a few years and then turned to television for redemption. Rather than grant an interview to a serious journalist at a newspaper, magazine, or television network, he agreed to a fee exceeding half a million dollars for a sit-down with the British celebrity interviewer David Frost. It was secured in part to promote Nixon's forthcoming memoirs. The former president thought he could dominate his softball interlocutor, but Frost surprised him with newfound evidence and an aggressive disposition. Nixon used the opportunity to create a new moment: he, Richard Nixon—yes, *that* Richard Nixon—expressed remorse. "I let the American people down," he said, "and I have to carry that burden with me the rest of my life." While this didn't count as an admission of guilt, it served as a nifty bit of mawkishness. In 1986, *Newsweek* published a cover story announcing "He's Back: The Rehabilitation of Richard Nixon," and in 1992 he appeared on CNN's *Larry King Live* to promote his new book, *Seize the Moment: America's Challenge in a One-Superpower World*. Nixon would never serve in public office again, but his reputation was salvaged enough for him to play the role of elder statesman until his death in 1994.

Nixon's career speaks to the primacy of optics in the age of liberal democracy. Television, like all media, unlocked new political rhetoric within the paradox. Some of this new openness was healthy from a democratic perspective, but much of it flooded politics with phony imagery. And that's sort of the point: every new media technology is a double-edged sword, increasing opportunities for free expression but also providing a means of exploitation. Senator Joseph McCarthy's rise and fall is instructive here. His rabid anticommunist campaign in the 1950s exploited old media such as newspapers and their reliance on wire services to gain prominence. When McCarthy hurled accusations about communist infiltrators in the US government without providing any proof, he had made sure to release them right before the filing deadlines. Neither reaction quotes nor fact-checking was possible; the press fell victim to its own objectivity. As Daniel Boorstin observed, "McCarthy and the newsmen both thrived on the same synthetic commodity" of ever more and more news to print.[6] McCarthy promised to deliver proof in the letters he would wave around at speeches and press conferences, but he never delivered. He simply moved on to newer accusations that were also dutifully printed. Though a Republican senator, Margaret Chase Smith, delivered a sterling speech in Congress assailing McCarthyism in 1950, she was mostly sidelined by her colleagues, who were afraid of the witch hunt.

Only in 1954, with television ascendant and backed by liberal norms, was McCarthy sunk. Edward R. Murrow's *See It Now* show on CBS demonstrated how the Red Scare was ruining people's lives, and Murrow condemned McCarthy in his editorial comments. The broadcasts also aired a montage of clips of the Wisconsin senator's speeches, which exposed him as not just contradictory but wholly unlikable—the kiss of death on television. McCarthy was afforded airtime on CBS thanks to the Fairness Doctrine enacted by the Federal Communications Commission, but he came off as agitated. He ran too hot for the coolness of the new medium. Then, a few months later, he was further undone as the televised congressional hearings he held revealed US Army lawyer Joseph Welch getting the better of him. When a frustrated McCarthy accused Welch of treason, the special counsel paused and delivered an epic moment of authenticity, an impression that sealed McCarthy's fate. "Until this moment, senator, I think I never really gauged your cruelty or your recklessness," Welch poignantly said. "Have you no sense of decency, sir? At long last, have you left no sense of decency?" The room erupted in applause, and the entire sequence was captured on television: all three networks—NBC, CBS, and ABC—broadcast that day's hearing live. McCarthy had lost the moment.

The medium seemed to galvanize the good in other ways as well. The rest of America would see the grim realities of Jim Crow as a young civil rights organizer, Dr. Martin Luther King Jr., threw a media spotlight on the brutality. He courted producers and videographers and made sure they were ready when peaceful protest marches began. The imagery of discrimination and violence was startling. In arranging the March on Washington, King made sure the optics were effective there too: standing in the shadow of the Lincoln Memorial, looking out over the Washington Monument, he delivered the celebrated "I Have a Dream" speech. While his repetition of the refrain is perhaps most memorable, far more important was King's ability to weave a narrative. The speech traced the story of American liberty, seeking to situate African Americans within that story. The Declaration of Independence, he said, was a promissory note that the oppressed now looked to cash. The Civil Rights Act passed soon afterward. Highlighting King here is not to suggest he was a cynical operator; he simply knew the logic of television and its effect on public audiences.

One politician tried to be genuine and honest on television, and it was a disaster. President Jimmy Carter benefited from a devastated Republican Party in the aftermath of the Watergate scandal to win the 1976 election. And his homespun shtick wasn't counterfeit; Carter was the real thing. He even put his peanut farm in a trust to avoid the appearance of impropriety. But his presidency was a mess, and two televised speeches in particular made things worse. In 1977, he addressed the nation while wearing a cardigan and sitting near a lit fireplace to report on the energy crisis, saying it was the moral equivalent of war. Carter asked for sacrifices from everybody: don't drive as much, use less heat in the winter. His address was sobering, not entertaining; there wasn't any projection of presidential strength. Carter's problem was his commitment to seriousness in the age of television, whose norms were governed by the cynicism of impressions and moments. Nixon hadn't killed televised politics so much as bequeathed a legacy that they must be performed artfully and consistently. Carter's reliance on television was further botched in 1979, when he delivered a speech on America's crisis of confidence. He again tried to be honest, with predictable results. While some newspapers awarded the president high marks for being straightforward, his speech didn't play well on television. The public would come to know this address as the Malaise Speech: Carter embodied the crisis of confidence he had sought to rebut. Television, to be fair, rewards honesty if there's a convincing narrative behind it. But as a medium of persuasion, it's driven by a branded image above all else, and Carter's optics were all wrong.

Ronald Reagan, the handsome former movie actor who supplanted Carter, understood media. Politics, he once boasted, were just like show business. He affected the impression of a Western hero, walking onstage with the swagger of John Wayne and wearing denim getups on his California ranch. During his and Carter's only presidential debate, he had cocked his head, smiling, before responding to the president's remarks on Medicare. "There you go again," he chuckled. America, Reagan promised, would once again become the city on the shining hill, a beacon of freedom for the world. It was an effective story promulgated by a celebrity hero. Infused with nostalgia, America would become great again. As president, Reagan played the statesman well. His commitment to conservative policies, ranging from tax reductions to religious values, was fierce, but it was the impression he gave of the presidential leader that mattered most. In this he succeeded, in addresses from the Oval Office, in Rose Garden talks with the press, and in speeches confronting the Soviet Union as the Evil Empire. His successes were matched, and even inspired, by Margaret Thatcher's rise as prime minister of the United Kingdom. She, too, promised her country a return to greatness. In their own way, each leader offered a universal rhetoric for the good of the individual at the expense of society, combined with combative foreign policy goals. What this amounted to was a conservative vision that largely benefited from the medium of television in the 1980s, just as liberals had in the 1960s. Both relied, above all, on the impression of standing firm in the face of change. This was particularly appealing at a time when Westerns began to fade as a popular genre of filmmaking. As if to fill this gap, the narrative of a lone cowboy restoring order to a lawless society was adapted to politics.

This swagger reached an apex with Oliver North. Facing allegations of misconduct in the Iran-Contra affair, North, a lieutenant colonel in the Marines assigned to the National Security Council, appeared before Congress in 1987 resplendent in uniform, wagging his finger. His opening statement to the senators and representatives of the committee investigating the affair was full of "you" language, blaming them for "fickle, vacillating, unpredictable, on-again, off-again policy."[7] The hearings themselves, he alleged, were what was causing serious damage to national security—not selling arms to Iran, a sworn enemy, and funneling profits to militias in Central America. Another moment was created, a new persona emerged. Defiance played well. North said he was proud of his accomplishments on behalf of the great president he served. In the end, he was indicted and convicted of obstructing a congressional inquiry by ordering the shredding of documents, but he didn't serve any jail time and his case was reversed on appeal. The $20 million he amassed for his legal defense fund through a direct-mail campaign after his congressional appearance served him well.

Despite Iran-Contra, which clouded Reagan's second term and that of his vice president, George H. W. Bush, Bush went on to win the 1988 presidential election. The cover of *Time* magazine's October 3 issue declared the campaigning a "Battle of the Handlers," and Bush's team counted among its top advisors Roger Ailes, who had worked on Nixon's 1968 campaign. The team played to racial fears with its television ads directed at the Democratic opponent, Massachusetts governor Michael Dukakis. Highlighting his program of prison furloughs, the ads depicted prisoners going through a revolving door as voice-overs suggested these convicts had unleashed a terror campaign of kidnapping and murder. Dukakis was thus portrayed as weak, but the ad that really struck a chord with the public chronicled Willie Horton, an African American convict who later committed armed robbery and rape after skipping out on his furlough. The story was true, but that didn't matter: the point was the impression made by an image of a scary Black convict stereotypically named Willie, even though he always went by his given name, William. Dukakis's troubles were further compounded by other campaign ads in which he was shown riding around in a military tank. He looked silly and feckless donning a helmet over his suit, and everyone knew it. Dukakis himself tried to contrive a television moment on an Arizona tarmac beside his campaign airplane, tossing a baseball around. This was after having failed to generate any coverage while playing catch outside an Ohio bowling alley. The Everyman routine wouldn't stick, though. The dividing line between phony and authentic was narrow and required expert navigation. Then, during a presidential debate, Dukakis was asked whether he'd support the death penalty if his wife were raped and murdered. He responded with honesty, saying no. His gravest sin here was exhibiting no emotion—not even a trace of anger at the thought. It was an unethical hypothetical question by journalistic standards, but this was a missed opportunity for Dukakis to capitalize on televisual rhetoric to create a moment of strength. He never shook the impression that he was weak.

Seen amid a host of other television content that shifts from shot to shot, scene to scene, and story to story, political ads are as fragmented and disjointed as the culture they speak to. There's little place for traditional oratory, and the possibility of any political discourse worthy of actual debate or deliberation is inhibited. The impressions of television advertisements render politics cynical as much as trivial. If the telegraph began the mediated collapse of time, network television condensed it. Only twenty-two minutes of every thirty are content; the rest is devoted to commercials. Political campaigns and their surrogates bought time, then as now, in thirty-second installments. Candidates have two options to choose from in effective television advertising: present a branded narrative, or go negative and slime the opposing candidate. The goal in any case is to present some idea, or some individual, that *appears* authentic while portraying the opposition as inauthentic. The medium thus encourages negative advertising. Thirty or sixty seconds isn't much time, but it's enough to tear down the ethos of the other candidate through ad hominem and straw man attacks. With a punchy, visceral ad, someone can cement a nasty impression of the opponent in the public's mind. In 1964, for example, President Lyndon Baines Johnson's campaign exhibited the Daisy ad, which showed a freckled little girl plucking a flower, counting its petals. The child pauses as a doomsday countdown is suddenly heard, followed by a nuclear explosion. With these images, the public was invited to fear the fanaticism of Johnson's opponent, Barry Goldwater, who would welcome the apocalypse. The ad played on Goldwater's Republican Convention speech, which was famous for the line "Extremism in defense of liberty is no vice."

Television also extended the universalizing qualities of previous mass media like the telegraph, cinema, and radio. The moments were collectively shared, the personages collectively embraced or reviled. Chaim Perelman and Lucie Olbrechts-Tyteca created a rhetorical framework of the universal audience. Their idea was that orators can call forth a like-minded audience of rational thinkers through arguments that "are self-evident, and possess an absolute and timeless validity, independent of local or historical contingencies."[8] In some ways, Perelman and Olbrechts-Tyteca attempted to rescue rhetoric from the superficial, relativistic charges it has endured since Plato. Rhetoric, they insisted, could proceed logically and with validity. It was the orator whose communication called forth the audience. The rhetorical objective here is a consensus of agreement, and television provided the illusion that this could continually be achieved, a hallmark of the liberal-democratic age.

Another perceptive rhetorical critic of the age, Walter Fisher, highlighted narrative: we are storytelling creatures, he wrote in 1987, and are persuaded to the extent that stories ring true for us. Processing political communication like this could only make sense in the mid- to late twentieth century, with television as the dominant medium. To Fisher, President Kennedy offered the public the opportunity to join a story of charting out into a New Frontier, an attractive narrative pitched into the future. President Reagan, in contrast, sought to restore the community honor of the past by allowing the public to join the mythopoetic Western hero in a journey up to a city on a shining hill.[9] And poor Jimmy Carter tried to reason with us. Fisher's point was that reason operates not on logic but story. What makes sense to us, more than anything, is narrative. In politics, this means citizens need to feel they are part of a story. Success is a function of politicians who can combine a telegenic ethos with a participatory campaign narrative. Television disrupted democracy with a bias toward imagery and branded narratives.

How, then, did the rise of television coincide with the heyday of liberal democracy? Two ways. The first is short and specific to television, the other more complicated and tethered to the media environment in general. Television was, for its first several decades, quite limited. It was much like radio in this regard. Only a few networks, or channels, were available; the signals of broadcast media were, as a consequence of being deemed public airwaves, tightly regulated. In the United States, the Federal Communications Commission had—and still has—the legal power to monitor network broadcasting. It demanded content in the public interest, and its Fairness Doctrine dictated that a reasonable effort be made to include both sides of a political discussion, given the scarcity of public airwaves. The Supreme Court unanimously upheld the constitutional viability of the doctrine for broadcast media in 1969. (The precedent of that case, *Red Lion Broadcasting Company v. FCC*, stands today, though the Fairness Doctrine was repealed in 1987.) The decision itself was juxtaposed to another unanimous Supreme Court decision a few years later, *Miami Herald v. Tornillo* from 1974. When the State of Florida attempted to enforce a right-of-reply statute against a newspaper and force it to run an op-ed from a subject of investigative reporting, the high court demurred, insisting that no such regulations could be imposed on print media.

Beyond the law, technology imposed its own constraints in the early days of television. With only three major broadcast networks holding court for several decades before the ubiquity of cable, public discourse could be *managed* by an elite gatekeeping force of executives, producers, and reporters. They determined what was carried live, what was covered, and what personages would be interviewed in their programming. Shows such as *Meet the Press* on NBC, *Face the Nation* on CBS, and *Issues and Answers* on ABC arose as the ultimate gatekeeping phenomena. The televisual press could talk directly to the public and decide whom the public would hear from on matters of importance. The gatekeepers thus set the agenda and, in doing so, exercised power over images. Politics may still have operated as a game, yet they were played on a circumscribed field with a defined set of rules. Liberal democracy relied on this framework to shape the contours of discourse and information. A universal consensus of facts was possible, but only because a culture of control was enjoyed by these elite gatekeepers. The public, as a result, could be steered in particular directions. This agenda-setting function of television news was far more powerful than any specific political bias it exhibited as a medium. What mattered was not so much the framing of events as the selection of which events or issues were prioritized. In the age of television, the public initially didn't have much choice to withhold trust.

Even the limited scope of televisual technology was an elite choice, as going with ultra-high frequency (UHF) could have expanded the spectrum of television channels in the 1940s. Instead, the government prevented new licenses for additional stations and opted for the very high frequency (VHF) system, which limited the diversity of television programming. The FCC possessed the directive and the authority to regulate, yet it consistently opted to reify, rather than contest, mediated power. And if Walter Cronkite was the most trusted man in America, it may be because he was one of the only men in America to be seen nightly on television. He blinked back tears when President Kennedy was assassinated, and he walked us through the moon landing. He was always … there. That famed moniker of trust, stemming from a 1972 poll in which Cronkite garnered 73 percent of the responses, might be attenuated in retrospect, given that 67 percent of respondents in the same poll trusted the "average senator."[10] Trust, in other words, reflected a faith in the broader cultural system of liberal democracy.

Television balanced the silliness of commercial advertising with the affectation of seriousness. This could be seen since the medium's earliest days, from NBC's *Camel News Caravan*, one of the first news programs, to Elizabeth II's coronation in 1953. Sponsored by the R. J. Reynolds Tobacco Company, the NBC show combined the marketing priorities of radio with footage resembling cinematic newsreels. The difference was the presence of a host, John Cameron Swayze, who presided over the affair with an air of trustworthiness, bolstered by a lit cigarette. The coronation, meanwhile, was broadcast live on BBC Television, with footage then flown to Canada and the United States for airing. Television demanded, at least initially, a certain calm and repose. While quiz shows, sitcoms, soap operas, and sports programming were offered up as entertaining content, news, which was limited nightly to half-hour local and national installments, skewed more formal. The sincerity of televisual news may have been a put-on, but such news did not, at first, attempt to compete against other programming of stimulating cultural entertainment.

In theory, this meant that government and politicians answered to reporting and the concerns of citizens. Media mattered—both as a conduit of information and as a persuasive force. Two consecutive American presidents stepped down from office, one amid a swirl of negative coverage and the other facing impeachment. Poor leadership and scandals had an impact; politicians had to behave according to established standards of decorum; social change was possible, even actualized on some occasions. But the period of liberal democracy relied on far more in communications than just television alone. The emphasis on imagery in the televisual age can easily distract us from what made liberal democracy work, to the extent that it ever really worked. How different media interact and intersect is what cultivates a cultural environment.

The controlling mechanisms of television certainly played a part in contributing to liberal democracy, yet print reporting across newspapers, magazines, and nonfiction publishing was lively and pervasive as well. Television bolstered competition from print as beat reporters aggressively pursued scoops, vying with other local and national competitors, while features writers pioneered fresh styles of long-form journalism. Dogged investigative reporting uncovered wrongdoing in Vietnam as Seymour Hersh exposed the My Lai massacre for the Dispatch News Service, which supplied the story to newspapers around the nation. Then the *New York Times* and the *Washington Post* fought the White House all the way to the Supreme Court in order to publish the Pentagon Papers. The revelations within those pages indicated how, and in what manner, the US government had lied to the American people in order to foment and sustain the war in Vietnam. When the Watergate story went cold and didn't play well on television, two young metro reporters from the *Washington Post*, Bob Woodward and Carl Bernstein, "follow[ed] the money" to unveil the startling corruption of the president. The phrase itself speaks to the ethics of journalistic duty, and through persistent shoe-leather reporting Woodward and Bernstein untangled the story. William Goldman, who wrote the script for the movie version of Woodward and Bernstein's *All the President's Men*, came up with the inspiring phrase. The reporters became heroes, portrayed onscreen by Robert Redford and Dustin Hoffman. It was a real high point for American journalism. Accountability seemed not just possible but absolutely essential. In this era, freedom of speech, press, and assembly were all distinguished characteristics of a First Amendment that facilitated democracy. They all contributed separately to the fulfillment of isegoria and the curtailment of concentrated, arbitrary power.

Some of the greatest contributions to journalism during this period could be found among the nation's magazines, later translated into nonfiction book publishing. The *New Yorker*, founded in 1925, evolved to showcase the finest feature reporting at the local, national, and international levels. It wasn't always objective or strictly political, but at a time when broadcast media sped news up, magazines like the *New Yorker* slowed time down and offered storytelling with depth. Outstanding early work included profiles by Joseph Mitchell, who highlighted the motivations of bearded ladies and homeless poets. In a more sobering capacity, John Hersey covered the aftermath of the atomic bombing of Hiroshima through the experiences of six survivors. The United States had won World War II by unleashing atomic weapons on another country, but Hersey was able to painstakingly detail what that power had wrought. He didn't espouse his views about the decision to drop the bomb; instead he chose to show, not tell, the harrowing stories on behalf of those who emerged from the destruction. Excerpts of his piece were published in newspapers, the entire article was read aloud on an ABC radio broadcast, and the book version has remained in print ever since it appeared in 1946. What makes the piece such a fine example of journalism is that it didn't need to moralize or speculate about political consequences; Hersey stuck with tracing the impact that official actions had on people's lives. These were the stories of others, and journalism qua journalism succeeds to the extent that it shares accurate, vivid accounts of human experience.

Not every work needed to be so grave. It was enough to chronicle the experiences of others—whether high or low—in the cultural arts, business, and politics. In 1950, Lillian Ross made waves by publishing a *New Yorker* profile of Ernest Hemingway. She received criticism for revealing a portrait of the real Hemingway, equal parts bombastic and cantankerous. Papa, to his credit, didn't seem to mind, but the story marked a departure. Print journalism, practiced at its highest level, would now seek to capture the essence of the person, place, or thing without deferring to the niceties of prominence. The *New Yorker* continued this undertaking through the 1950s supervised by its managing editor, William Shawn, and anchored by A. J. Liebling, who covered sports, politics, and the press. His three-part series about Louisiana from May 1960 profiled Earl Long, an idiosyncratic figure to say the least. Liebling's descriptions of the goings-on at the governor's mansion are outrageous, but he managed to capture the racial tensions, the politicking, and the cultural uniqueness of "The Great State," as the article series was named. For instance, guns are misplaced, great volumes of ice cream are consumed, and Earl, having just returned from a sanitorium, prepares for another election. The series opens with Liebling's reflections on covering Earl's brother, Huey, back in the 1930s, when Huey himself was governor and would meet reporters in his hotel room, pajama clad and scratching himself. In the issue the week before the series on Louisiana ran, Liebling had covered the American Newspaper Publishers Association convention for his Wayward Press series. The piece may be best known for his famous wisecrack, "Freedom of the press is guaranteed only to those who own one," yet Liebling's worries are consumed more by the "quickening of decimation" occurring in the newspaper industry.[11] Media consolidation that leads to monopolies, he argued, threatens news in general and journalistic practices in particular. His line about freedom of the press is followed up with a lament on how reporting freedom is exercised only with the permission of the paper's owner or publisher. Constitutional protections for the press created an inviting, unregulated market that encouraged businessmen to eliminate rival newspapers.

Liebling's concerns about the newspaper industry and the future of journalism were prescient for the time, but it would take decades for his warning to be heeded. Otherwise, the 1960s represented a pinnacle of success for print journalism, even during a period when television was considered ascendant. The *New Yorker* exerted even more of an impact as Rachel Carson's *Silent Spring* was, like her previous nonfiction books, first published in the magazine's pages. Carson's work exposed the harmful effects of pesticides like DDT and launched an environmental movement that would net the creation of the Environmental Protection Agency less than a decade later. In 1961, Shawn would send the philosopher Hannah Arendt on assignment to Jerusalem to cover the trial of Adolf Eichmann, a Nazi war criminal who had been captured in Argentina. The resulting series, published in the magazine in 1963, became a book of controversial renown for Arendt's banality-of-evil thesis. The trial itself was one of the first televised globalized events, and Arendt objected to the spectacle. Eichmann, she observed, was not some ideological bigot who had committed genocide in the throes of hatred; he was more of a bureaucratic functionary whose plainness represented the real danger or lesson to be derived from the Holocaust. Arendt's thought deserved more consideration, especially during a period of passive consumer spectatorship. The leftist intellectuals of the Frankfurt school, led by Max Horkheimer and Theodor Adorno, sounded similar alarms. Their famous essay from 1947, "The Culture Industry: Enlightenment as Mass Deception," argued that American media generated the same passivity as fascism, only under the guise of a commercial system ruled by advertising.[12]

Some intellectuals on the Right were just as worried about the fate of liberal democracy in a consumer culture. In 1960, Daniel Bell declared that we had reached the end of ideology. The political debates and the rise of mass culture had become, in his mind, exhausting but not necessarily deliberative. In 1972, Bell would write an essay, "The Cultural Contradictions of Capitalism," that charted how mass culture surmounted the legacy of the rural Protestant work ethic. It was hard to inculcate conservative values when capitalism simultaneously propounded ever-increasing consumerism. To Bell, society needed to choose one or the other, especially in a culture that relentlessly pressed forward. "The sense of movement and change—the upheaval in the mode of confronting the world—established vivid new conventions and forms by which people judged their sense perceptions and experience," he wrote.[13] The concerns over the pace of cultural change were more than justified. Revolutions in communications had never been as rapid or intense as they were in the twentieth century, and the sense of disruption produced an immense amount of backlash. Two French intellectuals of the Left, Guy DeBord in 1967 and Jean Baudrillard in 1981, questioned whether we could experience reality at all. For DeBord, Western culture was awash in spectacle—not just big, singular, momentous spectacles but the persistent succession of spectacles mediated through image and text. For Baudrillard, we had descended into a "precession of simulacra" in which reality was lost in a sea of mediated reproductions.

Both the Left and the Right had reason to bristle at the soft commercial core of liberal democracy, but despite its many faults, the openness of media was crucial to its ideological success in the Cold War era. While the East Germans had their listening devices and their Stasi network of informants and the Soviets had their communal loudspeakers, America relied on émigrés to help put together broadcasts on Radio Free Europe, Radio Liberty, and Voice of America that could reach populated swaths of Eastern Europe as well as cities in the Soviet Union. The CIA, meanwhile, subsidized literary magazines throughout Europe and Latin America, often unbeknownst to the writers themselves. The successful (and surprising) 1957 Soviet launch of Sputnik, the first artificial satellite, backfired, as it served no fundamental communications purpose and merely goaded the United States into creating NASA. Although NASA culminated with much televised fanfare in sending humans to the moon a decade later, the United States' more immediate goal was a system of communications networks. The agency began experimenting with radar systems and telephone lines to foster data transmission. Telstar was sent up in 1962, providing live television signals between America and Europe. Two years later, the United States and Europe founded the International Telecommunications Satellite

Consortium (INTELSAT) that would link real-time communications among the free world.[14] As a counter, the Soviets designed Intersputnik to connect with their communist brethren, but it wouldn't launch until 1971 and was limited to only a handful of nations. The dearth of personal communication devices among households in such countries also blunted whatever impact the system had hoped to achieve. Additionally, the US Department of Defense, along with university research centers, had designed computer networks that could share digital transmissions of information through the Advanced Research Project Agency Network (ARPANET), the forerunner of the internet. The advantage of such coordination for research and military planning proved decisive. Reagan, "the Great Communicator," may often be credited with singularly winning the Cold War, but these structural investments in communications played a massive role as well.

As we've continually stressed, though, an open communications environment is always a mixed bag. The cultural disorientation experienced in the 1960s bore this out in the United States. Free expression gave rise to a whirlwind of activism that fundamentally transformed the social and political landscape. When students at the University of California, Berkeley, attempted to raise awareness of civil rights issues in 1964, campus administrators shut them down. While one student was being arrested for distributing pamphlets, his peers surrounded the police car for more than thirty hours in protest. Another student, Mario Savio, stood on the car and delivered a speech on the rights of free expression. Two months later, in an organized protest that led to the arrest of eight hundred students, Savio spoke again. He noted how the greatest problem facing the nation, both on campus and among legislatures, was the unresponsiveness of bureaucratic control. The twin pillars of democracy, isegoria and holding power accountable, were thus exercised. University administration relented, and political activism has been a hotbed of campus cultures ever since. Democracies swing in both directions, however, and critical reactions to student politicking led in part to the rise of Reagan, who was elected governor of California in 1966.

During this same period, innovations among publications and publishing houses were equally disruptive. Betty Friedan published *The*

Feminine Mystique in 1963, which energized the Second Wave of feminism. The year before, Helen Gurley Brown had come out with *Sex and the Single Girl*, and in 1965 she began her long editorial run overseeing the magazine *Cosmopolitan*. Other weekly or monthly publications entered the fray, catering to specific demographics. The journalist I. F. Stone offered an influential eponymous weekly that challenged official stances from Washington—All Governments Lie was his motto. *Playboy* sought to supplement the literary taste, cartoons, and reporting of the *New Yorker* with the addition of pornographic photography. *Rolling Stone* appealed to its young followers with a blend of news on music, pop culture, and politics. Magazines were emboldened by New Journalism, a pioneering, subjective style in both reporting and writing. It was a counterstatement to the universal notion of consensus pursued by the mainstream press, offering glimpses of lived experience among subcultures. Chief examples of the genre from this time include Joan Didion's chronicles of California and Hawaii; Hunter S. Thompson's embedment with the Hell's Angels motorcycle gang in California and then among southern elites at the Kentucky Derby; Gloria Steinem's undercover work as a cocktail server at a Playboy Club; George Plimpton's experiences of failure in professional athletics; and Tom Wolfe's in-depth parade of race car drivers, hippies, and astronauts. Learning about the actions and motivations of others is a key element of reporting for a democratic culture, and New Journalism afforded opportunities of understanding outside the traditional limits of mainstream news and academic social science.

The inspiration for New Journalism, according to Wolfe, was Jimmy Breslin, a colleague from the *New York Herald Tribune*. Unlike most columnists who sat back and wrote their observations, Breslin got out into the world first and caught stories that captured experiences. He covered the funeral of President Kennedy through the lens of an Arlington National Cemetery gravedigger, a Black military veteran who made $3.01 per hour. The column is a sterling work of reporting, honoring the fallen president while highlighting a humble laborer. But the style of New Journalism, from its first-person reporting to its literary inventiveness, can be traced back farther. That honor should rightly go to Marvel Cooke, the first African American woman to work and write for a large-circulation daily newspaper. She began her work as a journalist in the 1920s writing columns for the NAACP's magazine, the *Crisis*, then under the editorial direction of W. E. B. Du Bois. In 1950, Cooke went undercover in New York City as a member of the "paper bag brigade" of Black women who stood outside department stores and waited to be picked up for a day's work of domestic duties. The series she wrote recounting the experience for the city's *Daily Compass* is a stinging portrayal of what women of color endured, even in the North. Cooke shows how they were subjected to withering treatment, from grueling manual labor to getting stiffed on agreed-on wages to a litany of patronizing comments. "I was not at peace," she reflected, standing one day in front of a Woolworth's. "Hundreds of years of history weighed upon me. I was the slave traded for two truck horses on a Memphis street corner in 1849. I was the slave trading my brawn for a pittance on a Bronx street corner in 1949."[15] A few years later, Cooke was hauled before Senator Joseph McCarthy's House Un-American Activities Committee hearings. The rest of her life was devoted to activist causes, yet her early work carved out a reporting style that offered a framework for the later New Journalists to follow.

Norman Mailer expanded New Journalism even further. His coverage of the 1967 March on the Pentagon in *Harper's Magazine* remains the longest magazine article ever published. Mailer, naturally, included himself as the protagonist in this great act of participatory journalism. A misogynist prone to violent outbursts, he was no stranger to the limelight. He publicly debated the conservative author and commentator William F. Buckley and appeared on his television interview show, *Firing Line*. Both men were contemptuous of liberalism, and each ran vanity campaigns for mayor of New York City. Buckley founded the magazine *National Review* in 1955 and at first supported segregation, writing in a 1957 article, "Why the South Must Prevail," how whites were the advanced race in possession of clear cultural superiority. Civilization, he argued, was more important than universal suffrage. He then shifted the magazine's tone in an attempt to offer a more respectable form of conservatism that eschewed the likes of the John Birch Society. That ultraconservative group comprised a well-funded network of publications and a speaker's bureau to oppose civil rights, the United Nations, and communism. When Buckley interviewed the presidential and arch-segregationist candidate George Wallace in 1968, he muttered, "For the first time, I feel like a liberal."

Wallace had lost his 1958 gubernatorial race in Alabama having shown some restraint on the racial question, but he wouldn't make such a mistake moving forward. He won in 1962, and in his inaugural speech proclaimed, "Segregation now! Segregation tomorrow! Segregation forever!" Degenerate liberals, he alleged, were seeking to persecute an international minority of white people. The speech served as prelude to a confrontation months later where he famously blocked the door to deny Black students from attending the University of Alabama. President Kennedy called in the National Guard, and the students were admitted; but Wallace's stand would later net him close to ten million supporters, five southern states, and forty-six electoral votes in the 1968 presidential election. Running again in 1972, Wallace was shot several times by an assassin, Arthur Bremer, who had been motivated by fame rather than ideology. Mass media had apparently obsessed him, as evidenced by a diary entry he recorded: "TV radio the big books more books and more masturbation sex fantasy daydreams of the father reading newspapers looking at my parents."[16] He was the inspiration for Robert De Niro's angry, frustrated character, Travis Bickle, who plots an assassination attempt on a presidential candidate in the 1976 Martin Scorsese film *Taxi Driver*. Out of some desire to honor that movie and impress its other star, Jodie Foster, John Hinckley Jr. shot and wounded President Reagan and his press secretary, Jim Brady, in 1981. These violent outbursts were grounded not in ideology but in media attention, foreshadowing the mass shooter crisis of the twenty-first century.

The fame-obsessed assassins of the seventies and eighties marked another turn. President Kennedy had been assassinated by a Marxist who, after serving in the US military, went to live in the Soviet Union. The subsequent conspiracy theories surrounding the Dallas shooting were themselves ideological, suggesting a right-wing network of operatives plotting to kill him. When Kennedy's brother Bobby ran for president in 1968, he was shot and killed by a man of Palestinian origin who objected to the senator's support of Israel. That same year, an avowed racist assassinated Dr. Martin Luther King Jr. in Memphis. After the Civil Rights Act had passed, King turned in a more traditionally leftist direction, vehemently opposing America's involvement in the Vietnam War and demanding social justice. Economic equality, not just civil rights and liberties, defined his later rhetoric. King had been in Memphis the night before his murder to support a sanitation worker strike in the city. His speech that evening, "I've Been to the Mountaintop," encouraged African American supporters to boycott banks, insurance companies, and businesses with records of discrimination, such as Coca-Cola. His goal was to inspire "a dangerous unselfishness" that could be harnessed by the Black community to facilitate equality beyond the scope of politics and the law. It's notable, then, that King was killed not while lobbying to expand voting rights but having led a new social movement against the arranged forces of oligarchy. The campaign did not rely, like the previous one, on reaching a universal audience and was more narrowly tailored to persuade a specific group with a call to action. Ideology did matter, but not in the sense that it automatically translated to popular support and political responsiveness. The Martin Luther King celebrated and remembered today is the specter of the universal audience, who fought for civil rights and cared about the content of character rather than the color of skin. King thought that race mattered, and while he may not have drawn from polarizing eloquence like other legendary Black orators of the time—Malcolm X and Stokely Carmichael, for example—he was dedicated to improving the lives of African Americans, not just securing their rights. Such a legacy of misremembering is unhelpful, obscuring an important message delivered on the cusp of his death.

Historically, though, the misremembering fits—especially given the rise and successes of conservative politics that ensued over the course of the 1970s and 1980s. This conservatism was sparked in America by fusionism, an organizing principle that tied together religious values and libertarian economics. Such a synthesis had been discussed before 1970, but it required the fall of Nixon and the Republican electoral losses of 1976 to gather strength. It also relied on a more general reactionary pushback against the social change of the 1960s, which advanced briefly into the next decade as President Nixon approved the creation of the Environmental Protection Agency; signed his approval on both Title IX legislation, which ensured gender equity in education, and the Equal Rights Amendment (ERA); and nominated justices to the Supreme Court who led a majority in deciding *Roe v. Wade.* The first element of fusionism was marked by Protestant evangelism's return to the public sphere. While at the start of the decade only 14 percent of Americans told pollsters that religion was important in their lives, by 1978 nearly half had done so.[17] Evangelists were buttressed by television in particular, as figures like Billy Graham merited coverage and influence while televangelists like Jimmy Swaggart, Pat Robertson, and Jerry Falwell harnessed the medium with their preaching and fundraising. Jimmy Carter was himself evangelical, yet it was Reagan who unlocked the rhetorical code to speak effectively to evangelicals as a coveted political demographic.

The social movement had an effective spokesperson in Phyllis Schlafly. She toured the country denouncing women's liberation, even comparing it to a disease. Schlafly opposed feminism, but she paid particular attention to political organizing, marshaling support to persuade state legislators to oppose the ERA. A similar approach was used with respect to reproductive rights, blaming women's liberation on a broad, moral scale and then lobbying local officials to encroach on specific rights with legislation. Social conservatism discovered and drew from this delicate blend of mediated activism and legal challenges, an approach that energized and dramatically altered the National Rifle Association (NRA). At its 1977 convention in Cincinnati, Second Amendment maximalists wearing orange hats orchestrated a coup that ousted long-serving NRA leadership. The previous executors had viewed themselves as heading an organization from the nineteenth century that represented veterans, Boy Scouts, sportsmen, and conservation interests. It was primarily in the business of arranging shooting contests and affording its members useful information in a relatively staid publication, the *American Rifleman.* Gun control regulations, like those passed in 1968, weren't considered onerous and even drew the backing of then-governor Reagan. One of the leaders of the 1977 revolt was Clifford Neal Knox, a journalist and editor for various gun magazines. The new leadership challenged the long-held collective understanding of the Second Amendment that tied its final clause, "the right to bear arms," to its opening clause, which spoke of "a well-regulated militia." Not until the Supreme Court's 2008 decision in *District of Columbia v. Heller* would this interpretation ever be formally codified. The success of the NRA in the thirty years between the Cincinnati revolt and *Heller* is no accident. Social conservatives in general adapted remarkably well to this new media environment, harnessing all the opportunities that a democratic society of open communication offers.

Still, social conservatism would never have been able to carry electoral power nationwide all by itself. The ability of social conservatives to fuse with libertarian economics was the key to Republican success. It helped that the 1970s were also defined by economic downturns, urban decay, and energy shocks. Democrats, for their part, embraced neoliberal policies of deregulation, a choice that haunted the party for decades. But the big point we want to stress here is that fusionism required a media-savvy vehicle to bring these separate spheres together. Carter, as we pointed out earlier, tried to address the malaise too forthrightly. That brand of sanctimonious rhetoric had run its course, which is why Reagan was the perfect vessel. He beat out George H. W. Bush in the 1980 presidential primary despite being accused by Bush of practicing Voodoo Economics. Taking Bush on as a running mate, given their initial animosity, showed he was a good sport. But Reagan's real power was television. Fusionism offered an ideological backdrop for him to play the part of president. He was warm, telegenic, self-assured. The ideology of the Reagan administration was easily transcended by his affable public presence.

Reagan's success also benefited from a shifting cultural landscape. The morose seventies were a perfect time for the auteur in filmmaking and television, from gritty realism in cinema with the likes of Francis Ford Coppola and blaxploitation pictures to edgy humor on the tube with *All in the Family* and *Sanford and Son* and the debut of *Saturday Night Live*. The mood changed in the eighties. Television shows exhibited ostentatious wealth, like *Dallas*, and white-suburban comfort, like *ALF*. Blockbuster movies benefited from product placement, as in *ET*'s Reese's Pieces and *Top Gun*'s Pentagon subsidies to showcase F-14 dogfights. A slick tycoon in *Wall Street*, meanwhile, affirmed that greed was good. These movies could be seen in the comfort of home through a VHS player, and one could also listen to synthetic New Wave pop with a Sony Walkman or boombox while decked out in the bright, garish fashion of the decade. It was good to be American. Orson Welles, the great filmmaker and Shakespearean actor, had closed out his career shortly before his death by contributing to the 1986 animated film *Transformers*. "You know what I did this morning?" he told a confidant. "I played the voice of a toy. Some terrible robot toys from Japan that changed from one thing to another."[18] The arc from his *War of the Worlds* broadcast was complete, as he now played a planet that gobbled other planets in a cash grab to hawk a new line of children's stuff. And he wasn't alone. Oprah Winfrey could go from local radio to earning an Academy Award nomination in a serious, literary cinematic adaptation of the Alice Walker novel *The Color Purple* to hosting a wildly popular daytime talk show on first-run syndication. One of her more prominent guests of the period, Donald Trump, represented its showy new-money ethos. The man was a real estate developer, casino mogul, and football franchise owner. While on her show, he floated the idea to Oprah that he might run for president to combat the pernicious competition of the Japanese. Our supine politicians didn't know how to handle them, but he, the big-time businessman, did.

Cable and satellite television opened the possibilities of the medium with new channels and programming. An endless loop of nonstop athletics coverage could be found on the Entertainment and Sports Programming Network (ESPN), and nonstop commercial and syndicated programming could be had through the Turner Broadcasting Channel (TBS). The latter's owner, Ted Turner, had graduated from the advertising and radio business to television. In between consolidating media companies and expanding their reach during the 1970s, he had purchased the Atlanta Braves and broadcast its games on TBS. Turner then charged into another media dimension in 1980 by creating the Cable News Network (CNN), a twenty-four-hour channel promising endless reporting from across the globe. This was a boon for democracy, in theory: it was more information for more people delivered more quickly.

Coverage of the Falklands Islands War showed Great Britain rediscovering its greatness by bringing the ruling Argentinian military junta to heel. Democracy arose as the decade-long dirty war in that country came to an end. Next door in Chile, a 1988 plebiscite removed the long-time dictator, General Augusto Pinochet. Such success was surprising and could be attributed to a sunny, hopeful television ad campaign that consolidated support among the typically fractious opposition parties. A 1981 coup attempt in Spain was thwarted as television captured images of military officers spraying rounds of submachine gun fire in the Cortes Generales chambers as that deliberative body was about to enshrine its second prime minister after the Francoist dictatorship ended. The king went on live television after midnight denouncing the insurrectionists, who yielded without harming the hostages. The Second Spanish Republic, and democracy itself, had been saved. The outgoing prime minister, Alfonso Suarez, remained a paragon of calm, stoic dignity throughout the affair, and resigned as promised after it was over. A Kennedy-like figure who had overseen the previous dictatorship's control of Radiotelevisión Española, Suarez knew that "it was no longer reality that created images, rather images that created reality."[19]

Over in the Soviet Union, a far less telegenic figure, Mikhail Gorbachev, took over as general secretary of the Soviet Communist Party in 1985. He instituted the twin reforms of perestroika, which promised structural changes to Russian society, and glasnost, which translates as "openness." The latter proved more decisive than the former. Media had been tightly controlled throughout the Soviet era, not just in the closed production processes of state-sanctioned propaganda but also in terms of access to technology itself. The Soviets hoarded all the nation's typewriters and even imposed a ban on photocopiers. What they feared, above all, was the proliferation of self-published samizdat. Photocopiers were locked behind steel doors and guarded, available only to government ministries. Students, engineers, and medical professionals could wait in long lines on limited occasions to reproduce their work, but only after having those documents officially inspected and recorded by machine counters. By the 1980s, the policy became superfluous with the rise of computers. And in the aftermath of the obvious disinformation surrounding the Chernobyl disaster, journalists grew more aggressive, the public more alert. A military hard-liner coup attempt in 1991, similar to the Spanish experience, was exposed and failed. Gorbachev did not just resign but dissolved the Soviet Union altogether just a few months later.

It was all but over for communism by that point anyhow. Global communications and a widespread belief in liberal democracy had already deteriorated the Soviet system. Two years after Reagan told Gorbachev to tear down that wall in Berlin in 1987, the world watched as young East Germans chopped it down with sledgehammers. A Velvet Revolution succeeded in Czechoslovakia soon after as support galvanized for a jailed dissident, Václav Havel. The playwright had come to notoriety during the Prague Spring of 1968 when, under the press freedoms opened by First Secretary Alexander Dubček, Havel delivered a series of radio addresses opposing Soviet intervention. "We are hungry for news of any expression of support that comes from anywhere in the world," he said in a riff on the importance of free access to transistor radios. "Every such expression strengthens us, and we are grateful for each one."[20] The hope of that moment dissipated as the Soviets barreled in and removed Dubček, but the resilience paid off two decades later. Mobilized protests secured Havel's release and communism receded, ending the one-party state. Havel himself became interim president and addressed a joint session of the US Congress in 1990 to ringing applause. The promise of democracy, he told the Americans, was that it relied on freedom of speech, free elections, and a prosperous market economy.

Global communications and free speech were seen increasingly as constituent features of liberal-democratic culture. The 1989 protests in Beijing's Tiananmen Square had young activists staring down communist tanks, and China even signaled a willingness to open itself to market reforms. In South Africa, Nelson Mandela was released from his decades-long prison sentence in 1990, a sign that the country's apartheid was buckling under international pressure. Slovenia and Croatia held referendums on declaring independence from Yugoslavia in 1990 and 1991, respectively. The citizens of each republic registered over 80 percent approval, and though Slovenian independence was greeted by Yugoslav forces from Serbia with a brief ten-day conflict, the expedition relented. Across the globe, liberal democracy was on the march as the twentieth century closed, highlighted by expanding free expression facilitated by open media.

As it turned out, the story wasn't over. Sisyphus's boulder was about to tumble downward once again. But it's worth pausing here to clarify a crucial point. Television dominated this part of the story for good reason; it was the dominant cultural medium for the second half of the century. But the key thing about this era of politics is that the entire media system—television, radio, and print all together—functioned as an arbiter of liberal-democratic values. We all agreed "the media" existed, and it served to maintain some semblance of a check on power. It was hardly a perfect system, as some used it cynically to manipulate and distract the public. Yet the presence of gatekeeping institutions meant that standardized journalistic practices were enforcing the rules of the game. Nixon's up-and-down career perfectly illustrates this dynamic, proving if nothing else that effective journalism still brought consequences. If we're right, liberal democracy is fundamentally a culture that only works to the extent that norms like fair play and truthfulness are respected. The union of commerce, television, and news remained something of a game, but the system survived because there were still boundaries of fair play. The rules of that game could always change, though, much like democracy itself.

We saw a test run of this tenuousness in the 1970s as Indira Gandhi, the prime minister of India, declared a nearly two-year Emergency that tamped down on freedoms of speech and press, jailed dissidents, and forced sterilization. She had been found guilty of campaign violations, and now she could rule by decree. The independence of the judiciary and the press was but a trifle. Gandhi's father, Jawaharlal Nehru, had served as the first prime minister of India, presiding over a new constitution for a multiethnic democracy after having been imprisoned by the British. Maybe it was his legacy, or the resiliency of democracy itself, but eventually Indira relented and agreed to new elections. The Emergency ended, and she promptly lost her seat. Democracy was restored, and Indian newspapers and politicians to this day solemnly reflect on the Emergency every June 26, the date from 1975 when it was declared. Yet, as Gyan Prakash has argued, far too much belief in the triumph of democracy emerged in the wake of the Emergency, as it had with Watergate. In both cases, we were led to believe that all was normal again because of the enforcement of certain norms and procedures.[21] What should have been an opportunity for introspection was overshadowed by an enduring misplaced confidence.

The truth is that democracy lurches from one emergency to the next, often gasping to sustain itself. The dangers are invited and lurk continually below the surface. Liberal democracy, with its focus on norms and tolerance, papered over many of those dangers. We were perhaps lulled into thinking that the rules of the game would always be enforced. When new technologies began to dissolve those boundaries, the global culture of communications began to split apart. And the fragmentation wasn't just political; it was epistemological. The gatekeepers lost control. Tribal impulses were suddenly amplified by a chaotic information space in which every truth claim, every story, was up for grabs. This has radically altered the practices of democratic politics, and the pace of change has outstripped the capacity of our institutions to keep up. The transformation would not be immediate but slow and then sudden. In hindsight, it should have been more apparent. The paradox suggests as much.

THE DEATH OF LIBERAL DEMOCRACY

HAVE WE GOT FAKE(D) NEWS FOR YOU

We could hardly see it happening in real time. Reality shifted beneath our feet. This was supposed to be the information age, with various new media providing a coherent, stable understanding of the world. Facts were instantaneously accessible. First we could click on a television remote for twenty-four-hour cable news, then we could click on a desktop mouse to run a search through algorithmic engines, and now we can swipe our smartphone screens wherever and whenever we want. Such advances in communications technologies promised to fulfill the Greek theory of *doxa*, ensuring that common knowledge could be established for more accountability and responsiveness between accurate public opinions and governments. What we got instead was the paradox of global para-doxa, a crisis characterized by alternative facts, fragmentation, and misinformation. Identity supplanted information as news has become curated, consumed, and enjoyed as a function of personal political preference. Faced with the tattered remains of a liberal-democratic cultural environment of communication that no longer exists, we find ourselves experiencing a collective failure in that we're inhabiting a serious case of denial—insisting that reality can be factually mediated in good faith. We need to acknowledge that what transpired over the past few decades has been the slow then sudden death of liberal democracy as a cultural historical period. New media arose, bad politics descended.

The universal ideals of liberalism were grounded in fairness and neutrality, featuring an impartial legal system devoted to right and wrong; objective journalism, which could inform public opinion with facts; a multicultural emphasis on tolerance and cosmopolitan ethics; rationally minded consumers and citizens; and a series of political norms respected by Right and Left alike. But as new media styles, technologies, and structural pressures opened up a networked world of instantaneous participatory communication, exploitative appeals to identity and power overwhelmed democratic societies. Only the most naked forms of mediated partisanship, it turns out, can cut through the morass of "communication abundance" we have at our disposal.[1] What we have experienced, then, is a return to democracy as such. It marks one of the crueler tricks the paradox has ever leveled. Liberal democracy put on a happy face and believed in progress. It was no match for a swarm of angry trolls seeking to win at all costs and yelling in us-them tones. We erred in fantastical thinking, assuming the contradictions between communication and politics had been solved once and for all. Yet here we are, basking in the chaotic glory of a new sophistic age characterized by communicative abundance and base appeals to identity and power.

Our collective blindness was understandable. The proliferation of more and more media, from cable and satellite television's twenty-four-hour news to the internet and smartphone-driven social networking, provided a legitimate reason for thinking that democracy could be protected from its worst impulses through the freedom of communication. But liberal democracy's ability to manage information through an elite gatekeeping class that constrained political passions could only last so long in such an environment. The hyper-commercialized and fragmented media landscape created epistemological bubbles, and "the people" weren't being irrational in revolting against the elites. Their lack of commitment to liberal democracy stemmed from a dissatisfaction with the unstable and unequal world that liberalism had wrought.

The international goodwill inspired by the 9/11 attacks in 2001 was squandered by the American- and British-led invasion of Iraq in 2003, based as it was on a mirage of allegations concerning weapons of mass destruction. When the operation degenerated into sectarian violence, a new rationale, based on spreading democracy, was promoted. Such cynicism suggested that democracy could be forced at gunpoint or was something to be casually invoked as a cover for a mistake. Over in Europe, most nations opposed the invasion and were busy constructing a supranational body, the European Union, to oversee economic and social matters for the Continent. Flows of people and the new euro as the common monetary unit, beginning in 2002, would effortlessly cross borders. Compared with the bloodshed of the preceding century, it was a good deal. Although the Americans and the Europeans didn't see eye to eye on military matters, their elites—liberal and conservative alike—affirmed a world of global markets and free trade, flexible labor, and exotic financial instruments. China had not fully liberalized yet but seemed pointed in the right direction. It had welcomed the handover of Hong Kong and respected the Basic Law, which granted liberalism if not democracy to the protectorate. It was to be "one country, two systems" working in harmony. Former Soviet Bloc countries along with Russia held their own elections. All those cheap goods and rising incomes and media innovation would surely translate into permanent political reforms. As for the Global South, its nations could join the party so long as they adopted policies in tune with the Washington Consensus and could adequately service their debts owed to the International Monetary Fund. The system hummed along imperfectly but reasonably until the financial crash of 2008.

For all the damage of the Great Recession, nothing much changed. The officials issued some stern warnings in a series of new, hardly exacting rules. But it was all still a game, proceeding in obliviousness to the anger of its fans. They remained in the stands, though, instructed to accept the austerity of the accommodations. The players and coaches and commissioners didn't anticipate that the stadium was outfitted with wi-fi, with all the new platforms in social networking connecting spectators to one another in real time. Fans then coordinated to cheer on incautious upstarts and flashy, no-talent veterans who were unafraid to play dirty and throw deep. If the rules were allowed to be broken, if only discreetly—off the field and hidden from view—it seemed to follow that an advantage could be found among those players willing to openly flout the customs and traditions of play. Everyone in the stadium, except perhaps the reporters in the press box, seemed to understand that the "good sportsmanship" of this game was as contrived as professional wrestling matches. In that case, fans figured they might as well lean into the spectacle of it all. If nothing is on the level, the rank amateurs at least provided a better show. The defiant attitude with which they played was, for many, refreshing. These newcomers were also willing to win at all costs. What they wouldn't do was play for a draw or get bogged down in the appreciation of a solid buildup of possession and field position.

Liberal democracy perhaps deserved to lose. It took its victories in the 1980s and 1990s for granted. Democracy's third wave suggested that the good times of political freedom would last forever. The defeats of 2016 and beyond sting because liberal democracy got run out of the stadium by an even more corrupt and undisciplined squad. The losers thought, wrongly, that the grand traditions of the sport mattered, that they had to be honored, discussed, revered. In thinking that democracy could only be played a particular way, they penalized themselves. By contrast, the winners liberated the field of play and exhilarated the fans. This game recap isn't a story of how democracies die; it's a story of how democracies are won.

The cultural conditions of communication had changed, a structural evolution of open media set in motion long before 2016. It was this dynamic that ultimately encouraged and rewarded models of political behavior that openly violated traditional norms. What we ought to recognize is that democracy provides no mandate to be fair, or kind, or accurately represent public opinion. Democracy only has to facilitate open communication. Unfortunately, that openness can lead to the consolidation of autocratic and oligarchic power just as easily as it can lead to more representative political systems. The tumult of 2016 and the wave of populist politics are proof of that.

But the shift in global politics didn't emerge from a vacuum. The paradox of democracy has always promised chaos and disruption. Liberal democracy shielded us from the paradox for a time, but transformations in media culture have a way of surfacing contradictions. While journalistic scandals of fabricated news could be found during this period—NBC's *Dateline*'s rigged GM truck explosions, Stephen Glass's falsifications in the *New Republic*, Jayson Blair's concoctions in the *New York Times*, CBS's phony Bush documents—the more decisive problem was the structures of media convergence, both economic and technological. The former promised unimagined synergies among the open communication processes of democracy, the latter abundant consumption patterns of expression and information. Each got out of hand, as the paradox would suggest. Economically, media organizations were encouraged to consolidate. The growth of ever-larger corporations would provide ever more content amid ever more business efficiencies. That was the theory, yet in practice this meant the very structure of the news had been faked long before "fake news" became a thing. First came the newspaper chains as Gannett, Tribune, News Corp, and Hollinger upended the staid private ownership model of family-run newspapers.

Bigger was supposed to be better, and advertising and subscription revenue looked good in the 1990s. The *New York Times* wasn't above getting into the act, purchasing the *Boston Globe* for over $1 billion in 1993. The once level-headed McClatchy chain joined the game in 1997, acquiring the *Star Tribune* in Minneapolis for $1.4 billion and then, in 2006, notching the Knight Ridder chain for $4.5 billion, assuming some $2 billion in debt. Even alt-weeklies—free city newspapers known for their edgy, independent reporting in urban spaces—consolidated. The *New Times* and the *Village Voice* began acquiring other alt-weeklies around the country. By 2000, Wall Street investors took a stake in the *Village Voice* chain, and then the *New Times* parent announced a merger in 2005, creating Village Voice Media.

All that bigness sapped local reporting of its energy. The rise of news deserts—communities with no access to journalistic reporting— resulted in a net loss of two thousand local newspapers between 2004 and 2020, with fifty million fewer print readers. Cut positions and reduced competition didn't lead to success either, as newspapers became something of a financial albatross. The timing was awful as well. Because of the advent of cheap online ads, by 2010 newspaper advertising revenue dropped below what it was in 1950. The *Times* sold the *Globe* for just $70 million in 2013, the same year Rupert Murdoch, bowing to investor pressures, divided his corporate empire into print holdings, as News Corp, and television and film, with Twenty-First Century Fox. In 2014, Tribune Media spun off its print holdings to a separate entity later called Tronc and saddled it with $350 million in debt. The *Village Voice* ceased publication in 2018, its merger with the *New Times* having lasted until just 2012. McClatchy filed for bankruptcy in 2020.

If the chains and their investor priorities were bad for journalism, the next wave of newspaper ownership, led by hedge funds and private equity firms, was even worse. These entities have a taste for not only layoffs but stripping the underlying real estate assets of newspaper offices and printing presses. Alden Capital runs Digital First Media, which controls over fifty newspapers and in 2021 bought out Tribune Publishing, which mercifully shed the Tronc appellation. Another of these firms running over a hundred newspapers, Gate House Media, is controlled by the New Media Investment Group under the umbrella of the Fortress Investment Group, which is itself owned by a Japanese financial conglomerate, SoftBank. When Gate House acquired Gannett and its holdings in 2019 thanks to a $1.8 billion loan from another private equity firm, Apollo Global Management, the new entity kept Gannett's name and became the owner of more than 250 daily newspapers and hundreds of weekly publications. The announcement of the merger was accompanied by a promise that $300 million in annual savings would soon be realized. Translation: expect more dramatic cuts to newspaper staffs.

Newspapers, the lifeblood of democracy since the eighteenth century, soon represented a fraction of the overall media ecosystem. They had competed with magazines, radio, and television throughout the twentieth century, and they managed reasonably well. In the twenty-first century, newspapers have been confronting the rise of twenty-four-hour cable news and (relatively) free online content such as news sites, blogs, and social networking platforms. These changes alone provide stark competition, but American democracy allowed its pumping heart to keep beating at a disadvantage due to the economic pressures of consolidation. A congressional hearing might have been nice. A political party suggesting a subsidy system, or even the prevention of such mergers, would have been welcome. Instead, there was hardly a whisper of complaint. No one realized that these media corporations were strangling news-gathering methods while also pumping out, by any standard, faked news. That is, to survive in a competitive environment, print media began relying on "custom publishing" full of "photo-illustrations," which edited images for contrast and style, and "advertorials," which offered promotional materials disguised as news articles.[2] Legally, these stories had to include a "Paid Advertisement" disclaimer, often inserted in a small type size. Within the larger sphere of economic convergence, we witnessed the practical convergence blending advertising, journalism, and public relations. The George Bush administration secretly paid opinion columnists like Armstrong Williams hundreds of thousands of dollars to write and speak favorably of its education reform effort, No Child Left Behind. Neither custom publishing nor paid opinion syndicates were a balm, as they both damaged journalistic credibility and failed to cover for print's losses to digital. The online world would service fake news better and for cheaper besides, with "native advertising" and "sponsored content" that continue to grace the sites of even the most respected news organizations.

Beyond the structural and self-inflicted problems facing print media was their being dwarfed by the emergence of even larger media conglomerates combining broadcast television networks, film studios, and internet service providers. We return to 1989, near the apex of victory for liberal democracy, when the first vaunted merger between Time Inc. and Warner Bros. was completed just in time to promote the blockbuster release of *Batman*. The markets responded in a positively giddy fashion. "What you've got," a financial analyst told the *New York Times*, "is a company that will be the largest magazine publisher in the country, the world's most profitable record company, a cable television entity with more than 5.5 million cable subscribers, one of the world's largest book-publishing operations and the country's largest suppliers of pay-cable programming."[3] This was but a prelude to Time Warner's 1995 merger with Turner Broadcasting, which delivered the Cable News Network (CNN), among other cable holdings, under its umbrella. And that merely whetted the appetite for America Online's $165 billion acquisition of the behemoth in 2000. Here was convergence in all its glory: AOL Time Warner could supply cable television and internet service and publish books and magazines while also creating an endless panorama of entertainment and news. All this media could then foster consumer interaction on AOL's chatroom and instant messaging platforms. Such a horizontally structured corporation may not have constituted an authoritarian dictator's dream of controlling "the media," but AOL Time Warner's scope was close. Investors, to their credit and discredit, tend to care more about the bottom line than anything else, and sure enough the heavy debt load and general mismanagement required spinning off the music division and cable systems and even AOL itself. By 2016, AT&T, which responded to the Ma Bell breakup of the early 1980s with effective investments in the mobile phone market, acquired what was left of Time Warner to join its control of DirecTV satellite television service. Almost immediately, Time's publishing assets were divested and scrapped for parts by the Meredith Corporation. AT&T then spun off DirecTV and Warner-Media in 2021.

Such deal-making is not isolated. In 1995, Disney executed a take-over of Capital Cities/ABC Inc., which handed it control of a major television broadcast network as well as the top cable channel, ESPN. The synergies were lovely across amusement parks, hotels, a cruise line, retail, sports, movies, and news. Disney spent millions in the nineties lobbying for stringent copyright protections, and then a decade later it devoted billions to the intellectual property rights for the Marvel Comics and Star Wars universes, followed by the archive of Twenty-First Century Fox. Comcast, by 2011, was the largest revenue earner in all American media based on its cable and internet service subscriptions alone. That year, the FCC under the Obama administration approved Comcast's acquisition of NBC Universal from General Electric. However, no matter which political party occupies the White House, networks that broadcast on public airwaves are just another asset to be bought, sold, and profited from as part of a corporate strategy of convergence. The terms of this norm were set in the late 1990s with the giveaway of the digital spectrum of the public airwaves without much debate. Senator John McCain raised some concerns but was ultimately defeated in his opposition to the Telecommunications Act of 1996.

McCain had joined then Representative Bernie Sanders as part of only a handful of legislators to oppose such sweeping changes to the American media system. The act's stated rationale was "to promote competition and reduce regulation in order to secure lower prices and higher quality services for American telecommunications consumers and encourage the rapid deployment of new telecommunications technologies."[4] It really did a masterly job of following through in its intent to prioritize deregulation and treat American citizens as little more than consumers. Section 202 of the act, signed by President Bill Clinton, took a hammer to the regulatory power of the FCC, tasking the commission with "eliminating any provisions limiting the number of AM or FM broadcast stations which may be owned or controlled by one entity nationally" (202.a); "eliminating restrictions on the number of television stations that a person or entity may directly or indirectly own, operate, or control, or have a cognizable interest in, nationwide" (202.c.1.A); and "permit[ting] a person or entity to own or control a network of broadcast stations and a cable system" (202.f.1). While there were some limited local restrictions, this was attenuated by subsection (h), titled "Further Commission Review," which allowed such scant regulations to be repealed or modified if they were considered no longer in the public interest. Turns out, subsection (h) had been inserted at the behest of two News Corp lobbyists. It didn't so much empower the FCC as encourage media conglomerates like Sinclair and News Corp to challenge restrictions in court to consolidate their holdings even further. To their subsequent delight, a series of legal decisions deemed the regulations applied by the FCC "arbitrary and capricious." One set of scholars concluded a decade later that section 202(h) was a "successful legislative ambush" that offered "broadcasters an assured opportunity to seek greater ownership deregulation on a regular schedule."[5] Under 1994 rules, broadcasters were limited to owning no more than 36 radio stations and 12 television stations nationwide, and they couldn't possess more than a 25 percent reach in any one medium. After 1996, Clear Channel soon amassed over 1,000 AM and FM radio stations spanning conservative news-talk, country, and Top 40 formats. Since being overrun by debt in a private equity deal from 2008, Clear Channel has since changed its name to iHeartRadio and remains content with a leaner, 800-station lineup. Sinclair, which owns television broadcast affiliates, ran eight stations in 1994; by 2020, it had owned close to 300.

Then in 1997, in *Reno v. American Civil Liberties Union*, the Supreme

Court unanimously struck down portions of the Telecommunications Act that had to do with regulating "harmful" online content. The decision was rightly (in our view) cognizant of the implications for restricting free speech, but the high court said nothing about the restriction of freedom of the press caused by concentrated ownership. It also didn't comment on section 230 of the act, which provides immunity to online platforms for interactive communications, meaning that host sites wouldn't be liable as press publishers. At first, section 230 inadvertently created the first rule of the internet: *Don't read the comments.* Comments sections became so fraught with polarized discourse because there was zero incentive for moderation, by posters or the sites themselves. Social networking sites like Facebook, Twitter, and Reddit owe their existence to section 230, which shields them from litigation. What these sites amount to is a global comments section. While this has triggered the creation of propaganda and the sharing of misinformation on a pervasive scale, section 230 can at least be justified as furthering the possibilities of expression (for good and ill). Less can be said about concentrated media ownership. The US government did not, for instance, ban the Dixie Chicks from having their music played on country music stations after they spoke out against President George W. Bush at a London concert in 2003. But Clear Channel, which owned a great swath of country music stations on the FM dial, could. Likewise, the US government didn't demand that hundreds of local television news stations play "must-run" commentaries by Boris Epshteyn, a political commentator and former advisor to Donald Trump, from 2017 to 2019. But Sinclair did.

To be fair, in *Reno* the Supreme Court ruled narrowly on a very specific element within a larger work of legislation with considerable implications for free speech. Yet a broad conflation of expression to include both speech and press ignores their enumerated protections. That very fusion of speech and press would later warrant the majority decision in the 2010 case *Citizens United v. FEC*, which deemed money as speech and granted corporations the First Amendment rights of citizens. The original case concerned a political pay-per-view documentary against then presidential candidate Hillary Clinton. However hackish such work might be, and no matter how it was produced, we should agree that the piece should have been allowed to air on television. The Supreme Court could have left it at that. But it asked for another round of legal arguments expanding the underlying scope of the case and arrogated to itself the power to reject limits to financial contributions in politics altogether. An underappreciated tragedy of *Citizens United* is its defanging of press rights in the name of corporate power, meaning that basically, no distinction can be made between news media organizations and other corporate entities. The press clause of the First Amendment was, essentially, voided. Whereas free speech, as the legal scholar C. Edwin Baker wrote, reflects "a vital element of individual liberty," a free press "presumably refers to institutionalized structures or legal entities."[6] *Citizens United* has been criticized for equating money as speech. That aspect of the decision may be unsightly, facilitating quasi corruption, but that pales in comparison to an outright negation of the press clause of the First Amendment.

While only so much can be done to "manage" information and persuasion in a digitally connected global system, economic media convergence welcomed such a poisoned body politic. That's because talk is cheap, and the press can reach efficiencies only when news consists of endless commentary and speculation about politics. We could take the easy way out and blame this all on Rush Limbaugh and Fox News. And to their credit, twenty-four-hour conservative news-talk stations did pioneer an American rhetorical platform for ethnonationalist identity politics. But democracy's requirement of open communication allows for the existence of demagogic entertainers who ingratiate themselves with the public. What ought to concern us is not Limbaugh's noxious soliloquies or great personal wealth, but how that sum was amassed at a relative bargain when compared with funding journalistic programming that reports on actual news across local, national, and/or global contexts. All Limbaugh had to do was speak into a mike. The larger problem is how closely the rest of the news media landscape, beginning in the 1990s, came to resemble Limbaugh's form of infotainment—not in terms of his crude xenophobia or endless rants against feminazis, but in terms of just filling airtime with commentary. If more respectable broadcasts were produced with a gentler tone, they nonetheless remained limited to aimless talk.

The danger here was the focus on commentary itself, not its partisan nature. This wasn't journalistic reporting so much as conjecture and speculation. We would rightly be considered hypocrites to denigrate mere commentary. It is, after all, a form of political expression. Though its influence as a more destructive, sensationalist brand of journalism didn't mature until the 1990s, in 1982 CNN developed a new program, *Crossfire*, which endeavored to showcase partisan commentary pitting liberals against conservatives. *The McLaughlin Group*, appearing on PBS stations nationwide, emerged the same year with a similar format. A topic is introduced, the hosts or guests bicker with one another and try to spin the news to their advantage, they cut to break, and they come back to a new topic. This format would have been fine if it remained the same as it had evolved to on PBS: a limited, specific show of political punditry balanced by a larger predominance of actual journalistic programming. But that's not what happened. Television, particularly cable news, became a repository for facilitating endless spin about political matters. Reporting on the consequences of politics—what some might reasonably call governance—took a backseat to tracking the personalities and strategies of politics.

The mainstream press became infatuated with coverage of close political contests and the political implications of news. Campaign consultants became prized sources, even media figures in their own right, and flash polls were treated as something resembling statistically significant social-scientific data. James Fallows, among a few select journalists at the time, warned that this "relentless emphasis on the cynical game of politics threatens public life itself, by implying day after day that the political sphere is mainly an arena in which ambitious politicians struggle for dominance, rather than a structure in which citizens can deal with worrisome collective problems."[7] This is a strong point that holds up a quarter of a century later. Kathleen Hall Jamieson, a political communication scholar, also cautioned back then how "a focus on strategy invites viewers and readers to see themselves not as voters but as spectators evaluating the performances of those bent on cynical manipulation."[8] These warnings were ignored. We might point out that it's the politicians' job to figure out how best to appropriate communication to their advantage and leverage power. That's the game. And politicians, for their part, are compelled to play it. The news media, whatever it chooses to do, can never erase this part of the process.

However, if the sum total of liberal democracy stood for anything, it was adding something new to the legacy of its Greek and Roman forebears: a Fourth Estate that would employ new tools of media to push back against the exercise of political power, to set the record straight on behalf of the public. To Plato, rhetoric rendered democracy dangerous and wrong; it had to be replaced with the logical distillation of truth. Yet democracy can't survive under such conditions. It requires the open communication of persuasion. The rise of the press promised a remedy to Plato's critique. News delivered a daily or weekly arrangement of information that could index political rhetoric against the record of public officials and the needs of the community. It could also solicit and share opinions, the acts of rhetoric themselves. Both information and opinion are possible; but while the rhetorical power of political communication will always accompany, even imperil, democracy, effective news coverage is a choice that can help democracies remain democratic in the face of paradox.

But if all that mainstream journalism can offer is a platform for politicians and their parties and their public relations specialists, it may be an open press, but it is by no means a free press worthy of the responsibilities of a Fourth Estate. News is best served by mediating between the actions (or inaction) of power and the effects they exert on the public. Jay Rosen's public journalism model in the early nineties was a movement to promote direct coverage as more impactful, local, and relevant to citizens. It was, sadly, helpless against economic convergence and horse-race political coverage swamping the media environment. We shouldn't begrudge all reporters for obsessing over politics, but when they avoid scrutinizing policies and impacts on the public, the press indeed surrenders its own power. Democracy's new sophistic age emerged because it was encouraged by a news media focused solely on politics as sport, not the movements of power. The press by this point had tried to serve as a neutral referee, but in doing so it gave up any meaningful sense of reporting. Commentary remains cheap whether the host thoughtfully and fairly mediates a discussion between both sides or regales the audience with rhetorical bromides.

The rise of a separate journalistic function, fact-checking, admits to this underlying failure. Its very existence suggests that the rest of news reporting ought not to be taken seriously. If the news is faked in how it's assembled and distributed, with its focus completely devoted to power politics, no amount of facts will transcend the onslaught of information weaponized by partisan forces. Figures like the former House Speaker Newt Gingrich didn't spring from a void. If the press is going to limit its focus to political strategy, it's a rational response for politicians, movements, and parties to work the refs and scream bias at every turn. The partisan turn was invited—a natural response to the environment's obsession with the game of politics. What did we expect? Of course a party and its politicians were going to adopt a ruthless, zero-sum approach to deliver only for their fans. It was a reasonable response to the conditions set forth by the media gatekeepers themselves.

This wasn't entirely the fault of "respectable" journalists and mainstream outlets. If the focus on political strategies and personalities was lamentable, it was, at least, pursued with some semblance of serious commitment. The same can't be said of the increasing pervasiveness of sensational tabloid infotainment. Highlighting and spotlighting news of celebrities, crime, and racial conflict were the dominant methods of the local press, particularly on television. This wasn't accidental. As news affiliates experienced concentrated ownership, broadcasts were dictated to by consultant agencies, which insisted on an action-news style in which reporters appeared on camera live from the scene of crimes and fires. This provided, as the journalism scholar Neil Henry observed, "an illusion of immediacy, sensation, and responsiveness to the community."[9] Anchors were instructed to engage in as much chatty "happy talk" as possible. To cut down on costs, these local affiliates ran video news releases (VNRs) to fill up time. They tended to be national stories lacking relevance to the local communities for which they were aired. The George W. Bush administration gamed the system, creating VNRs that were surreptitiously run to support its new Medicare legislation.

Nationally, *Inside Edition*, *A Current Affair*, and *Hard Copy* began in the late 1980s as syndicated "newsmagazine" television programming. Bill O'Reilly was a star anchor for *Inside Edition* until evolving to host his own "no spin zone" on Fox News for two decades. While Fox's partisan mission may command all the obvious attention, its methods rely on the pure sensationalism handed down from this type of programming. The partisan slant is largely subsequent to the style. Fox News itself had been primed by the increasingly racialized and tabloid nature of the news before the network's existence, which came to a head with video footage of Black motorist Rodney King being beaten in Los Angeles by police, the acquittal of the officers involved, and the ensuing riots. Then we had the arrest and trial (and acquittal) of O. J. Simpson. An African American professional athlete turned broadcast and film star, Simpson was charged with murdering his white ex-wife and her boyfriend in the Los Angeles neighborhood of Brentwood. His guilt was presumed. His "Dream Team" of defense attorneys weren't shy in attacking the racist detective who investigated Simpson and perjured himself, or in taking advantage of a bungled prosecution that sought a first-degree murder conviction despite obvious evidentiary problems. CNN broadcast the trial daily, and B-roll footage in the aftermath of the not-guilty verdict played up the racial dynamics as much possible. In so many ways, the "trial of the century" prefigured the peculiar mix of infotainment and identity politics that would define news reporting in the early twenty-first century.

Small wonder, then, that satirical fake news began filling the programming gaps in the 1990s with television shows like Comedy Central's *The Daily Show* in the United States and the BBC's *Have I Got News for You* in the United Kingdom. Such humor has become a sobering and necessary correction as the news media transformed into a comic farce of conflict-fueled political pantomime. There's a dark bent to these shows, one that serves as a despondent reflection of democracy itself. If mainstream journalism is unable and unwilling to reveal the news behind the politics, these shows expose that failure. On *The Daily Show*, Jon Stewart confronted the hosts of CNN's *Crossfire* during the 2004 presidential election, telling them that they were "bad for America." He laid it out pretty clearly: the debaters, including

Tucker Carlson, were hacks engaged in the spectacle of mere theater and, most damningly, complicit in the political strategies of those in power. They *could* debate real issues facing citizens, as might be hoped for in a democracy, but instead they offered only the parlor game version of politics. The jocular hosts of *Have I Got News for You* didn't affect any seriousness in their work, but their silly interrogations of British politicians sadly indexed the paucity of public discourse more broadly. And well before we worried about living in a post-truth world, Stephen Colbert, in the 2005 premiere of his cable news parody, *The Colbert Report*, had confidently boasted he stood for "truthiness." That he identified this gut-reaction reflex as the sine qua non of mediated politics in the twenty-first century at a time when Twitter didn't exist, YouTube hadn't been bought out by Google, and Facebook was limited to those with .edu addresses is remarkable. What's more, he anticipated how much worse public discourse could become once the online world of tech ramped up its reach.

The technological convergence of media was no saving grace, only serving to accelerate the underlying problems of economic convergence. The early internet of search indexes, message boards, and blogs connected through modems comprised networked redoubts of sharp opinion and aggregated news. The blogosphere initially served as an edgy complement to a smug, satisfied mainstream press that serviced platitudes and horse-race political coverage. These were often partisan sites, but they emerged as a threat to traditional gatekeepers. The Drudge Report website was first to release the full Starr Report, detailing President Clinton's White House affair. A conservative blog took down a lion of television news, CBS's Dan Rather, by exposing the fraudulence of documents reported on *60 Minutes II* as allegedly showcasing gaps in George W. Bush's military service. And it was liberal news sites like Salon that offered some of the only serious questioning of the Bush administration's rationale for the Iraq War. Web 2.0 then changed the online world with streaming audio and video platforms and e-commerce linked through high-speed fiber-optic cables. Wi-fi, social networking newsfeeds, and smartphones soon followed, connecting everyone and everywhere. Facebook and Google grew through advanced algorithms offering their wares for free in exchange for geo-cached data footprints that could be sold to the highest bidder. These tech companies—including Amazon, which started as a bookseller—pioneered a risky business strategy, a gamble that what they lost in revenue they would gain in drawing investors through sheer growth. Eventually, they made money by consolidating market share. All they asked of citizens was to log online as consumers and provide the free labor of content and clicks to fuel sophisticated data collection engines. Traditionally, the mass media model had been based on advertising to reach demographic segments of a population. There was consumer behavior research, but it lacked precision. Media planners would buy "time" in broadcast formats or "space" in print. The shift to digital involved something altogether different: cheap exactitude based on geopositioning and behavioral tracking. We searched and we shared, but in the process we were searched and we were shared.

Mass media could never offer corporations and political campaigns microtargeting at this level. The sheer volume of online interactions mixed with the compression of digital space ensured a revolution in how communications were created, networked, and monetized. How people interact—and thereby how they are persuaded in their consumer choices and voting patterns—fundamentally shifted. Information had become commodified long before the internet; that wasn't new. What was new was the complete and utter fragmentation of the public sphere brought about by what the media scholar Zizi Papacharissi calls the "technological architecture" of convergence.[10] This shift uniquely facilitated misinformation. Disinformation, the creation and coordination of propaganda, has been a product of modern society that stretches back to the very beginnings of mass media. It has been, and will likely remain, a permanent feature of political culture. From corporate entities to politicians and their parties, the goal is to move the public. The twenty-first century added the new variable of misinformation through social media, enabling citizens to create and share propaganda among themselves at warp speed. This pivot, from disinformation to misinformation, expanded propaganda as more pervasive and unruly. Through social networking platforms, the public could exercise the powers of dissemination once exclusively reserved for publishers and broadcasters. Citizens no longer passively accepted flows of information and persuasion but were activated as prosumers who created and shared public discourse. If economic convergence tarnished the reputation of the news media as peddlers biased by sensational info-tainment and political preference, technological convergence robbed them of their privileged status. Everyone could become a gatekeeper now, yet citizens were under no obligation to conform to corporate priorities or professional ethics.

The digitally converged world is simultaneously hot and cool, real and faked, commercial and nonprofit, entertaining and political, inter-active and passive—it blurs and melds everything together. Our infinite commercial choices and personal expressions are layered through complex networked relationships among media. Images and text and audio and video and news and opinion and entertainment all hang to-gether like a plate of loose lasagna. Algorithms and up-vote/down-vote recommendations cater to what they think we like and in the process help carve out our echo chambers of like-minded souls, but we can't ig-nore the demand-side problem here. People are getting what they *really* want. The invasive and monopolistic tendencies of tech are regrettable, and reversing their power is nearly unthinkable at this point. The scale is just too large. But what if their policies and practices were ethical? What if they couldn't trade on your data and identity? Would their more personalized experience of consumption remain preferable to the limited, liberal-democratic monoculture that reigned through the mid- to late twentieth century? We can't possibly know because that's not the world we have. And even if things had unfolded differently, we would still be experiencing the cultural chaos of fragmentation that displaced the comfortable universal norms of appointment television. We shouldn't bemoan this switch, misinformation and all. What we have truly lost—for better or worse—is the utilitarian pretensions of a liberal culture that can satisfy everyone at the same time on the same thing. We now have better entertainment programming, with serial-ized shows, than ever before. The online world also offers a surfeit of courageous, informative long-form reporting. It's genuinely good to connect with others through digital spaces across the physical places of the globe. Mark Zuckerberg, the founder and CEO of Facebook, is right in his defense of social media—but for all the wrong reasons.

In fairness to the techno-utopians, they had some reason to relish the democratic possibilities of our connectivity. They found inspiration in the new waves of democratization before the millennium, which coincided with the emergence of the new mass medium. With social networking, we witnessed the sharing of the 2008 YouTube music video *Yes, We Can*. It mashed up and synthesized a primary campaign speech by candidate Barack Obama in an inspiring fashion, helping him become the first Black president in the history of the United States. Then came the Twitter Revolutions, supporting the Iranian protests for democracy in 2009 and the Arab Spring in 2010, itself touched off by a Tunisian's act of self-immolation in response to WikiLeaks. Even movements as diverse as the Tea Party, Occupy Wall Street, Kony 2012, Black Lives Matter, and #MeToo suggested that authentic, grassroots political mobilization was possible. In each instance, we had "viral" activities on social media activating new mobilizations. Yet the incessant sharing and virtue signaling among social media users weren't enough to actually challenge power. Viral moments alone didn't save us or support democracy. At worst, such responses, as with the Tea Party, were co-opted as Astroturf campaigns, offering only the illusion of resistance. Other movements reliant on the social unwound into performances of collective kitsch, limited to the sharing of affected emotional resonance. At best, you would need to marshal actual strategies and specific campaigns targeting structural configurations of power. This can happen, but the process plays out, as in Egypt, against governments who can shut off internet access or erect, like China, a Great Firewall of censorship.

For although digital media possesses democratic potential, we find a world where power is exceptionally savvy at fighting back. Democratic openness remains a double-edged sword, and we should never expect utopia, least of all in the conditions of communication. From personal face-to-face interaction to online messages that are shared and liked, communication is messy. Our challenge is not our tribal instincts so much as our all-too-human capacity to sift through a world that publishes and broadcasts more mass-mediated information every forty-eight hours than all of human history up until 2003, as Google CEO Eric Schmidt once noted. Whatever rise in mediated quality has been exceeded by an exponential quantity of information and entertainment, and sleuthing for the good stuff is challenging. We don't just mosey on down to the agora or the lyceum to hear great orators hold forth; we log on, follow, and share. The extremely online world reflects an infinite capacity for volume, encouraging ever-increasing hot takes. Just as dosage is the most critical factor in determining toxicity, so our collective exposure to the hypermediated scaling-up of communication led to acute and then chronic sickness. We suffer from "the paradox of an era of information glut," Mark Andrejevic has written. "At the very moment when we have the technology available to inform ourselves as never before, we are simultaneously and compellingly confronted with the impossibility of ever being *fully* informed."[11]

Even so, the consequential social realities of hyper-partisanship and virtue signaling and trolling so present in digital media are, for whatever else one may say of them, a more democratic shift from the perfunctory artifice offered by the mass media of liberal democracy. We should recognize these overwhelming media changes as preferable to the stability once enjoyed and gleaned from the elite gatekeeping class and norms-driven journalists and politicians. The communications infrastructure of the lost mass society was, overall, more contrived than our layered spheres of convergence. The problem isn't some imaginary Matrix separating us from the Real; it's that reality itself is a jarring hybrid of the digital and the physical. The first and singular example of this was witnessed in 2010 as a computer virus, Stuxnet, wormed its way through Iranian digital networks to compromise the operation of centrifuges in its nuclear program. This wasn't some cheap malware designed to steal passwords and financial data. It collapsed distinctions between digital and physical space altogether. The computer language of hacking resembles democracy in this regard, full as it is of vulnerabilities and exploits. We find ourselves mired in multiple paradoxes, and we do not yet even inhabit that world of purely digital communication.

Perhaps the singularity of artificial intelligence does take over at some point. If so, we are a ways off. Our world remains far too human, rhetorically and structurally. We are likely stuck, as we have been since the 1990s, in the swirling realm of economic and technological media convergence. It is this layering of structures, and the fragmented blend of some old and some still not entirely new communications, that has given rise to actors practicing democratic politics in bad faith through weaponized information. If liberal democracy offered scripted formulas in politics, its successor has relied on the absurd conventions of reality television and the disruptive playfulness of the online lulz world. The biggest problem for politics in liberal democracy was bullshit, relying on the rhetorical concealment of what was true in norms-driven discourse. The largest problem we face in its aftermath is the excesses of overwhelming public discourse. The only way to stand out in this miasma has been appeals to identity and power. People cling to what they can as a way to deal with the overwhelming nature of our global culture of information.

The cultural disorientation that accompanied the triumph of liberal democracy was profound, from a globalized sphere of growing markets and media and security to the insistence of a more tolerant, multicultural world. We need not excuse the likes of Ted Kaczynski, Timothy McVeigh, Osama bin Laden, and Anders Behring Breivik to recognize their objections to contemporary society. Each of these terrorists, in their own way, perpetrated violence to combat the encroachments of liberal democracy. To do so, they all leveraged media to symbolically exaggerate, hence terrorize, people beyond those whom they harmed directly. Kaczynski, the Unabomber, objected to the increasing role of technology in society, targeting computer science and engineering professors as well as public relations professionals. In a letter to the editor of the *New York Times*, he offered to stop the bombings only if his manifesto on the problems of industrial society was published. (The *Washington Post* would run it in the fall of 1995; the next year, he would be captured.) McVeigh sought to avenge the misguided federal responses to the standoffs in Ruby Ridge, Idaho, and at the Branch Davidian compound in Waco, Texas. Both places served as redoubts of ethnonationalist identity. McVeigh and his gang turned the tables by blowing up a federal office building in Oklahoma City. The incident was quickly painted as the handiwork of Islamic radicals, but McVeigh, the white military veteran, was the one who had lit the proverbial fuse. Muslim extremists wouldn't be outdone, however, as bin Laden created al-Qaeda, a terrorist organization, to protest Saudi Arabia's tolerance of permanent US military bases. He offered an ethnoreligious political appeal, declaring war so as to link Muslims together in a transnational culture. His war declaration, even after bombing American embassies and attacking a naval vessel, was mostly ignored, though he had welcomed interviews with ABC News and *Esquire* magazine. The rest of the media world paid more attention after the 9/11 attacks, which resembled a disaster film whose footage looped endlessly. Bin Laden's goal had been destruction and death but also terrorizing and prompting an overreaction. Before 9/11, he had contended that the United States was leading a global war on Islam. His accusation suggested that liberal-democratic values were a sham. America then proved bin Laden's point, unleashing a war on terror that included two military invasions against primarily Muslim nations and suspending its commitment to domestic and international laws.

Al-Qaeda utilized the networks of the online world to organize its attacks and propound its message, something picked up by angry young men like Breivik, who trafficked on message boards and trained on video games to prepare for the slaughter of over seventy Norwegians. He, too, posted a manifesto, and other mass shooters like him—from incels to anti-Semites to racists like Dylann Roof, who murdered African American churchgoers in Charleston, South Carolina—blur the boundaries of reality in a wash of mediated violence and violent media. The alt-right essentially got its start from misogynist trolls who had harassed women during the Gamergate controversy in 2014. It was only a short leap from the toxic culture of video games to see this pattern emerge in political communication. We're certainly entitled to view these people as demented trolls drunk on their own resentment. Yet many of them also share a worldview remonstrating with liberal democracy's universal insistence on markets, technology, and tolerance.

Marshall McLuhan had predicted this reckoning some time ago, observing that emerging communication technologies would appear to the average citizen as the sky falling. He worried that new media would prompt a frantic search for lost identities and was likely to result in tremendous violence: "As the preliterate confronts the literate in the postliterate arena, as new information patterns inundate and uproot the old, mental breakdowns of varying degrees—including the collective nervous breakdowns of whole societies unable to resolve their crises of identity—will become very common."[12] The frequent eruptions of terrorism and digital harassment can be seen, then, as violent expressions of identity against a globalized world mediated by the conventions of liberal democracy. Yet while terrorism is a dangerous, powerful tool, it doesn't translate to the establishment or exercise of sustained power. Ethnonationalist populism countered liberal democracy just the same as terrorism, but it pushed back by more overtly expressive means. This savvy and unscrupulous network of characters and their parties have sought the implosion of democracy through the simultaneous use of identity and power through media. It feels so new and dangerous if only because liberal democracy left us unprepared while taking a languorous victory lap, richly content with more and bigger media as a new generation of malefactors took root. And it's why, with democratic global dissatisfaction reaching an all-time high of 57.5 percent in 2019,[13] such malefactors continue to benefit. In short, people who were bad news figured out how to rely on fake and faked news. Just as distributed denial of service attacks (DDoS) crash website servers by overwhelming them with data, so these figures and movements punish the system at large with a never-ending stream of activity.

The abundance of options means that politics, like everything else, become more personalized than universal. This is something the notorious postmodern thinkers had grasped long before everyone else. The French philosopher Jean-Francois Lyotard was already sounding the alarm in his 1979 book, *The Postmodern Condition*. He had diagnosed how human consciousness and society were caught in a cycle of representations and products, leading not so much to relativism as fragmentation. For Lyotard and others, the point wasn't that truth was dead or that knowledge was impossible; instead, we had lost a legitimate source of epistemological consensus. It's a good thing to scrutinize the processes of knowledge, and the subsequent scrambling of ideological lines—the fact that even the language of conservatism and liberalism now feels empty—suggests that Lyotard and the postmodernists were onto something.

Yet there was one big thing they missed. Grand narratives would not die out on their own or cease to function as society's nonpareil force of persuasion. Grand narratives can indeed be reduced to language games of representation, but they also form the basis of democratic politics. We communicate through narratives, not facts; that's how we make sense of the world. The postmoderns may have been impenetrable, but their best insight was simple enough, arguing that reality was socially constructed and that truth was unstable. The liberal-democratic project, descended as it was from the Enlightenment, relied on the illusion of reason. Oddly enough, postmodernism was an intellectual movement from the Left that identified the Achilles' heel of liberal democracy. It was a dark prophecy about the precariousness of epistemology, and it largely went unheeded when it wasn't being mocked. If anything, postmodernists didn't foresee how their anti-foundationalist critique could be transformed by a political project. If all social phenomena could be reduced to identity and power, then embracing this insight could help create a partisan platform on the auspices of identity and power. Grand narratives may be faked, but in that case there remains only the incentive to fake it as well as possible.

For the illiberal encroachments remind us that democracies are historical constructions, as vulnerable to change as anything else. They are never secured or achieved so much as maintained and managed. Because we lived for so long under the stability of liberal democracy, we assumed that that stability was permanent. We assumed that periods of disruption were the exception, not the rule. We assumed that liberal democracy was democracy as such, that the system was grounded in immutable norms and ideals. But none of these assumptions held up. Like the child who discovers that the world isn't ready-made after all, we can see that democracy is flux and that the so-called pathologies of democracy—demagoguery, populism—are features, not bugs.

Hence, it's so important to not reduce democracy to a bundle of institutions or procedures, like cyclical elections or peaceful transitions of power. Democracy is an open field, always caught between the processes of becoming and unwinding. And the culture of any democracy is shaped by its tools of communication: how people acquire information, how that information is distributed, and how persuasion takes place. To be clear, this is not the only account of democratic life.

Any number of material factors shape a political culture—like wealth distribution or government corruption or demographic shifts. But the media environment is crucial insofar as it colors not just what we pay attention to but also how we think and orient ourselves to the world. This has an enormous impact on which identities get activated, which voices are heard, and what citizens are willing to tolerate.

You can't say that we weren't warned. Surveying the self-satisfied global landscape in 1997, Fareed Zakaria cautioned that democracy was vulnerable to illiberal sources of power. "The problems of the twenty-first century," he predicted, "will likely be problems *within* democracy."[14] Whereas constitutions exist to limit power, democracies empower citizens and politicians alike through open communication to accumulate and exercise power. Achieving balance is ideal, but that is no simple trick within the paradox. Zakaria's concern was that elections would become the defining feature of democratic society, with civil liberties treated as an optional accoutrement. Yet going back to the initial Athenian experiment in democracy with isegoria as free speech, civil liberties ought to be seen as fundamental, even preceding elections. The open communication inherent to democracy can diffuse power and limit arbitrary rule, but it's no guarantee. What concerned Zakaria at that time was how the new wave of democracy had become just another means by which power could be concentrated. He was particularly troubled by the "power vertical" erected by Russia's then-president Boris Yeltsin, following the shelling of parliament in 1993 and the new constitution that consolidated his authority. Zakaria hoped that Yeltsin's successor wouldn't exploit such concentrated power.

As we all sadly know, appeals to nationalistic identity and autocracy increased in a time of considerable media fragmentation, and it was all started by the machinations of a guy named Vladimir. But wait—not *that* Vladimir. Long before Vladimir Putin's campaign of fake news in Russia and elsewhere, another Vladimir had set his sights on democracy: one Vladimiro Lenin Illich Montesinos Torres, a disgraced Peruvian military man turned political fixer turned intelligence chief. What occurred in Peru in the 1990s presaged the demise of liberal democracy globally in 2016. Montesinos, the other Vladimir, first played an outsize role during the 1990 Peruvian presidential election, which pitted the celebrated novelist and Nobel laureate Mario Vargas Llosa against Alberto Fujimori, a Peruvian of Japanese descent. The election took place amid serious economic decay and the violent insurgency of the Shining Path. Vargas Llosa represented classical liberalism, promoting cosmopolitan values and free-market policies. He seemed to be a shoo-in, too, with good poll numbers and a million-dollar American campaign team that had recruited a pop singer to star in ad spots. Fujimori, another relative newcomer to politics, wasn't necessarily camera shy. For a couple of years in the late 1980s, he hosted a television program devoted to agricultural issues. On the campaign trail, he wore traditional Japanese garb and held a samurai sword. At other times he drove a tractor, signaling his solidarity with rural voters. While it may seem odd that a minority figure can run as a populist insurgent, Fujimori's success owed to Montesinos's political strategies, which protected Fujimori from investigation and painted Vargas Llosa as an out-of-touch elitist. One of the advantages of populism is that it outflanks opponents on the Right and the Left, exposing the gooey mush of the political center as riven with capitulation to a consensus that excites no one.

Fujimori had another advantage during the election: the support of the *prensa chicha*, tabloid newspapers that trafficked in crime, vulgarity, and polling. These publications, which had become prominent in the 1980s, wallowed in the horse-race coverage of personalities, blending the sensationalism of popular culture with politics in a stew of convergence. Naturally, they loathed stuffy, self-important figures like Vargas Llosa, who wanted to be seen as above the dirty fray of politics. After Fujimori won, however, it was time to consolidate media support beyond the praises from the *prensa chicha*. Montesinos helped by bribing television networks for favorable coverage. Your average dictator may threaten or buy off politicians and judges, and Fujimori's regime wasn't above that. Montesinos's trick was in figuring out how bribing media is more valuable: his payments to television stations were calculated as one hundred times larger than those dispensed to the legislative and judicial branches of government.

At first, things seemed okay. Montesinos and Fujimori, two scholars of Peru wrote, "maintained the facade of democracy—the citizens voted, judges decided, the media reported."[15] Then in 1992 Fujimori executed an *autogolpe*, or self-coup, that dissolved Peru's congress in the name of restoring democracy. With Montesinos shifting from mere political strategist to the nation's top intelligence chief overseeing a network of assassination teams, extrajudicial massacres were ordered and a Peruvian reporter of international renown, Gustavo Gorriti, was kidnapped, jailed, and exiled. A selective law threatening a ten-year sentence for journalists who revealed "secret information" was imposed. Yet all the while, Montesinos enjoyed millions of dollars in funding from US intelligence services; for this he secured American gold mining interests and "contributed" to the nation's war on drugs. Turns out, he sold weapons to the Revolutionary Armed Forces in Colombia, a rebel group, and amassed hundreds of millions of dollars in foreign bank accounts. Montesinos and Fujimori remained steadfast in propping up the imprimatur of democracy in their decade of arbitrary rule. "Without functioning institutions, the public sphere housed idle critics who posed no threat at all," Catherine Conaghan has written. "In fact, this situation was a boon to the coup, as Fujimori quickly discovered how useful freedom of speech sans institutions could be in his public-relations offensive."[16] A few years later, Montesinos even boasted how he didn't so much as bother with little newspapers like *El Comercio*, which dated back to the nineteenth century, and its sister television network, Channel N. He would bribe only the biggest and best TV stations, and he would secretly record himself making the bribes.

The strategy worked for about a decade, during which the pair created and sustained Fujimorism. Some of their business was considered unseemly, but to the international community the economics were sound and the terrorist threat of the Shining Path had been removed. Breaking eggs to make an omelet, and all that. Still, just as democracy is always vulnerable to exploitation, so some semblance of freedom of expression and press can shine a light and make an impact. Media giveth, and media taketh away. The luck of Fujimori and Montesinos ultimately ran out in 2000 as Fujimori stood for another election. Channel N, so little it didn't even merit a bribe, unearthed a cache of

Montesinos videos showing him paying off congressmen and journalists. The Vladi-videos, as they were called, marked the end of Fujimori and Montesinos. Both men fled and Fujimori resigned by fax from Japan, but each was eventually returned to Peru to stand trial and face conviction.

Although it ultimately failed to sustain itself, Fujimorism became a model for politicians and parties to retard democracies from within. It's a process of not just violating norms but leaning into the paradox, and every instance of this scourge begins with a legitimate gripe with some failure of liberal democracy. Peru also showed that even against hurdles of corruption and state terror, some kernel of free expression and press allows democracy a chance to correct its course. That hope is potential, though, and in Peru's case Fujimori, as a minority president, tended not to resort to explicit appeals to identity.

Peru was something of an outlier in this, for the 1990s had witnessed the rise of ethnonationalist rhetoric and violence well before its acceleration by social networking in the twenty-first century. The increase in radio bandwidth and new television stations accompanied this rhetorical turn, fueling identity as the basis of political meaning. This dangerous relationship could be seen throughout the decade, first in the Balkans with the siege of Sarajevo and ethnic cleansing and then with the Rwandan genocide, which began in 1994 soon after its president was killed in an attack that brought down his airplane over Kigali, the nation's capital. Hutus slaughtered close to a million people of the ethnic Tutsi minority, propelled by a Hutu Power movement and a radio station, RTLM, that started broadcasting the year prior. While a dispute remains over who had launched the missile at the presidential aircraft—a Belgian investigation found Hutus responsible; a French judge accused Tutsi rebels led by Paul Kagame, who later became president—Hutu rhetoric simultaneously dehumanized the Tutsi and complained of their own lack of power. That not just paramilitary forces but average citizens can be so easily driven to murder their neighbors suggests something dark about human nature. This also speaks to the interactive dynamics of mediated communication: ancient hatreds, racism, and systemic acts of violence aren't essentialist reflections on humanity; rather, they are consequences of our intersubjective reliance on communication. One *learns* to discriminate, in prejudicial behavior or cultural taste. Not all appeals to ethnonationalist identity lead to genocide, but in a fragmented environment of communication, the persuasive mechanisms of identity and power can galvanize unsettling calls to action.

Take India. Since independence, the world's largest democracy has continually negotiated the representation of its Hindu majority with its minority Muslim population. Aggressive forms of Hindu national- ism had been tempered for decades, but a fast-growing media in the early 1990s led to greater prominence for the nationalism espoused by the Bharatiya Janata Party (BJP). When members of its paramilitary branch burned down the Babri Masjid mosque in northern India in 1992, riots ensued between Hindus and Muslims. The BJP benefited politically from the chaos, leading to the rise of Narendra Modi, who became the chief minister of the Gujarat state. A decade later, he pre- sided over, or merely tolerated, another riot and massacre over the status of the former mosque site, which some believe was the birthplace of the Hindu god Ram. Modi's Hindu nationalism eventually propelled him to the prime minister's office in 2014. After his 2019 reelection, a new citizenship law was enacted that excluded Muslims; amid the ensuing chaos and riots, Modi's government shut off the internet in parts of the country, sent protesters to detention centers, and revoked the autonomy of Kashmir, India's only Muslim-majority state. In a rally to defend such actions, Modi demanded "respect [for] the people elected by the people."[17] Though it is neither terribly unusual nor un- democratic to issue discriminatory laws and rationalize them through traditional political means of rallies and television, Modi also relied on an online army of BJP trolls to pump out fake news through Facebook and its messaging service, WhatsApp. Mass text blasts falsely accused oppositional figures of rewarding terrorists and lobbying for special Muslim rights. While the calculus of such propaganda is layered across so much media, the politics are simple arithmetic: some 80 percent of India is Hindu, and the BJP seeks to consolidate power through appeals to the identity of the majority.

This is where we are, globally. But it is also where we have been for some time. The ethnonationalist populists take a fractured media infrastructure and exploit the polarized political environment to undermine the press even further. Israel, another democracy that like India was forged in the 1940s, is no different. Its genesis may be shrouded by the plight of Palestinian refugees who were forcibly removed from their land, but Israel at least sought to balance the practices of liberal democracy with free expression and press along with rights for its Arab-Israeli minority. The nation had encountered criticisms both deserved and unfair over the decades. Then, following the Oslo Accords of 1993, a two-state solution and peace seemed possible. Such hopes withered in the face of ethnonationalist violence, first in 1994, when an American-Israeli citizen murdered dozens of Muslim worshippers at a West Bank mosque, and then in 1995, when Israeli prime minister Yitzhak Rabin was assassinated by another Far Right nationalist. The opposition party, Likud, had portrayed Rabin as a traitor. He was deemed responsible for selling out the security of Israel for a peace deal with the Palestinians. Benjamin "Bibi" Netanyahu, who had risen to international fame and glowing media profiles in the 1980s as Israel's ambassador to the United Nations, led Likud at the time. His rallies stirred resentment against Rabin for abandoning Zionism and caring more about Palestinian rights than Israel. After the assassination and in the face of increased terrorism and a breakdown of the peace process, Netanyahu narrowly won the 1996 election. While his style had worn thin by 1999, having lost that year's election, Netanyahu remained determined, concluding, "I need my own media."[18]

It took some time to happen, but Bibi would develop a communications infrastructure of his own by 2009, when he again ran for prime minister. With the help of the casino mogul Shelden Adelson, then one of the largest conservative donors in the United States, *Yisrael hayom* (Israel today), a free daily newspaper, was born. The goal was influence, and it was worth the investment, becoming the most read news source in the country. Netanyahu served as prime minister for over a decade. By 2014, he appointed himself head of the Communications Ministry, and in the lead-up to his 2015 reelection campaign he allegedly offered to bribe the publisher of *Yediot Aharonot* (Latest news) with reduced circulation in Adelson's paper in exchange for favorable coverage. This bribe is "alleged," as Netanyahu has not been proved guilty in a court of law. As prime minister, he escaped trial for this and other cases, such as that involving Walla, a news site whose publisher was offered beneficial terms for his telecom interest in exchange for, again, favorable coverage. The investigations forced Netanyahu to step down from continuing to serve as his own communications minister in 2017, yet his basis of power remained grounded in ethnonationalist appeals and hostility to the judicial system and the press. He prevailed at the polls in 2015 by fomenting fear that Arab citizens were illegally voting, barely survived three close elections in 2019 and 2020 while facing indictment, and then finally lost his post in 2021. Bibi is neither the first politician to rhetorically exploit the public nor the last to consolidate power and corrupt his office. Sadly, these actions have become all too common. But while it may be asking too much of democracy, let alone human communication, to tame political rhetoric once and for all, the practices of democracy can identify corruption and arbitrary power. Free expression and free press are designed to allow for this, yet only as an opportunity, not a guarantee.

We are not so naïve as to insist that democracy necessitates good governance or fairness. Nor are we persuaded by complaints that democracy always devolves into mob rule. Yet if bribery and corruption continue to persist in the face of open communication, and when executive power serves no other role than tearing down deliberative, journalistic, and judicial checks on such power to rule by fiat, then the real danger is that democracy is irrelevant. The phrase "nothing matters" increasingly hints at the pit of despair democracies face because of the paradox. The problem is not that these populist outposts have descended into majority tyrannies; it's that in many of these cases, there's no possibility for democratic publics to challenge power in any meaningful way—that power continues to be exercised in a wholly arbitrary manner. All citizens and politicians have a right to complain about the press as well as their opposition. Democracy allows everyone a say. The lack of any guarantee that what you want will materialize is what makes it so frustrating, and that frustration can always be exploited.

While this antidemocratic scourge has most recently manifested on the right side of the political spectrum, Venezuela's Hugo Chavez

proved that ethnonationalist mediated power from the Left is not impossible to obtain and consolidate. After two failed coups in the early
1990s, it should have surprised no one that this man was hostile to a
free and open society. But the liberal complacency of the Venezuelan
power elite underestimated his appeal and even released Chavez from
prison, hoping he would play nice. Like other ethnonationalist figures,
his initial rise benefited from appealing to both the Right and the Left.
Having dispatched, among other candidates in the 1998 race, a former
Miss Universe, Chavez conjured a renewed Bolivarian Republic, even
going so far as changing the official name of the country after his victory. "The national soul," he proclaimed the night of his election, "has
been reborn."[19] His plans were not just symbolic but tactical. By the
turn of the century, he and his supporters had issued a new constitution
and dissolved Venezuela's congress and Supreme Court. He cracked
down on the press, demanding censorship in the name of truth. As a
cheap, entertaining substitute for the public sphere, Chavez offered his
own weekly television show, *Aló Presidente*, which could last for hours
as he performed comic routines, lectured on history, and interviewed
other heads of state.

Though his 2006 United Nations speech earned mockery for calling
President George W. Bush the devil, the lack of decorum wouldn't have
shocked his television audience back home. Earlier that year, Chavez
had filmed an episode in a barnyard. With cows as a backdrop, he dared
the American president, whom he called a donkey named Mr. Danger, to invade Venezuela. In 2012, a reporter from the *New York Times*
couldn't help but notice how Chavez relished using a catchphrase,
"Exprópiese!," which translates as "Expropriate it," much like another
reality television show host had marshaled "You're fired!" to so much
media notoriety.[20] Before Chavez's death in 2013, he had taken a shine
to Twitter. It was there that his inflammatory rhetoric could dictate
public discourse by calling the opposition fools and tweeting in global
solidarity with such respected world leaders as Libya's Muammar al-
Gaddafi and Syria's Bashar al-Assad. Throughout this convergence of
mediated politics, Chavez left Venezuela tattered from ruinous socialist
policies. His charismatically deprived successor, Nicholas Maduro,

somehow made matters worse while eliminating even more of what was left of democracy in Venezuela.

Reflecting on her time as the US secretary of state, Madeleine Albright concluded that Chavez had "conceived of politics as spectacle, a rollicking exhibition of good guy vs. bad guy entertainment."[21] This, more than anything else, is what we're talking about when we talk about populism in the early twenty-first century. It's the ongoing, exhaustive politics of communication as entertaining spectacle, which transforms power into a show and a show into power. Populism is a rhetorical style pitting the people against the elites, and given the crest of liberal democracy, its return was justified and necessary. But given all of what we know of the past three decades, invoking populism becomes just a lazy synonym for bad manners, as Benjamin Moffitt has argued.[22] Ideally, populists would have to earn the title by actually doing something, democratically considered, on behalf of the public. The populists during this period who politically succeeded, Right or Left, evinced a particular talent for absorbing and maintaining attention in the convergent media landscape.

Starting in the 1990s, Italy dealt with the rise and fall and rise and fall of Silvio Berlusconi, a former cruise ship crooner. His bad manners were sublimated as a form of charisma, whether he was comparing his sacrifices to those of Jesus Christ, promoting himself as the best politician in the world, or attacking the press (he didn't own) and the judiciary. His political success also owes to a structural understanding of communications infrastructure, from his 1980s investments in a cable television conglomerate, Mediaset, to acquiring the prized A. C. Milan football club. Like Netanyahu, Berlusconi used his high office as a shield against prosecution. While his rhetoric was outrageous, he wasn't exactly keen on transformative illiberal change. His brand of clownish conservatism was relatively harmless. Perhaps not coincidentally, this explains why Berlusconi and his right-of-center party were eclipsed by the rise of two right-wing parties more staunchly ethnonationalist in scope, the League and the Five-Star Movement. The former was wrapped in a regional, anti-immigration bow, while the latter, founded by a popular blogger-comedian, Beppe Grillo, tended toward pure antiestablishment, Euroskeptic rhetoric. In both his blog and his political movement, Grillo sensed something: amateurs were taking over the political world, which he was quick to boast about. Yet he left the Five-Star just before the 2018 elections, when both parties claimed victory and agreed to a compromise candidate for prime minister. It didn't appear that Five-Star had any real plan for governing, and Grillo abandoned the League as well to join up with a left-of-center party. All this chaotic political turmoil reveals the degree to which ethnonationalist populist parties require figureheads.

The show must have a star, an individual vehicle through which power can be embodied. Some authoritarian types would grow into such a role, like Recep Tayyip Erdoğan of Turkey. At first a mild-mannered conservative, Erdoğan began his time in the nation's capital of Ankara seeking reforms to qualify the country's entry into the European Union (EU). However, he also sought to reverse the strict policy of secularization in place since the establishment of modern Turkey under its first president, Mustafa Kemal Atatürk. As the mayor of Istanbul during the 1990s, Erdoğan had been jailed for reciting a religious poem at a public gathering. By the turn of the century, the citizens of Turkey, a nation composed largely of observant Muslims, were reasonably fed up with the corruption and the ongoing battles between the militarist Right and the secular elite. The country had been mired in an economic crisis preceding the 2002 elections, when Erdoğan's Justice and Development Party, the AKP, received only a third of the vote but two-thirds of the national legislative seats. Even so, Erdoğan's first term as prime minister was innocuous: he steered the country toward meeting some of the EU's membership requirements, and he didn't deploy heightened Islamic rhetoric to antagonize the military. "Democracy," he affirmed in 2004, "is a dialogue of tolerance and reconciliation."[23]

Everything was lining up nicely. Extreme military interventions that thwarted the democratic will would no longer be tolerated. The foreign investment money that accompanied EU accession talks would modernize the economy. Turkish citizens and politicians would have a little more leeway for religious expression, but with Erdoğan they had a responsible leader offering a strong contrast to militants in the age of al-Qaeda. His AKP forged a relationship with the Gülen movement, a peaceful Islamic sect that supported civil society projects such as schools, hospitals, and mass media. Its *Zaman* newspaper, an Istanbul-based daily widely read in print and online, provided a valuable source of information. Elsewhere, rapprochement with Turkey's Kurdish minority seemed possible, and Erdoğan demonstrated leadership that suggested a facility to mediate ongoing disputes in the Middle East, from Israel to Iraq. Surely, this ought to have been a win on the global stage.

Then came the cold feet as the leadership of some EU member states, despite Turkey's progress, floated the idea of limiting the EU's relationship with the country to that of a "partnership." The military blanched at the idea of having Abdullah Gül, a religious former prime minister, serve as president. The Turkish Supreme Court annulled Gül's 2007 election, held by parliament, on a technicality. Frustrated, Erdoğan decided he had more to gain as an autocrat. He insisted on nominating only partisan figures from the AKP as judges, then he went after media figures and protesters. Having called snap elections that year and increased the AKP's majority in parliament, Erdoğan counseled his fellow Turks that any citizens not supporting Gül should consider renouncing their citizenship. To celebrate the political victory, the government promptly seized *Sabah*, a newspaper critical of the AKP, and sold it to a crony minister who henceforth pushed laudatory coverage of Erdoğan.

Things only got worse from there as Erdoğan and his allies politicized the intelligence services, media, and court system during the Ergenekon-Sledgehammer investigations. In fairness, information agents of the state, journalists, and judges should be held accountable for transparency and critique. Lord knows they have committed their fair share of wrongdoing in just about every society. Turkey went well beyond healthy critique, though, as a wave of allegations of coup attempts by a "deep state" conspiracy led to indiscriminate arrests and imprisonments of military personnel, journalists, and members of the political opposition. Generals leading the army, navy, and air force resigned in protest after the 2011 elections but to no avail. "The tyranny of the elites is over," Erdoğan proclaimed.

Comparable to other autocratic regimes, whatever populist edge an ethnonationalist leader possesses often conceals corruption within his inner circle. Facing just such a probe in 2013 for enriching his cronies, Erdoğan swiftly removed police and judges deemed unfriendly. In addition, more investigative journalists were jailed. Erdoğan dodged every probe and sought to distract the public with plans to erect a gorgeous mosque in Gezi Park, next to Taksim Square in Istanbul—the secular epicenter of Turkish civic culture. Millions of citizens came out to protest this Ottoman-style fantasy, creating a public fervor not unlike the Occupy movement. To Erdoğan, these were simple hooligans, so he vowed to press forward. In 2012, he had seen firsthand the power of gaudy architecture when appearing at the opening of Trump Towers Istanbul with Ivanka Trump. And in 2014, after three terms as prime minister, he further consolidated his power by winning the presidency. "The biggest theft, the biggest corruption," he warned that year, "is the theft and corruption of 'the will of the people.'"[24]

Quite so. In fact, the ethnonationalist populist is not above signaling personal guilt. And so it went for Turkey: to consolidate public opinion around Erdoğan, in 2014 and 2015 the AKP ran a sophisticated pro-government Twitter campaign, harassing journalists and the political opposition. Turkey was one of the first countries to weaponize social networking. The AKP took the culture of trolls and transformed it into fake news by creating fake accounts of opponents with fake quotes. The party also created bots for trending, spamming, and hacking purposes. Such antics distort the communication environment and poison the trustworthiness of information. Everything is contested and nothing can be believed—except, maybe, the person in the position of highest authority. This problem was especially acute in Turkey, where online trolls and their AKP-supported politicians warn endlessly about foreign plots to destroy society from within. Erdoğan and other ethnonationalist autocrats fully recognize the paradox of democracy, and they trade on such intimate knowledge. Yet these types are nothing if not thin skinned and overly sensitive; Erdoğan himself made use of a ludicrous Turkish law allowing a sitting president to sue citizens for insults. This he did over twelve thousand times between 2014 and 2017 alone.[25] One benefit of democracy we'd like to think is uncontroversial is the ability to critique, even satirize, one's leaders. Yet even that simple exercise of expression has been forbidden in Turkey.

By the time the Gülen movement, known as Hizmet, finally began to question the consolidation of power and corruption in AKP leadership, it was too late. The Turkish government officially labeled Hizmet a terrorist group. This designation was tested in July 2016 during a coup or something approximating one. Military members purportedly linked to Fethullah Gülen, himself a US resident, blocked bridges in Istanbul and rolled tanks through Ankara. The Turkish public broadcaster, TRT, aired an empty set. Parliament was bombed from the air, and rebel jets locked in on Erdoğan's presidential plane. Over two hundred people died. Those are some of the facts, yet the motivations and players behind the coup are still something of a mystery. Whether it was the most ham-fisted revolutionary plan ever or just an incredible false-flag operation, Erdoğan, the populist hero, hopped on Facebook Live from his plane and broadcast a message of resiliency. Millions took to the streets to oppose the rebels. All of a sudden, no matter the coup's provenance, it was over.

Which created another pretext to seize unfriendly media outlets—more than 150 of them—and fire or imprison more academics and journalists. *Zaman* was raided and shuttered in a brutal televised spectacle. The state broadcaster was robbed of its independence and reduced to conducting its reporting at the pleasure of the AKP, as was the Anadolu Agency, the country's wire service. Within this new milieu for Turkey, in 2017 a national referendum, narrowly and controversially decided, changed the constitution to create even more executive power for the presidency, which Erdoğan could now inhabit until 2029. After Istanbul defied the AKP in a 2019 mayoral contest, the government dismissed the results and ran another election. After his party lost again, Erdoğan deigned to accept the results. Whether this leads to some measure of democratic accountability and renewal in Turkey remains to be seen. For that you need not just elections but a modicum of respect for freedom of expression along with an actual desire to limit political power. As it is, the disrespect for liberal democracy is so overwhelming that Erdoğan's security detail, visiting Washington, DC, in 2017, felt comfortable beating up American protesters at a public park in broad daylight. Turkey earned its own embarrassing disrespect the next year as Saudi Arabia saw fit to kidnap, execute, and dismember a Saudi journalist and American resident, Jamal Khashoggi, in its Istanbul consulate.

By this point, liberal democracy had become a laughingstock: too corrupt and weak to avoid disappointment, too craven and ineffectual to defend itself. The paradox has always rendered democracy vulnerable from implosion, but never has its contradictions in communication been so easily exploited. Liberals served democracy on a platter to ethnonationalist authoritarians, practically inviting them to feast on the public. Such was the case in Hungary, where Viktor Orbán and his Fidesz Party have consolidated authority since 2010 without much pushback from other democratic leaders and states around the world. Yet long before his autocratic turn, Orbán had been a young man opposing Soviet influence as a member of a George Soros–funded student group. Fidesz itself stood for the Alliance of Young Democrats, and in 1989 Orbán was its representative onstage in Heroes' Square for a commemorative reburial of a Hungarian prime minister who had been executed during the failed 1956 revolution. Before a quarter of a million people in attendance, with many more watching on live television, Orbán demanded the removal of Soviet troops and free elections. If we believe in our strength, he told the crowd, Hungary could become an independent democracy. That it did just two years later, and Orbán climbed the ranks to become prime minister in 1998. His first term was mostly preoccupied with EU accession preparations and his country's becoming a new member of NATO. By 2002, Hungary had at long last joined the liberal galaxy of nations.

Though Fidesz and Orbán were more nationalist than most mainstream European political parties and politicians, they played nice in the game of liberal democracy. In losing national elections in 2002 and 2006 to a liberal-leftist alliance, Orbán became an opposition figure delivering more caustic speeches in front of crowds as staged media events on the new right-wing network, Hir TV. He was given a gift after the 2006 elections when a secret recording of the sharp entrepreneurial prime minister, Ferenc Gyurcsány, was leaked to Magyar Radio. "We have screwed up. Not a little: a lot. No European country has done something as boneheaded as we have," he was heard admitting to fellow party leaders. "It was totally clear that what we are saying is not true."[26] The talk was sprinkled with vulgarity and made it clear that the country's leadership relied on both political tricks misleading the electorate and infusions of international capital. Almost immediately, and not undeservedly, mass protests formed outside parliament.

Gyurcsány resigned in 2009 amid the global financial crisis. The timing of Orbán's campaign against liberal democracy in general and the EU in particular was apt. Fidesz—seemingly reasonable compared to anti-Semitic rhetoric emanating from its right-wing cousin, the Jobbik Party—scored a supermajority in 2010. Soon enough, Hungary had a new constitution limiting the power of the judiciary and expanding executive prerogative. This fresh legal and political framework was meant to serve Fidesz, since parliamentary elections were gerrymandered, media licenses were centralized and handed to pro-government personages, and public broadcasters had become mouthpieces for the party. Despite piloting Hungary's accession to the EU in his first term, Orbán, the Euroskeptic, has shown little reservation in accepting billions of euros in annual subsidies and rewarding a network of party minigarchs, as they have been called, with largesse. Beyond cronyism, he oversaw a cultural shift of legislation and media through the prism of Hungarian nationalism, funneling politics through the collective memory of betrayal, resentment, and chauvinism. Orbán presented himself as a leader redeeming Hungary by symbolically liberating the nation from the painful Treaty of Trianon in 1920, the Nazi takeover, and Communist rule. Miklós Horthy, the regent during the interwar period, has been lionized, as has Hungarians' purported distinguishing characteristic as a Turkic people of battle-tested marauders. This notion of Turanism seeks to establish a Hunnic birthright coursing through the blood of contemporary Hungarians; it's expressed through popularized symbols of Rovás, an ancient Hungarian script. The meanings don't matter as much as their very presence as a marker of ethnonationalist identity.

After reelection in 2014, Orbán began promoting the new Hungarian reality of illiberal democracy. He articulated the contours of such a state as grounded in Christian culture, the family, and opposition to immigration. Such steps were necessary, Orbán observed, to combat "the consequences of a civilizational phenomenon in which the world has become a huge global village."[27] Orbán has read his McLuhan, apparently. Like other ethnonationalists during this period, amid a cultural cascade of disorienting change, he justifies autocratic turns through blood-and-soil rhetoric. He loves his country, he said, and he would not allow anyone to change Hungary from the outside. The critique is understandable, but the rhetorical trick is that it was *his* ethnonationalist party's policies that fundamentally changed Hungary.

It was fine for Orbán to criticize Europe and the West more generally as offering liberalism at the expense of democracy. He was right to point out that European elites had failed, and he was right to call out hypocrisy. But Hungary's attack on liberal democracy was far from being some principled stand on managing change. It was little more than autocratic consolidation of power under one man and one party. You find corruption and propaganda all the way down. These are explicit political choices too. Denmark and Australia, for example, have legislated strict immigration policies, yet they have not lapsed into autocratic or authoritarian rule. Democracy, even without liberalism, affords for differences of opinion and policies; what it cannot and should not countenance are increasing concentrations of power combined with a denigration of the ability to critique and report on power. One should be able to see through this, but Orbán's success, to the extent that it redounded to him and not the public, relied on exercising a spread of contradictory arguments. On the one hand, he promoted Turanism, a historically twisted anthropological basis for Hungarian nationalism; on the other, he positioned himself as the only leader in Europe willing to defend Christian culture. He acknowledged that he doesn't care for preserving the beliefs of Christianity so much as its way of life, which he characterized through the concepts of dignity, family, and nation. The only real way to effect such a vague political program is to offer cheap identity appeals and an ever-increasing power vertical.

Securing such goals meant that by 2018, Fidesz had replaced Jobbik as the country's true Far Right party, the latter having seen through the inherent corruption of its erstwhile ally. Soros, the Hungarian Jewish philanthropist, became the continual target of political attacks that trafficked in anti-Semitic tropes. Having fled the Holocaust as a child and supported Orbán's rise as a student leader, Soros was repaid thirty years later by Orbán's jettisoning his Central European University from Budapest. In response to the COVID-19 pandemic, in 2020 the government handed Orbán the authority to rule by decree indefinitely to deal with the emergency. The paradox was made whole by a man who in 1989 had stood courageously against a concentrated system of power and for democracy. As Anna Szilágyi and Andras Bozóki sadly note with regard to Orbán, "Thus, the revolutionary rhetoric that had once been used to initiate a transition to democracy is now used to complete a constitutional coup d'état against an established democracy."[28]

Ethnonationalists played the paradox and won. They watched liberal democracy discredit itself, then took advantage of the cultural vacuum of communications in its wake. This was very much the path followed by that other Vladimir—Putin, of Russia. Unlike Orbán, Putin hadn't been some freedom fighter for democracy in a past age. He had been a KGB agent stationed in East Germany who witnessed the fall of the Berlin Wall. The breakup of the Soviet Union provided the great calamity of Putin's life, not because of an ideological fidelity to communism but because it compromised Russia's identity as a world power. That humiliation was then exacerbated by the cultural and political chaos sowed in the 1990s while Russia moved in a more democratic direction. Putin would not let Russia or himself be so debased again, and in the process he would prove that liberal democracy's victories were pyrrhic.

His formative experience with media culture might help us understand Putin's politics. Back in 1973, while he was studying law at Leningrad State University, the Soviet Union had been transfixed by a new television show, *Seventeen Moments of Spring*. Most communist creative media had been social realist schlock, but here we had a genuine hit—a riveting series about a Soviet agent who had infiltrated the Nazis during World War II and thwarted a separate peace between the Americans and the Germans. Tens of millions of Russians watched, crowding into private and public spaces alike. The series was broadcast annually across Eastern Bloc nations in order to celebrate Russia's victory. Vyacheslav Tikhonov played the lead character, Max

Otto von Stierlitz, who infiltrated the Nazis through his charm, stealth, and duplicitousness.

The implication of *Seventeen Moments* was that Russia had won the war on its own through the guile of the KGB. The institution was to be celebrated instead of feared and disowned. Young Vladimir was convinced, joining as soon as he graduated and working his way into a German field office. Of all the consequential public decisions in Putin's life, this was perhaps the most important: the choice that launched his foray into politics—particularly democratic politics. After the dissolution of the Soviet Union, Putin worked in the mayor's office of Saint Petersburg, which had just restored its original name. A filmmaker spotlighted Putin, who resembled Tikhonov, and had him reenact scenes as Stierlitz. The connection was made, and it would stick. In 1999, the year before Putin's first election as president, an opinion poll in the newspaper *Kommersant* asked readers who among Russia's historical and fictional personages they would like to see serve in such a role. The answer was resoundingly in favor of Stierlitz, and the persuasive influence of a constructed image wasn't lost on Putin as he indeed became president. Such propaganda power didn't need to be overtly ideological. For Russian political leadership, it only required a steely, nationalist presence that projected confidence, cunning, and pride.

These are attributes that Putin's predecessor, Boris Yeltsin, lacked. He was a corrupt politician who oozed incompetence. The man who had stood down a military coup at the end of the Soviet era almost immediately sowed disarray with his "shock doctrine" of economic policies. Encouraged by leading minds in the West who conflated democracy with free markets, the idea was to open the floodgates of capital into Russia. The currency wouldn't have to change, civil society protections wouldn't have to be managed: it was all good, so long as the West could pronounce victory as the free market reigned and NATO expanded. The shock doctrine became a nightmare as incomes couldn't keep pace with prices set by mafia-like distributors who consolidated industries and supply chains. Communism may have been a bankrupt ideological system, but ordinary Russians found capitalist democracy to be a scam abetted by open communication. An example of this could be found in the popular television character Lenya Golubkov, an avuncular schlub who puttered about the house and on his tractor. His personage represented the new democratic face of Russia, and it praised the cheery potential of investing in shares of MMM, a financial company that promised 30 percent returns. When exposed as a Ponzi scheme, the contributions of millions of Russian citizens were erased.

If Putin represented Stierlitz, Yeltsin was like Golubkov. That sufficed in the 1990s at least, for Yeltsin had benefited electorally from being the lesser evil compared with the political alternatives. These included facing a fascist-like figure, Vladimir Zhirinovsky, in 1993, and Gennady Zyuganov, who sought a restoration of communism, in 1996. The 1993 campaign was followed by Yeltsin's order to dissolve the legislature, prompting an impeachment vote against him in the Duma, whose leaders barricaded themselves inside and encouraged violent protesters to take over the Ostankino public broadcast network. In response, Yeltsin had the parliamentary White House fired upon and raided. The new constitution shaped the power vertical that rendered the Duma inconsequential. When that deliberative body asked Dmitry Kholodov, an investigative journalist for *Moskovsky Komsomolets*, to testify about corruption at the Ministry of Defense in 1994, he was blown up at the offices of the newspaper before he could appear.

By 1995, the vaunted loans-for-shares program had begun to crystallize the culture of kleptocracy and oligarchy that Russia continues to negotiate decades later. It prized growth, crony privatization, and concentrated ownership at the expense of open competition. One emerging oligarch was Boris Berezovsky, an auto salesman turned oil magnate who assumed a major stake in Ostankino. Advertising revenue was embezzled so frequently that the television network had to halt paid commercials. The decision was greeted with the assassination of Vladislav Listyev, a popular and respected national figure who hosted a game show, a newsmagazine series, and an interview program on the network. Listyev had been gunned down in his apartment stairwell. Berezovsky then transformed the network into ORT, which offered itself as a campaign conduit for Yeltsin in the 1996 contest. New oligarchs hatched a plan, aptly named the Davos Pact, to support Yeltsin. Another major Russian network, NTV, was also brought in. Following the election, Berezovsky crowed, "Now we have the right to occupy

power in the face of a postindustrial society. He lamented that the Soviet state underestimated the importance of communications systems, and his vision outlined a more high-tech society, with a focus on computer science and telecommunications networks. Russia would not become a second edition of the United States or the United Kingdom, mind you, where liberal values have deep historical traditions. Putin had in mind something different, a commitment to making sure that "Russia has been and will remain a great country." All he would have to do was wait until March for the presidential election.

Two days later, Yeltsin recorded the televised address traditionally delivered on New Year's Eve by Russia's head of state. But just as the production crew wrapped, he asked to retape the talk. When the cameras rolled this time, he resigned, effective immediately, and ceded power to Putin. Within twenty-four hours, the new president was filmed dressed in camouflage on the front lines in Chechnya. In the months to come, Putin would campaign by piloting both a fighter jet and a submarine. His main opposition by that point had been reduced to only the tired, defeated communist rear guard. About the only moment of pause in the entire fait accompli was a puppet sketch in January on the NTV satire program, *Kukly*, in which a fairy resembling Berezovsky cast a magic spell on an ugly dwarf to make the townsfolk think he was beautiful. The spell represented the media, and the dwarf was understood, ostensibly, as Putin. The reaction was swift: even before the election, Putin had ordered an investigation of NTV and its parent company, Most Media. *Kukly* continued with other skits lampooning Putin, and just days before the election another NTV program had questioned the FSB's role in the bombings from the previous year.

Putin won, of course, and the first order of business following the inauguration was attacking the offices of Most Media. A month later, the CEO was jailed without charges and forced to sell NTV for his freedom. The shakedowns continued that first year as Berezovsky balked at his protégé's legislative initiatives that sought to control local and regional governments. Putin signed the series of bills "strengthening vertical power," in his words,[30] and Berezovsky wound up fleeing to England. ORT's Dorenko dared to report critically on the *Kursk* submarine sinking and lost his gig, and soon there was new ownership as Channel One Russia. Joined by the new NTV and others, Russian media have devoted fawning praise to Putin in a blizzard of sensational infotainment ever since. The power vertical remains intact, stronger than ever, buoyed by an ethnonationalist rhetorical impulse that privileges the leader as the custodian of Russian identity. Putin made a good show of letting Dmitri Medvedev serve as president from 2008 to 2012, but Russia was and is defined by arbitrary rule, in business as well as in information and politics—from who controls what to who owns what. The constitution was amended in early 2020 to let Putin stay in power until the 2030s.

Press freedom, political opposition, and protests are tolerated until they are not. The entire culture, in that sense, is chilled. Anna Politkovskaya, an indefatigable journalist reporting critically on the war in Chechnya, was murdered in her apartment elevator in 2006, the same year that Alexander Litvinenko, a defector and former FSB official, was poisoned to death in England. Members of the band Pussy Riot were jailed in 2012 for their provocative performances protesting Putin and Russia's LGBTQ+ policies. Berezovsky was found strangled in 2013, and in 2015 the liberal politician Boris Nemtsov was assassinated on a bridge within sight of the Kremlin. It had been his plan for the next day to lead a protest march through Moscow. His monograph-length text, *Putin. War,* had yet to be published. Nemtsov had argued that the Russian invasion and appropriation of the Crimean Peninsula in Ukraine was a cheap, nationalistic ploy to shield Putin from domestic troubles regarding corruption and a poor economy. In 2020, opposition leader Alexei Navalny was poisoned in assassination attempt; after returning from his medical recovery in 2021, he was promptly arrested and sentenced to a two-year prison term.

Like Erdoğan's Turkey but on a global scale, Putin's Russia weaponized an online troll army to harass others and overwhelm the cultural system. Keep in mind that fake news isn't powerful because it's false; it works by inundating an already overleveraged media environment to the point where nothing truly can be believed. The key to such disinformation is volume, adding more and more blur to a culture deprived of clarity. Putin is not the first dictator to enjoy fawning coverage, and to the extent that he succeeds, it owes to the convergence of classic and new styles of propaganda. The old approach is not, by itself, completely effective; anyone can be revered. Putin's real skill is mixing the leadership principle of a dictator with bots and trolls who question anything and everything. In a culture marked by media saturation, only power and identity stand out.

The internet had been created by the US Department of Defense to thwart Russia. Creating and opening media were largely how the West had won the Cold War. Now those tactics would be used against the West—specifically, liberal democracy. At Putin's behest in 2016, Russia's military intelligence service, GRU, hacked the Democratic National Committee servers and spear-phished the email account of Hillary Clinton's campaign chairman, John Podesta. GRU then timed the laundering of such information to maximize media attention and exert political damage. The first dump launched right before the Democratic National Convention, the weeklong televised spectacle culminating in Hillary Clinton's formal acceptance of her candidacy for president. The second was meted out in drips beginning the night of October 7, only a few hours after the *Access Hollywood* tape transcript had been published by the *Washington Post*. The recording had captured candidate Donald Trump bragging about his star-powered ability to grab women by their genitals. The revelation rocked the campaign for about a week, commanding all sorts of media attention and high-profile calls among Republicans for Trump to step down. Then the press moved on, demonstrating balance by eagerly playing up conflict within the Clinton campaign based on the WikiLeaks revelations. Reddit's message boards gleefully dissected the language of the hacked emails for conspiracy theories, such as Pizzagate, which suggested that Clinton was part of a child sex-trafficking ring. Eventually, the GOP got back in line. The strategic legal and political function of WikiLeaks is that Julian Assange's outfit mediated some distance between Russia and Trump surrogates. A conspiracy could not be proved, as the former only provided WikiLeaks with the stolen documents, and the latter, knowing the timing of the American election cycle, optimized the publishing cycles.

Russia's state-sponsored troll factory, the Internet Research Agency (IRA), had been tasked with flooding Facebook and Twitter with fake accounts and false news. At first the idea was to sow social discord, hence Russian trolls were posing as such divergent groups as Blacktivist, United Muslims of America, and @TEN_GOP (the Tennessee Republican Party). The latter two had over one hundred thousand followers by the time their accounts had been deactivated in 2017 by Facebook and Twitter, respectively. The IRA also used social media to divisively inflame immigration issues, promoting exaggerated crime stories and organizing rallies in places as far removed as Germany and Idaho. A change came over the bots and trolls by the summer of 2016, switching to endorse Brexit and Trump. They planted false news stories that could be liked and retweeted and shared for misinformation purposes. This creative media and rhetorical environment motivated Macedonian teenagers and American college students to get in on the act, reporting that the pope endorsed Trump and that phony ballots were being trucked into Ohio.

But understand this: while Russian disinformation inspired the fake news misinformation that may have tipped the scales in two close elections, blaming Putin and WikiLeaks and the flirtations of the Vote Leave and the Trump campaigns with Russia is far too simplistic an explanation for why such widescale support for both those campaigns existed in the first place. The elections of 2016 did not signal the death of democracy so much as the final decoupling of liberalism from democracy. The Brexiteers peddled fictions about how much money Britain stood to make in leaving the EU and how the departure would stem a violent swarm of Muslim immigrants. On the campaign trail, Trump promised to lock up his opponent. Without question, this rhetoric was dangerous. A week before the Brexit vote, Jo Cox, a Labour member of Parliament from northern England, had been assassinated by a right-wing nationalist who yelled "Britain First" during the act. Trump himself encouraged violence against protesters at his rallies on the campaign trail, and he floated the possibility that "Second Amendment people" could take matters into their own hands if Clinton was elected. It was all so terribly uncouth. Surely voters would reject this assault on our vaunted political norms, right? From the Remain supporters to the Clinton campaign and the mainstream press, it was assumed that citizens would continue accepting the status quo.

They didn't. Instead, liberal democracy lost a battle of asymmetrical political warfare characterized by weaponized information and rhetorical invective. None of it would likely have worked had liberal democracy recognized its shortcomings and been more responsive to the people it represented. The conventional response, from elites in any case, was to focus on the chaotic new media landscape, on the trolls and the Russians and the alt-right provocateurs. But these features were not so much new as newly prominent. A blur of faked news and populism had coursed through democratic societies across the globe for decades, and members of the great Anglo alliance weren't innocent bystanders. Boris Johnson, a chief proponent of the Vote Leave campaign, had begun his public career as a journalist for the *Times* of London, which had been acquired by Rupert Murdoch in 1981. Johnson was fired for fabricating a historian's quote in a 1987 article about King Edward II's love affair with another man. A gross violation of journalism ethics such as this dooms most reporting careers, but Johnson's splashy style was picked up by Conrad Black's *Daily Telegraph* soon after. Tasked with covering the fledgling European Union talks from Brussels in the early nineties, Johnson colored his dispatches with something less than objective circumspection. By ridiculing stuffy European bureaucrats and their onerous regulations on everything from condoms to cucumbers, he discovered a weird sense of power from, as he put it, chucking rocks over the garden wall. The French politician Jacques Delors, president of the European Commission at the time, was a particularly inviting target. In a 1992 article, Johnson intimated that the man planned to rule Europe by himself. The accusation was seized on by Danish opposition groups, fueling Denmark's rejection of the Maastricht Treaty that same year. Chris Patten, a former Tory cabinet minister, has said of Johnson, "As a journalist in Brussels, he was one of the greatest exponents of fake journalism."[31]

As a reward for his efforts, Johnson got a plum columnist gig back in London. Here he could spout off on anything that pleased him without dirtying his hands reporting on actual news. His inflammatory comments outraged polite society, but the floppy-haired pundit was considered a harmless distraction, another in a long line of Fleet Street blowhards. Yet Johnson understood the intersection of media convergence and politics, appearing frequently as a good-natured target of humor on *Have I Got News for You* and considering a political career. Eventually, Black handed him the keys to edit another of his media holdings, the *Spectator* magazine. By 2001, Johnson had become a member of Parliament while continuing to edit that publication and maintain a weekly column in the *Telegraph*. This Tory stood for nothing politically except a vague spirit of Britishness and a hostility to fellow members of the press, dismissing their (accurate) revelations of his adultery as "an inverted pyramid of piffle."[32] The flexibility helped him become mayor of London in 2008. Boris was seemingly everywhere, even becoming, somewhat outlandishly, the chief mascot of the 2012 London Olympics. He just wanted to have fun and playfully dabble in ethnonationalist populism and let the underlings take care of business. There were no policy priorities, just spectacle.

When Prime Minister David Cameron decided to hold a referendum on Brexit, he seemed confident that the result would put Euroskepticism in its place once and for all. Clearly, the British would see the benefits of the EU relationship. In the early days of 2016, Johnson, for his part, hadn't even made up his mind on whether to support Leave. Then, on a whim, he threw in with the Brexiteers. While ol' Boris was the establishment face of the formal Vote Leave campaign among traditional media, Leave.EU ran a more hostile, racially tinged digital communication movement. This last was overseen by Arron Banks, a businessman, and drew support from Nigel Farage, a politician from the ethnonationalist United Kingdom Independence Party, which opposed EU membership from its start in the early nineties. Leave.EU was unrelenting on social media, trafficking in memes and fake news warnings of immigrants overrunning Great Britain. While serious leaders seriously warned that Brexit would be an economic nightmare, the Brexiteers promoted Leave as an opportunity to take back the country. The British press loved the unfolding drama, likely confident in poll numbers that suggested Remain would win. But when democracy as such was put to the test against liberal democracy, the Brexiteers triumphed with 52 percent of the vote.

To be clear: there is a fundamental difference between the results of Brexit and the 2016 US presidential election. The Brexit outcome reflected the democratic will of the people; the Electoral College awarded Trump the presidency despite his losing nationwide by almost three million popular votes. While Trump as president was handed the keys to the entire executive branch and the power to appoint federal judges with the added advantage of Republican majorities in both branches of Congress, the Brexit debate hadn't been won so much as just begun. Would it be a clean break with the EU? Would there be another referendum? After almost four years and considerable parliamentary resistance, Great Britain had finally negotiated a "deal" to leave Europe. Johnson had by that point transitioned from foreign secretary to acting prime minister and then scored a resounding parliamentary election victory in late 2019, just before finalizing the deal. The people wanted Brexit, and they got it behind Boris's playful populism. It wasn't a clean break as the Leave.EU folks had hoped but a compromise of necessity: the Brexiteers could say they had won, and some ties with Europe would remain.

Like Johnson, Trump had made a name for himself by publishing something in 1987. His best-selling book, *The Art of the Deal*, laid out his vision of communication for the next several decades in public life. "I play to people's fantasies," he wrote. "People want to believe in something that is the biggest and the greatest and the most spectacular."[33] The book, like his persona, was a construct—largely ghostwritten to cement Trump's image as a cocksure businessman with an aura of unbridled success. This was despite his having been seeded great wealth from his father's real estate assets and having already cratered a professional football league, the USFL, by persuading it to file an antitrust lawsuit against its larger competitor, the NFL. But Trump had always understood the media ecosystem. From books to television to Twitter, he excelled at priming the celebrity apparatus of a culture fascinated with buzz and glamour and conflict. Even before his best seller, Trump had planted stories with the tabloid and the financial press as his own alter-ego publicist, John Barron, who lionized his real estate deals, inflated his net worth, and leaked details of his sexual prowess. The man created not only his own mythos but his own reality.

And he was feted at the trough of the new infotainment landscape. Television appearances and tabloid fodder gave way to influence, and in 1989 he placed several advertisements in New York City newspapers calling for the reinstatement of the death penalty. The basis for the ad was retribution for the Central Park Five, a group of minority teenagers who had been coerced into confessing to the rape of a woman. (The young men served over a decade in prison until their convictions were vacated, having been exonerated by DNA evidence.) On a family ski trip to Aspen, Colorado, Trump invited his then mistress to town. When she and Trump's wife inevitably confronted each other, the row was front-page tabloid news back in New York.

By 1995, the jig seemed to have been up. Creditors had cut Trump off, as his three casinos had filed for bankruptcy. His father's complex network of shell companies, along with his illegal scheme to purchase and dump casino chips, could not perpetually cover his son's debt payments and operating losses. What did Trump do? He went public, literally. An initial public offering appeared ridiculous given his financial position, but a publicity campaign centered on Trump as a brand wound up generating some $300 million in investments, half of which were issued as junk bonds. He paid himself millions plus expenses as CEO, and brokered real estate deals wherein Trump Hotels & Casino Resorts, Inc. purchased his distressed properties. The much-needed infusion of liquidity prompted another book, *The Art of the Comeback*, in 1997. In it, Trump dispensed such brilliant advice as tips on playing golf and securing prenuptial agreements. Despite these theories of leadership, Trump's corporation would lose, all told, over a billion dollars under his leadership, which ended in 2009 after the second time it filed for bankruptcy protection. The first Chapter 11 restructuring was in 2004, not so much a bailout as a lifeline of credit to stay afloat.

Trump's real bailout came that year with the start of a new reality television series, *The Apprentice*. The show aired on NBC, the broadcast network then run by Jeffrey Zucker, the future head of CNN during Trump's presidential campaign and presidency. The show's creator, Mark Burnett, had made his name in the reality television genre with *Survivor*, a successful program of ruthless competition set in exotic, hostile terrain. "The tribe has spoken," the host would say at the close of each episode when losers were voted off by fellow cast members. *The Apprentice* didn't have such democratic aspirations. The program pretended to be set in the cutthroat world of New York City business, and each episode culminated in The Donald telling a contestant he or she was fired. The winner of each season was promised a job working for Trump. *The Apprentice* was a major hit for NBC. It aligned so neatly with Trump's public image—the straight-talking, no-nonsense executive. Combining the business brand with the authoritarian television personality was a clever bit of marketing. The Donald was shown in a limo, a helicopter, a jet, a boardroom. Not that he did much. In fact, he generally ignored contestant performances and pursed his lips to iconically intone, "You're fired," to whomever he felt like saying it. This caused postproduction editors to scramble and rework footage to show the losing cast member in the worst possible light.

Trump's understanding of reality TV culture formed the basis of a political ideology. *The Apprentice* sold a narrative about America in the same way he sold the *idea* of himself as a successful businessman. Politics is not about what a politician says or does but rather how a person engages a spectacle of conflict, just as it is in professional wrestling— the audience suspends disbelief just enough to enjoy the theatrics. They know it isn't real, but they're encouraged not to care. The simulated cruelty is too much fun. The conflict glamorizes winners and disgraces losers, rewarding figures who supposedly speak their mind. Trump, the embodiment of this reality competition, appeared as himself multiple times in World Wrestling Entertainment events. He was the perfect heel and eventually was inducted into the organization's Hall of Fame.

In wrestling, the heel antagonizes the faces, or good guys, to the delight of cheering crowds. Trump parlayed this role into the presidency. First, having been an early adopter of Twitter, he harassed President Barack Obama with the Birther campaign. In the "reality" spectacle that liberal democracy had become, Obama was the ultimate face. Born in Hawaii to a white mother from Kansas and a Black father from Kenya, he attended Harvard Law School and chose to become a community organizer in Chicago rather than secure a cushy corporate gig. He had come to public attention as a guest speaker at the 2004 Democratic National Convention. Not even yet a senator, he cut through the polarizing election-year discourse with a soaring address that negated the disharmony of red states and blue states. Obama's

2008 presidential campaign was based on hope and change, promising to heal the divisions of an America caught in a quagmire of overseas military operations and a global financial crisis. As president, Obama would realize the liberal-democratic dream of pure universality, delivering a post-racial America where difference no longer mattered. Only comity and reason would flourish in this new world. But while Obama managed the fallout of the Great Recession with the help of an elite class of economists and passed health-care reform legislation modeled on a market-based plan created by a right-wing think tank, this didn't stop conservative detractors in Congress and on Fox News and talk radio from pillorying him as a Marxist. American politics had become zero sum by 2009 as Senate Minority Leader Mitch McConnell, a Republican from Kentucky, announced that his chief goal was to make Obama a one-term president by denying him any bipartisan support—for anything.

Trump's timing was impeccable, because American democracy was a polarized, hollowed-out shell as he entered the political scene. The Birther campaign itself offered something new and different from the pure power politics of gerrymandering and filibustering and Super PACs. The ongoing drama of ethnonationalist opposition to Obama—not the man but what he represented—was certainly racist, yet also motivated by an abject hatred of liberalism. Fueled by anger over the financial crisis and the prominent rise of a Black man, some Americans wanted a symbolic show of force to take their country back. At first this was expressed through Glenn Beck's ranting convergence of book publishing, talk radio, and Fox News. He became the putative head of the Tea Party, which promoted less government spending—a most curious demand in the middle of a recession. As Beck's extremity ran afoul even Fox, which removed him, and the Tea Party devolved into nothing more than a humdrum, corporate-backed lobby for new congressional representatives, Trump offered ethnonationalist conservatives a high-profile media campaign to entertain and launder their resentments.

Trump's central insight was figuring out how to decouple conspiracy from theory within the scope of politics. Whereas conspiracy theories traditionally attempted to uncover secret facts to explain events and power relations, Trump discovered how reactionary assertions

attributed to mystifying sources can command attention and get promoted amid the swirl of media convergence. A broadcaster like Beck
genuinely wants to convince you of the facts of a conspiracy. He is the
consummate true believer. The advantage of a guy like Trump is he
doesn't care whether what he's saying is true or false, or whether you
actually believe it. The affected pose of the style is the thing. The Birther
campaign was never about proving Obama's Kenyan birth or remov-
ing him from office. As Russell Muirhead and Nancy L. Rosenblum
have pointed out, when it comes to conspiracies, "the power to make
people affirm the message is the power to impose reality."[34] Trump,
the celebrity of celebrities, was uniquely positioned to harness such a
power. He used social networking to blast updates on his investigation
of Hawaiian birth records, tweeting on August 6, 2012, "An 'extremely
credible source' has called my office and told me that @BarackObama's
birth certificate is a fraud." Trump also solicited calls from television to
earn free media airtime about the matter. If his ridiculous allegations
were more amenable to hosts of Fox News than those on *The Today
Show*, *The View*, *Morning Joe*, and CNN, the differences were erased in
the overall commitment to the buzz of his presence. As long as he was
retweeted and interviewed, this new reality of ethnonationalist antago-
nism was affirmed. Obama's White House eventually released his birth
certificate to disprove the conspiracy, as if doubting the veracity of the
existence of the document was ever the point. Trump subsequently
claimed victory for bringing an end to the questions about Obama's
origins. The goal all along had been to humiliate the country's first
African American president into acknowledging the conspiracy.

Trump then took his newfound ethnonationalist celebrity and combined it with the red-meat style so common among conservative media
personalities, from Rush Limbaugh and Michael Savage on the radio
dial, to Sean Hannity on cable television, to Sarah Palin's campaigning
in 2008, and to the emerging alt-right framework of Breitbart and
Gamergate. He successfully adapted to the grand convergence of all
things, which we should have expected. This new sophistic age finally
reached its apex when Trump ran for president. It was destiny, and the
man even called his shot. In 2013, a group of Republican operatives
approached Trump about running for governor of New York, but he

declined. He told them they'd be useful when he ran for president a few years later. "I'm going to suck all the oxygen out of the room," Trump reportedly said. "I know how to work the media in a way that they will never take the lights off of me."[35] Shocked, the attendees told him that a presidential campaign requires massive amounts of television ad spending and basic retail politics, such as attending events at little Pizza Ranches dotted across the country. You couldn't become president on earned media alone, they insisted. Trump rejected this, explaining to those present, "It's really about the power of the mass audience."

It was a bit of a risk entering the race in June of 2015. It was a long time before the first caucus would be held the next January, in Iowa. But Trump calculated that he could turn the slow summer television cycle into a fount of coverage. So he descended the golden escalator, cheered on by paid guests jamming out to Neil Young's "Keep on Rockin' in a Free World," and declared, "The U.S. has become a dumping ground for everybody else's problems."[36] He bemoaned Mexican immigrants who brought drugs and crime and were rapists—though some, he said he assumed, were good people. He blamed the Chinese for bamboozling the United States with bad trade deals and for stealing jobs. The Japanese were bad because they refused to drive Chevrolets in Tokyo. And ISIS earned money from Iraqi oil that Americans should have confiscated. Trump promised to build a wall on America's southern border, and his negotiating prowess would get Mexico to pay for it. This was all highly inflammatory stuff, and perfect for a mainstream press captured by celebrity, racial conflict, and sensationalism. Members of the press couldn't look away, and they immediately jockeyed for position to host Trump for interviews. The conservative media of radio and cable news loved this bold truth telling about foreigners, having espoused similar talk for decades. Finally, here was a presidential candidate willing to eschew the careful tone of respectable Republican politicians. The liberal press was horrified by the comments on immigrants, sanctimoniously insisting that such divisive rhetoric could never work on *this* grand a political stage.

Both sides appeared to miss an underlying premise that Trump had marshaled in his campaign announcement speech. His ire had also been directed at American politicians. They were losers in thrall to lobbyists, he alleged, and morally corrupt. They sold the country out through bad wars and bad trade deals and piss-poor legislation, like Obamacare. The rising stock market was a bloated bubble. Only he could make America great again—because America needed a cheer-leader. He would be that cheerleader, cutting through the bullshit to generate jobs and wealth and winning. So much winning. For a lot of Americans, this candidate was worth a shot. The respectable politics of the status quo had led to massive inequality and messy foreign en-tanglements. Even under President Obama, the great hope of liberal democracy, wealth continued concentrating and the US military re-mained bogged down in the Middle East. Why were we supporting Saudi Arabia's war efforts in Yemen?, Trump had asked. If nothing ever changed, nothing would change. Trump offered Americans a new political show, executed better than before, as well as an opportunity to break the wheel of liberal democracy. It was not going to be nice, but it was going to be different.

Luckily for Trump, he was able to run against two persons whose names reflected the last several decades of failed policies and national ruin. In the primaries, the Republican establishment front-runner was Jeb Bush, a son and brother to former presidents. He was a former governor and had amassed a campaign war chest of over $100 mil-lion. His campaign was run by all the conventional consultants, who blanketed television ads across the important primary states. This was to be Jeb's turn—unless it was to be Hillary Clinton's turn. She said the nation was "Stronger Together," a decent platform of unity for the age of liberal democracy. But such sentiments had become old hat by 2016. Her campaign, like Jeb's, thought Trump would destruct and be easily countered through television ads. Clinton's spots showcased Trump as a bully, unfit to serve as president. Little did she and Jeb and their highly paid politicos know that they were affirming Trump's main attraction, that the values of decorum so dearly held in the age of liberal democracy had vanished. That reality had passed its born-on date. Pennsylvania, Michigan, and Wisconsin—which served as a "blue wall" for Democrats in every presidential election since Bill Clinton's in 1992—changed direction. Hillary won by almost three million votes nationwide, but she lost by eighty thousand in these states.

The apparent madness of Trump's campaign operation was not illogical. The people around him targeted the right audiences at the right time with the right messages. That's just good political rhetoric. With Paul Manafort as campaign chairman, Trump had a man used to backing unsavory characters around the globe. Before Manafort had to step down owing to revelations of his financial dealings with pro-Russian Ukrainian oligarchs, for which he would later serve jail time, he had suggested elevating Indiana governor Mike Pence to the ticket to help keep religious voters in the fold. After Manafort left, Trump chose campaign cochairs Kellyanne Conway, an extraordinary prevaricator perfect for television "news" interviews, and Steve Bannon, the then editor-in-chief at the online news site Breitbart. Brad Parscale, a web guru from San Antonio, served as head of the digital campaign, mining the psychographic data gathered by Cambridge Analytica to skillfully target Facebook users in swing states. When, during the campaign, stories were about to leak implicating Trump in affairs with a Playboy model and a porn actress, his legal fixer, Michael Cohen, arranged for both to be paid off to keep silent. Cohen funneled Trump's money through a shell corporation to pay off the porn star, and he worked with American Media Inc., which published the *National Enquirer*, to practice a "catch-and-kill" technique with the Playboy model. This infamous journalistic method purchases the rights to a story and never reports on it so as to spike the contents from public view. Cohen's schemes were not just unethical but illegal violations of US election law. He was imprisoned as a result of the subsequent federal criminal probe, with the then president of the United States listed as an unindicted coconspirator, "Individual 1," on court documents.

Most Americans voted in 2016 unaware of any of this, but they were aware that FBI Director Jim Comey had reopened the investigation into Clinton's emails. Comey, along with high-profile media outlets who were keyed in, chose not to disclose the open investigations into the Trump campaign related to Russian interference. "F.B.I. Sees No Clear Link to Russia," a *New York Times* headline had proclaimed just days before the election. The salacious details of the dossier compiled by the counterintelligence specialist Christopher Steele would not be published by Buzzfeed until the following January. The Clinton campaign, which had funded the opposition research, had elected not to dump it. All these revelations and non-revelations may not have mattered that November, because nothing seemed to matter. Yet it is a particular irony that the big players of liberal democracy—the state intelligence apparatus, the mainstream press, the Clinton campaign—showed ethical restraint in not tarring Trump with the accusations.

When, way past midnight, the returns were final and the president-elect arrived on the stage for his victory speech, he seemed surprised, even gracious. His words that night were colored by platitudes associated with liberal-democratic norms. Trump had, over the course of his campaign, threatened to open up the nation's libel laws, jail his opponent, and ignore the voting results. But that night was different. Hillary had served her country well, he said. He would reach out to those who didn't support him to rebuild the country—every race, religion, and background would be included in the effort. The nation's infrastructure would be second to none, he asserted, a political priority typically associated with the Democratic Party. In his dealings with the rest of the world, Trump said the United States would seek common ground, not conflict or hostility. These dulcet tones suggested maybe, just maybe, now that he had been elected president, Trump would change. He was the ultimate chameleon, having reinvented himself many times before and adopted so many political positions over the years. In the primary and general election campaigns, he had outflanked both the Republicans and the Democrats to the Right and the Left. He was probably one of the few national figures who, as president, could have actually drained the polarized, special-interest swamp that is the nation's capital. All that media attention could have been parlayed into something, finally, different.

When President Trump used his inaugural address—a civic ritual traditionally reserved for a rhetorical occasion of unity and healing—to highlight "American Carnage," it was, in many ways, refreshing. The commentariat of pundits were appalled, but there could be a benefit to dispensing with the emptiness of tired clichés. Here was some tough talk about how American elites had failed the people they were supposed to represent. "A nation exists to serve its citizens," Trump said, noting that he would cater to the slums of urban Detroit and the windswept plains of Nebraska alike.[37] If liberal democracy had died, perhaps it had found a worthy successor who would not go down the road of ethnonationalist autocracy.

Alas, it took less than twenty-four hours for Trump and his administration to show their cards. The day after the inauguration, the new president assailed the news media in a speech delivered to the CIA, deeming journalists "as among the most dishonest human beings on Earth."[38] Trump's press secretary, Sean Spicer, then lied to those gathered at his first news conference about the attendance figures for the inaugural address. The administration was particularly upset about photographs comparing President Obama's crowds to Trump's. Kellyanne Conway, who had become a special advisor to the president, appeared on NBC's *Meet the Press* the following day to defend Spicer, declaring that the new administration would rely on "alternative facts." Whatever promise President Trump may have offered to represent the people evaporated, as his detractors had predicted, into the ongoing spectacle of the Trump show.

The news media could have responded by ignoring the publicity stunts and morning rage tweets of the new president and returned to the basics of journalism. They could have trained their reporting focus on government agencies and local and state developments that affect the day-to-day lives of the actual public. Journalism could have deprived Trump of the oxygen of attention he so desperately craved, and needed, to thrive. But no. Instead, reporting at CNN and the like became increasingly caught up in the force of Trump and the horse race of politics. Jeffrey Zucker, CNN's president, was delighted in early 2017 that his roster of political pundits, both for and against the new president, served as "characters in a drama."[39] The opportunity was lost. The national press could have been liberated by the end of liberal democracy, returning to what it's done best historically. While it demonstrated a willingness to fight back and expose lies, the onslaught of pundits and polls and hot takes continued without any introspection. It was the Great Trump Chase, and in outrage or in affection, various media simply couldn't get enough. The fake news moniker applied to misinformation propaganda in 2016 soon became Trumpian shorthand for the mainstream press. The twist was cynical but not undeserved.

All these populists rely on identity appeals and propaganda to consolidate power and politicize the impartial practices of institutions. Their rhetoric is ethnically divisive, but at bottom they don't care for representing the will of the majority so much as thwarting a democratic culture in general. Their goal is a complete lack of accountability, often to enrich themselves and avoid legal exposure. They don't care if people get hurt or humiliated in the process. One imagines 2016 playing out differently, not politically but across the mainstream press. The top story of that year could have been the Panama Papers, a networked investigation that revealed international corruption on a grand scale. The reporting demonstrated how the power of those with wealth and the wealth of those with power concealed their assets from accountability. The revelations took down the government of Iceland but didn't go much further, other than the tragic 2017 assassination of a Maltese journalist, Daphne Caruana Galizia, who had investigated the matter. What was considered more important was the continual horse race of power politics, and this is where propagandistic fake news and convergent faked news met. The mainstream press was always shocked, but it never looked away from its obsession with the game.

Perhaps the saddest thing is that we can't even account for the scale of the death of liberal democracy as a time period. The story we have to tell only scratches the surface of the disrespect and dissolution democracies have faced since the 1990s. There are so many more autocrats we could cover, so many more corrupt leaders in Africa, Asia, Europe, and Latin America who concentrated their power. Sham elections, journalistic harassment, corporate surveillance: this is what had become of the global village.

8

DEMOCRACY, IF WE CAN KEEP IT

We can't be "post-truth" because we were never pre-truth. And we certainly never lived *in* truth. What we had instead was a liberal order in which media gatekeepers dictated what passed as truth, but that system has unraveled. And even if it still existed, public trust in elite institutions has so eroded that it wouldn't work. So now the unruliness of a real democratic culture of open communication stares us in the face. Indeed, the past decade has been a reminder that democracy has no essence or shape; it is simply open society and its consequences. Which is why the existentialist obsession with uncertainty, with the lack of any definite end point, is such a useful framework for thinking about the paradox of democracy. It's because nothing can be decided in advance that everything is possible. It's because of the openness of democratic society that everything is permitted. To assume, as so many have, that democracy tilts inexorably toward liberalism was always to misunderstand its defining feature.

Admittedly, there's something unsatisfying about the paradox. But the goal of this book is to try to clarify what democracy actually is and how, specifically, it works. We grant the democratic pessimism of Plato and Walter Lippmann, and agree that a reasonable demos is a phantasm. We even agree that democracies will invariably fall into disorder, especially when the communicative environment is reshaped. And yet these critiques aren't fatal if we recognize that a reasonable demos isn't the point of democracy. To justify itself, democracy need only do two things: provide space for free expression and the opportunity to check power. Autocracies offer the virtue of stability at the cost of freedom, necessitating arbitrary rule. Oligarchies degenerate into corruption and can't provide the basis for an active civic life. Only democracy offers a form of life compatible with human liberty and capable of dissolving power hierarchies.

Every democratic society is perpetually in an existential crisis, and that means it will require existentialist commitments from the public. The centrifugal forces that undermine democratic legitimacy—concentrations of wealth, racism, and so on—will always seek to consolidate their grip on power, through lobbying or propaganda or subterfuge. In late capitalist culture, as many conservatives and postmoderns have warned, the enemy of political dynamism is often consumerism. If human consciousness is trapped in a cycle of stupefying entertainments and misinformation, it will never be easy to mobilize the citizenry. But in a free society, the opportunity to challenge these power structures is always there, always beckoning. In 2020, this took the form of Black Lives Matter social justice activism after a video emerged of the extrajudicial killing of an African American man, George Floyd. Millions of citizens took to the streets demanding reforms to law enforcement. It can also look like the hundreds of thousands of protesters in Minsk demonstrating against the president of Belarus, Alexander Lukashenko, who remained in office for more than a quarter of a century after presiding over another questionable election. By the same token, mobilizing citizens and challenging power can also resemble the digitally coordinated QAnon conspiracy, which alleges that deep-state operatives and Democratic Party officials are involved in a child sex-trafficking ring. There's no rule or law specifying that the freedom of open communication must rely on accurate information and righteous causes. A democracy permits every available means of persuasion, and people determine for themselves what facts they consider accurate and what causes they consider just.

The focus on choice and engagement is deliberate. Plenty of people, especially centrists, insist that our problems are largely structural, that if we reinforce our political and legal institutions we can get back to "normal." But that's naïve. Of what use are "institutional guardrails" if the electorate doesn't care about them? These things matter, but citizens must be invested in them. We need to reflect more on the cultural foundation of our political institutions, which are only as reliable as the people who make them up. And the people who make them up are citizens. We often think of institutions as bundles of rules or protocols, but they're part of a much broader geometry of cultural practices and beliefs. You can set up the finest election laws or enact an independent judiciary or any number of constitutional restraints. None of that will change the reality that in a democracy, all of it sits on a razor's edge: people and parties seek to win power in order to exercise power.

Consider North Carolina. After the 2010 election handed Republicans full control of state government, the GOP studied ethnic breakdowns of voting patterns to create gerrymandered congressional maps and voting hurdles for minority citizens. The policies were rationalized as upholding the Voting Rights Act and protecting against voter fraud, yet a federal appeals court would later deem this as "the most restrictive voting law that North Carolina has seen since the era of Jim Crow," one that targeted "African Americans with almost surgical precision."[1] In 2016 Roy Cooper, a Democrat, was elected governor. Shortly thereafter, the outgoing Republican governor, Pat McCray, called a special session of the legislature under the pretense of aiding victims of natural disasters. The legislature frantically passed a series of bills that neutralized the incoming Democratic administration by limiting its power to appoint cabinet members and granting control of the Board of Elections to Republicans. In 2018, the election of a Republican in the Ninth Congressional District was invalidated due to fraudulent ballots procured by conservative consultants. The GOP would get a do-over and win the special election the next year.

The conventional view of these actions is that they serve as a brazen attack on the very idea of democracy. They were certainly attacks on liberal democracy, on the norms undergirding our constitutional system. And the actions are a clear repudiation of the rules both sides had abided for a long time. That these steps were carried out in the light of day against the popular will is all the more galling. But the Republican power grabs in North Carolina offer a glimpse of democracy shorn of liberal restraints. GOP officials exploited the powers of the legislature with respect to voting, then the lame-duck sessions to their absolute limits, then the sanctity of an election, without any regard for conventions. The results were antidemocratic, and yet the acts reveal how vulnerable democracies are to the pursuit of power, especially when the institutions that enforced constitutional norms have eroded. Indeed, this is what the face of democracy looks like when it isn't anchored by an ethics of prudence or forbearance. In the end, Republicans did what they thought they could get away with, and it worked. But the problem runs much deeper. As President Trump demonstrated at the national level, the US Constitution is just a document and the law is just a construct. No democratic system contains a final trigger, some guarantee that it will self-correct. The custodians of the Constitution or state laws have to affirm them, or they cease to matter.

The debacles in North Carolina remind us that abandoning liberal-democratic norms in pursuit of power can work—at least in the short term. And the freedom of democratic cultures permits, even invites, this kind of illiberalism. There was an obvious institutional failure in North Carolina; the rules of liberal democracy were inverted by a party pursuing power as a zero-sum game. At the same time, there's a sociocultural problem facilitated by communications technologies. You have Republicans and Democrats occupying opposing epistemological worlds, each armed with their own "facts" and "talking points." The result is just enough confusion to muddy the waters and ensure a winner-take-all political climate, exposing the chaos of a free democratic culture.

Norm-breaking shouldn't be surprising, since playing by the norms is always a choice made by the actors participating in the system. Again, liberal-democratic norms were never binding in the way so many supposed. The politics of a democracy are like an iterative game that runs on the goodwill of its players. What the public is willing to countenance hinges largely on the culture of communication. If voters are entrenched in partisan information bubbles, politicians and their parties will feel accountable only to the voters who supported them. When the political culture is sufficiently poisoned, shame or some amorphous fidelity to "the rules of the game" is no longer an operative constraint.

In the case of American politics more broadly, the problem isn't that a majority of citizens reject constitutional principles; it's that their beliefs scale with their loyalties. As Ezra Klein put it, "People's opinions on democracy lie downstream from their partisan identity," especially in a world where news consumption is fragmented along ideological lines.[2] Timur Kuran, an economist, has argued that the real threat isn't a lack of trust in government but rather in each other.[3] We live in what Kuran calls two intolerant communities: one composed of "identitarians," who are concerned with issues like racial and gender equality, and "nativists," those preoccupied by the threats of immigration and cultural change. These communities live in different worlds, desire different things, and share almost nothing in common. And these alternative universes are reinforced by a partisan media environment that delivers news like any other consumer product and sorts people into virtual factions. Is it any wonder politics are hopelessly marred by tribalism? Is it any surprise that every political contest becomes an intractable existential drama, with each side convinced the other is not just wrong but a mortal enemy? In 1960, 5 percent of Republicans and 4 percent of Democrats objected to the idea of their children marrying across political lines. In 2010, those numbers jumped to 46 percent and 33 percent, respectively. A 2014 Pew Research Center study concluded something similar: "In both political parties, most of those who view the other party very unfavorably say that the other side's policies are so misguided that they 'threaten the nation's well-being.'"[4]

For many centrists, this is a catastrophic problem for American democracy. Yet the solutions won't come merely from better legislation or institutional reforms or more virtuous politicians. We'll have to reestablish a healthy culture of democracy by improving the communication environment. There are lots of ways to do this, but none of it will matter without a media-literate citizenry. It's an old idea that communication skills and media literacy ought to be introduced in secondary education. Marshall McLuhan was calling for this as far back as 1968, echoed more recently by the former *Washington Post* editor-in-chief Marty Baron. Yet such calls haven't been taken seriously. These subjects, more than any test-based metrics in preexisting courses, should form a common core curriculum and be required as part of matriculating toward a high school diploma. Our children should not be studying English or language arts limited to grammar and literature alone but communications from the time they are in middle school. The public speaking and media courses offered at colleges and universities as general education requirements are, in any case, too late. Citizens are surrounded by communication technologies and bombarded with bullshit from an early age; they need tools to discern their environment as they mature.

In a consumer world rife with choices, everyone must be their own intellectual self-defense system. There's no way around this in a democratic society; ultimate responsibility falls to the people. Public opinion is perpetually vulnerable to hysteria and mass manipulation—from opportunistic politicians, from attention merchants, from corporate media. And now it's subject to its own self-induced misinformation. We need an educational model that will help citizens guard against the onslaught of disinformation that awaits them in the public sphere. That means more than just crying bias or fake news at every turn. The quality of information in a free society only matters to the extent that voters can recognize and apply it. Educational reform won't come close to solving all our problems, but there's no path forward that doesn't involve rethinking how we prepare citizens to fulfill their democratic opportunities. And if we as a society can't take this seriously, then we won't be able to effectively negotiate the paradox this book has diagnosed.

What we really mean by media literacy is a total understanding of communication technologies and the rhetorical techniques on which they rely. Again, democracy runs on persuasion, and so much turns on the ability of citizens to recognize when and how they're being influenced. Tremendous work has been done on the role of civics education in propping up democratic institutions, notably by the political theorist Danielle Allen.[5] But all the civics training in the world means nothing if people can't distinguish emotional appeals from dispassionate claims or recognize how media technologies discipline our bodies. To be a democratic citizen is to be continually at the mercy of a communication environment full of Sophists, swindlers, and tools of distortion. In a democracy, this comes with the territory—and that's okay. However, it follows that education in the arts, in the deployment and understanding of rhetoric, in media history, and even in public relations is far more important than conventional literary skills and social studies knowledge. The citizenry will have to save itself from the elites who have abandoned them and from populists who won't stop lying to them and from the tech industry which constantly surveils them. It's true that we've never been this free, but it's equally true that we've never been this monitored, this manipulated, this overloaded with information. The importance of discernment, of rejecting bad-faith appeals and recognizing corruption and propaganda, has never been so urgent. And these are skills—habits, really—that have to be taught.

One of the many casualties of our market-driven economy is the idea that an education ought to be more than preparation for the labor market. We've privatized education and shifted the costs from the state to consumers. States all over the country have slashed funding for universities, raised tuition, and abandoned teaching in favor of profitable or subsidized research. Education is no longer a right but an investment, to which our entire economic fate is tethered. Our massive postwar commitment to public education crumbled in the face of the neoliberal revolution that began in the 1970s, and the freedom to pursue education for education's sake has all but disappeared. For the working and middle classes especially, the prospect of a lifetime of student debt is simply too daunting. It's impossible to quantify the full impact of such a foundational cultural shift. There are signs of its effects: the world has grown more complex and more interconnected, yes, but the business of political action has been handed to lawyers and lobbyists and technocrats. When citizens don't understand what's happening and are increasingly alienated from the political process, the only affirmative act for the public in a system like this is to revolt. And this impulse toward negation is at the center of the appeal of antiestablishment populists like Trump.

The failure to cultivate civic agents means fewer and fewer people with actual skin in the democratic game. Calls for more media literacy or civic education usually produce lots of eye-rolls. Fair enough. A more media-literate citizenry or a better-educated public won't improve democracy by increasing knowledge. In fact, we know from the research of political scientists Christopher Achen and Larry Bartels that the most knowledgeable voters, the ones who pay the most attention to politics, are also the ones most prone to biased or blinkered decision-making.[6] And the reason is simple: most people make political decisions on the basis of social identities and partisan loyalties, not an honest examination of reality. So more knowledge is more likely to increase, not reduce, partisanship. This is not the sort of education we have in mind. Teaching people how bills become laws or encouraging them to follow the news more closely won't end our partisanship problem. Civics training by itself gets you more lobbyists and the zero-sum politics of a Mitch McConnell. We're thinking more about the sort of education that can lay the foundation for participatory citizenship; that treats democracy as a culture and not merely a form of government: that's focused on communication and ethics much more than on the priorities of scientism.

John Dewey, the American pragmatist, is instructive here. No one wrestled with the relationship between democracy and education as well or as deeply as he did. But Dewey never succumbed to Romanticism or apologetics. He looked democracy in the face, acknowledged its near-impossible demands, and asked how we might improve it. Culture and communication were at the center of his democratic vision. Let us return to a quote of his from our introduction: "A democracy is more than a form of government; it is primarily a mode of associated living, of conjoint communicated experience." Like any culture, it's always in flux, always a generation or two from extinction. To focus exclusively on economic output or voting results is not enough. To make democracy work, citizens need to negotiate their shared environment together. Only through communication is that possible, Dewey insisted, a point that approaches the philosopher Hannah Arendt's view of citizenship as an act of cocreation or world-building among free beings. Everything, even reality, is up for grabs, but that doesn't preclude communication ethics—it necessitates it.

John Stuart Mill made a useful distinction between active and passive citizens. By active, he didn't mean the kind of political hobbyism you'll find on Twitter. The reason for involvement, for Mill at least, wasn't merely to avoid the tyranny of the majority; it was also because meaningful participation in the political process is its own kind of education. It's only through political engagement, through discussion and action, that we transcend our individual existence and become a member of a community. This is why thinkers like Dewey and, more recently, Astra Taylor place so much emphasis on participation.[7] We've become a society of subjects in which the majority of citizens are interested in politics purely on transactional terms—in what they hope to gain or expect to lose. But a democracy built on participation is about inputs as much as outputs. Citizens collectively construct the values that shape policy decisions. Today, citizens are so removed from the process, so estranged from their communities, that apathy and animosity are understandable responses.

Problems related to education, communication, and participation have been amplified by concurrent shifts in the media environment. The deaths of both local journalism and the advertising model that supported it have been particularly devastating. Citizens trust local press more than national press, mostly because it feels more connected to their lived experience.[8] It's no wonder, then, that a 2014 study found a strong link between declining local journalism and decreased civic engagement.[9] As Alexis de Tocqueville observed in the nineteenth century, democracy depends on intermediary associations essential to civic society. Local newspapers have always been key catalysts for these informal mechanisms, providing a shared context and a starting point for deliberation and political action.

Another, perhaps less appreciated, consequence of the decline of local journalism is a flatter, more abstract discourse. As politics become more nationalized, as citizens turn to cable news and social media, the conversation is dominated by caricatured Right-Left narratives about remote issues that feed blind partisan allegiances. Recent data showing a spike in negative partisanship, or motivated hatred of the other party, are partly attributable to the collapse of local journalism as a consistent, reliable source of news.[10] It may sound trite to call for the restoration of local journalism, especially print newspapers, but it's critical if we want to restore public trust and facilitate dialogue among citizens. The biases of print media allow time for thinking and deliberation that the convergent, online media world we now inhabit does not offer. Though newspapers can be manipulated like other news media, print sources require clarity and are rooted in a sense of place. They serve as the bedrock without which modern democracies can't effectively operate. We have known this for over two hundred years but seem willing to consign newspapers to oblivion.

Access to local, decentralized print media should be seen as a right of all citizens—in the United States in particular, as it was the vision of the Founders. Research from both the historian Jeffrey Pasley[11] and the law professor Sonja R. West[12] document how the question for the early US government wasn't whether to subsidize the press but how much. The press clause of the First Amendment is not limited to a redundancy of free expression or simple protections from government. Its inclusion affords an affirmative and necessary right of access to newspapers, which has been lost in the twenty-first century. The early republic focused on nurturing a print-based culture through the postal service, with local news outlets spread out across the states. Its vision was the fusion of democratic dialogue and informative news at the local levels of all communities, not just metropolitan areas. Only print can do this. A new localized press, even with government subsidies, will never recapture its former role as the dominant form of news media, but we can still reestablish its place as a useful local nexus of information and dialogue. Both conservatives, who espouse an originalist interpretation of America's founding, and leftists, who decry corporate media consolidation, should come together to support such a structure. Again, we have no illusions about the challenges to reestablishing print media as the primary news source in the twenty-first century. But citizens can—and should—do everything they can to support print as a counterbalance to the fragmentary, polarizing impact of broadcast and online media.

The news business also plays a role in this new political climate and desperately needs to reassess how it operates. One benefit of the Trump era is that he exposed how incompatible the twentieth-century model of journalism is in the digital age. As president, he thrived on opposition, and the mainstream press consistently played into his hands, feverishly chasing every lie and half-truth he uttered or tweeted. In a real sense, Trump hacked the press by exploiting journalistic conventions and offering continual pseudo-events designed to hijack news cycles and dominate coverage. The communications scholar Whitney Phillips calls this the "oxygen of amplification."[13] The cliché is that sunlight disinfects; Phillips reminds us that sunlight also makes things grow. Because there is now so much disinformation, so much noise, journalists must realize that a decision to cover something is a decision to amplify it or, in some cases, normalize it. The reluctance to own this, to feign neutrality at all costs, has backfired. The decentralization of news admittedly limits the impact of such a course correction, but it's an important step in the right direction.

Although we can certainly bolster our democratic culture with a renewed emphasis on education and media literacy, improved news coverage, and a commitment to de-nationalizing politics and subsidizing local news, such efforts won't be enough. We live in a culture defined by immersive, self-indulgent technologies guided by commercial incentives. And we simply have to acknowledge that however disruptive Facebook or Twitter might be, there are limits to what we can do. We can seek ways to maximize their benefits, and surely there are regulatory mechanisms worth exploring, but they can never be rendered unproblematic or truly safe. Whatever we do, we must do it against this backdrop, and that will require something beyond policy solutions or even the law. If we're going to live as small-*d* democrats in a sprawling society like ours, we'll have to face up to the ineradicable contradictions of democratic politics.

The first is that democracy is a political culture without foundation. It's a throw of the dice, a hope that power will fall into the right hands. As Jacques Rancière has written, "The democratic scandal consists in revealing this: there will never be, under the name of politics, a single principle of the community, legitimating the acts of governors based on laws inherent to the coming together of human communities."[14] Such a scandal is precisely the challenging existential freedom that makes democracy so meaningful: to establish a ground for political power in the absence of any ground. It is also, crucially, an invitation to forge a political community out of thin air. But the shape and direction of that community are always up for grabs. Democracy is not a goal but a means, a potentiality—it's never fully achieved or secured or determined. And yet it remains our best, most preferable form of political life. In the end, democracy offers free expression and the possibility that power might be checked. Those opportunities may not be fully taken advantage of, but they constitute democracy's claim to superiority over technocracy or aristocracy or authoritarianism. Unfortunately, there's no guarantee of escape from communicative anarchy. There are some who hope that we can escape Plato's cave of ignorance, that reason and the right institutions are all we need. Yet there is no "outside world," no refuge from bad outcomes or dangerous demagogues—only the volatility of wide-open expression.

The history of democracy, we often forget, involves those in power seeking to limit popular participation or dampen public passions via mediating institutions and discourses. As the media scholar Robert McChesney once observed, "Democracy has never been handed down from elites to those beneath them in the social pecking order. Democracy must be proclaimed, organized around, fought for, and won."[15] In the twenty-first century, we face a communication environment without informational firewalls. Institutions that reinforce power hierarchies are still in place, but their ability to constrain the communicative space has been thoroughly diminished. Once again, the so-called crisis of democracy isn't really a crisis of democracy; it's the explosion of illiberalism and a loss of elite control over flows of information. This hasn't buoyed popular sovereignty or tipped the scales of power in any significant way (not yet), but it has reintroduced the chaos of an open democratic culture.

Take the debate over cancel culture and the illiberalism of the newly emergent cultural Left. An open letter published in 2020 by *Harper's Magazine* and signed by dozens of high-profile artists and intellectuals suggested that woke activism is destroying the space for free expression. But the reality is that our discourse is as open and democratic as it's ever been. Many will balk at such a claim. How could it be that speech has never been freer than it is today, given the wave of censoriousness washing over public life? If you imagine speech as inherently good or civil, the claim that speech is uniquely free today will sound absurd. And if you think free speech means uncontested speech, or speech that is shielded from costs, the current situation hardly appears free. When we say that speech has never been freer, we mean that there have never been fewer barriers to entry in public discourse. There are now more voices, more perspectives, and more platforms than ever before. One of the many consequences of this cultural environment is the struggle over where to draw discursive boundaries and what sort of social sanctions are permissible when those boundaries are transgressed. What was previously unsayable will become commonplace, and what was previously acceptable will be challenged and even culturally suppressed in favor of new discursive norms.

The problem of cancel culture is a problem *within* free speech; it is not a problem of free speech itself. This shouldn't surprise us, given the history of democratic culture going back to Athens. A culture of free speech has never been self-securing, and now we have been forced to negotiate the perils of such liberty in real time. All the speech policing, oddly enough, may not signal the short-circuiting of a free society so much as its natural outcome. To say that the age of liberal democracy is dead is to say that the liberal-democratic rhetorical style of discourse no longer reigns supreme. The *Harper's* letter speaks to a commitment to a *type* of inquiry as opposed to *free* inquiry writ large, and it's not so surprising to see it published in a magazine over 150 years old. That commitment may be noble, but free expression merely ensures a contest of persuasion, not the ultimate prevailing of any particular rhetorical style. Whereas the *Harper's* letter's liberalism endorses what was once the dominant mode or style of communication—in the mid- to late twentieth century, in particular—it now finds itself as but one option among many in a public sphere characterized by convergent media. And there are now more voices and styles competing for supremacy in the public sphere. The conceptual mistake, then, is to assume that freedom invariably leads to more liberalism, or that a free society will naturally reinforce the conditions that sustain it. We might look at various conservative state legislature bills in 2021 proscribing critical race theory as an example of an actual threat to free expression.

The reality of illiberal democracy brings yet another tension into view: there is no inherent normative dimension to democracy. The very nature of democracy implies that there can be no deliberative or rationalistic consensus—and we should cease striving for one. Starting with John Rawls's *A Theory of Justice*, published in 1971, political theorists have sought, in different ways, to anchor a commitment to liberal values to some democratic process that would float above contestation. But, as Chantal Mouffe points out, this is an attempt to insulate democratic politics from their natural consequences.[16] It's also a conflation of liberalism and democracy, two separate albeit compatible projects. For someone like Rawls, there's an overarching conception of "justice as fairness" that "all citizens may reasonably be expected to endorse in light of the principles and ideals acceptable to them as reasonable and rational."[17] The problem is that Rawls wants to ground political legitimacy on a form of public reasoning that does not exist in real life. The pluralism inherent to democratic culture obliterates the possibility of any such consensus. Rawls avoids this objection by divorcing private views about metaphysics or morality from the public realm, a separate domain grounded in a shared conception of justice. But again, that neat wall doesn't exist in practice, undermining the sort of "overlapping consensus" Rawls imagines. In any case, the collapse of media gatekeepers—and with them any reliable boundaries on discourse— leaves the public sphere even more vulnerable to conflict.

Rawls was operating in a wildly different context. The post–World War II consensus was defined by manageable inequalities, consistent economic growth, and robust labor unions. Racial and gender disparities were greater than they are today, but there was a stability to the postwar order that seemed almost eternal. And yet as Rawls was penning his great liberal opus, that postwar consensus was already beginning to crack. Liberalism, as Daniel Bell pointed out at the time, was already up against the wall. The countercultural revolution was still percolating in the background, and the successes of the civil rights movement were quickly subsumed by the realities of mass incarceration, urban decay, and deindustrialization. And the era of late capitalism was taking root, ushering in a wave of privatization and corporate excess that ravaged the middle class and rocked the foundations of American society. Rawls hoped that capitalism could be constrained, that the principle of liberty could coexist with the principle of equality. But it hasn't worked out that way. Liberal capitalism has instead given rise to historical inequalities and undermined the basis for the welfare state. And now that the media gatekeeping structures have imploded, the illusion of social consensus is impossible to sustain, and the contradictions of postwar liberalism are more apparent. All we have is the chaos of open society—in other words, democracy.

Unlike Rawls, the German philosopher Jurgen Habermas embraced the communicative challenge of democracy. Indeed, Habermas had complete faith in the power and potential of open communication. For him, the key question was one of legitimacy: if we could establish "communicative action," a deliberative space in which everyone participates freely and equally, where not just the rules of discourse but how they're applied and implemented are up for debate, where so-called private interests are bracketed and power disparities are transcended, and where the decisions reached are both equitable and unpolluted, the result would be a rational, fair process to which all citizens could assent. Habermas's ideal speech situation is just that—an ideal. The notion that open public discourse could be rational and free of coercion simply doesn't square with reality; any free society, by virtue of being free, will have its share of communicative contagions. To his credit, Habermas understood that there was no way for democracy to exist absent a public sphere. He knew that citizens would have to talk, would have to participate in civic life, and would have to do it in a space separate and apart from the state or the market. This was the arena of political action, the site of democracy itself. And Habermas tried to mark out the conditions that made such an arena possible. But if our thesis is right, the public sphere can't be controlled, and it structurally forbids rational consensus. Our communication environment today is as open as it's ever been, and yet precisely because of its openness, it's also honeycombed with attention merchants and demagogues.

The focus on reason has obscured an equally important question for democratic theorists: How can we construct an actual demos? Or how can we secure allegiance to democratic institutions—and not just democratic institutions in general, but the living institutions that form the basis of our collective political life? Because of the pervasive belief that liberalism and democracy are flip sides of the same coin, we've taken these sorts of questions for granted. We've assumed that good ideas will triumph over bad ideas, that truth wins out. The history unpacked in this book shows that democracy has always been a carnival of buncombe, as H. L. Mencken defined it, with novel media as the great catalyzing force. The public sphere has never been as accessible or as rational as we've wanted it to be, and it never will. Democracy *is* communicative irrationality—we have to own that. The fantasy of a perfectly rational or deliberative society has sent us on a fool's errand, looking for harmony and purity where we'll never find it. Instead, we need to return to Dewey's project and ask what it takes to propel democracy, not as a rational political system but as an evolving form of life built on participation and communication.

Hyper-individualism, cultivated by consumer culture and reinforced by media technologies, has accelerated the privatization of public life and eroded civic bonds. Every domain of life is governed by the laws of commerce. Without social connections, the very notion of taxes, of supporting a broader community, feels like theft. Meanwhile, we've witnessed the gradual destruction of unions, of organized party machines, even churches and other institutions that have traditionally served as buttresses of democratic activism. The great value of these institutions was that they connected voters to a larger political movement and helped structure political attitudes in coherent ways. As these elements have collapsed, political culture has simultaneously splintered and hollowed out. Without meaningful opportunities for civic action, people have instead turned to more toxic forms of collective identification, and these problems seem increasingly intractable as the population grows more polarized and fragmented.

There's no clear way out of this trap. Mouffe remains one of the more interesting theorists to attempt to map the way forward. She calls for prioritizing institutions, discourses, and forms of life that align with democratic values. Instead of worrying about establishing an intellectual foundation for some particular vision of justice or ethics, she argues that we must first realize that "agreements in forms of life" precede "agreements in opinions." This doesn't mean that common lifestyles will produce a consensus of core values; instead, she proposes an agonistic model of democracy according to which the goal is "not to eliminate passions from the sphere of the public" but to "mobilize those passions toward democratic designs."[18] The virtue of Mouffe's theory is that it dispenses with the dream of rational consensus. Gone is any

hope that mass deliberation will produce agreement about "first principles." And there's something worthwhile in asking, as she does, how
we might transform political enemies into "adversaries," people with
whom we disagree but nevertheless share a foundational commitment
to democracy as such.

But even that question seems academic against the backdrop of all
this political malaise. One of the great tragedies of contemporary politics is that so many people believe there are no practicable alternatives
to the status quo; the near collapse of the conventional Left-Right distinction points to this problem. The pretense of "third way" politics
pioneered by people like Bill Clinton and Tony Blair in the nineties was
that they went beyond categories like Right and Left. In reality, they
were a tacit admission that the world was in a good way and that we
ought to triangulate interests so as to preserve the present order. In the
post–Cold War world, liberal democracy became a globally hegemonic
ideology with no viable competitors and thus nothing against which
to measure itself. But then Western societies grew inert, grossly unequal, and increasingly unable to justify themselves. So when political
arsonists like Trump and other populists came along and promised to
obliterate the status quo, was it any wonder that so many citizens were
intrigued?

Such a revolt lacked any affirmative project, however. It was pure
negation, a middle finger raised to the established order and nothing besides. There was no answer to the question, What now? Since
hardly anyone believed that deep structural change was possible or
that political parties could deliver, the impulse for collective identity in
the form of racism or nationalism reemerged with a vengeance. Even
when politicians like Elizabeth Warren or Bernie Sanders spoke about
redistributing power and wealth, it fell flat; left-wing politicians have
been making these noises for years, only to be subdued or otherwise
absorbed by entrenched interests. It's impossible to weigh the full costs
of the desperation and indifference this failure has produced. Only in
the last few years, with the reality of a Trump presidency and Brexit,
have politics, and in some ways history, started up again.

For all her insight, Mouffe doesn't quite face up to the paradox. Her
focus on the opposing logics of liberalism and democracy obscures

the contradiction built into the very culture of democratic life. It's revealing, for example, that her book ends with a call to something like a democratic-socialist project. If democracy is agonistic in the way she suggests, if it's defined by a never-ending dialectic of struggle, there can be no ideological stability, no enduring outcomes. Mouffe never says socialism is the inevitable result of democratic politics, but there's a hesitation to acknowledge the unfinished—and unfinishable—nature of democracy. She may be right to claim that neoliberalism threatens democracy, but neoliberalism is nevertheless as compatible with democracy as socialism or populism or any other political project. The democratic road has many exits, of which liberalism, fascism, and socialism are among the many possibilities.

If democracy is going to survive the twenty-first century, it will have to adapt to the realities of life in a vast, technologically saturated society. Reinvigorating local journalism will help restore trust and center political discourse on flesh-and-blood issues, but it won't collapse America into a monolithic community. Besides, abandoning any attachment to the nation in favor of local politics exclusively amounts to a rejection of American democracy in any recognizable form. In addition to these challenges, we still face the enormous task of erecting a truly inclusive multiethnic society. To achieve any of these things in a climate as divided as ours is no small thing. So much of America's political stability has rested on the repression of dangerous or inconvenient voices. But now those voices have been let loose, and there's no shortage of opportunists looking to capitalize on them.

And then there's the problem of how identity and discourse overlap in our communication environment. The polarization of politics has led to an explosion of what the existentialist philosopher Jean-Paul Sartre famously called bad faith. However convoluted, the term is nevertheless useful. What Sartre meant by "bad faith" was a particular kind of thoughtlessness, a way of being in the world that reflected an absence of authenticity. In his 1943 opus, *Being and Nothingness*, Sartre describes a waiter in a Parisian café who is merely playing at being a waiter in a café, performing the role of a waiter in all the conventional ways. The man is acting in bad faith precisely because he's acting, because he refuses to acknowledge or consider the purpose of his actions. The waiter, like most of us, disappears into the role he thinks he's playing. It's a kind of self-deception that reduces action to posturing. The problem for Sartre isn't that the waiter is pretending to be something he's not; it's that he's bowing to social pressures and adopting false values as his own. Perhaps Sartre is too harsh here. The waiter is just a man doing a job the way it's supposed to be done. But his point is that the role of "waiter" is no different from every other role we assume in life—husband, mother, soldier, teacher, and so on. Our identities are rarely chosen in any meaningful sense; instead, we conform to expectations in ways that betray our freedom to choose who we are, what we believe, and what matters.

Now think about how most people take on their political identity. Do we not retreat into our roles as conservatives or liberals, Republicans or Democrats, just as the waiter succumbs to all those waiterly clichés? Some of this is unavoidable: everyone models their politics and worldview on what's around them. But this becomes debilitating in a communicative culture like ours, in which the issues we're debating are remote and abstract, divorced from lived experience and shaped by media narratives. The dominance of national politics infuses everything with an all-or-nothing furor that obliterates the possibility for compromise, because often the issues themselves are insoluble; it's mostly culture warfare and virtue signaling. Every public conversation is thus flattened and caricatured, processed through the lens of prefabricated political identities. And these identities reflect, increasingly, the partisan tenor of our commercialized mediascape.

This sort of politics amounts to a flight from the demands of democratic action. It's a refusal to take political freedom seriously and authentically form judgments about issues of public concern. To the extent that the nationalization of politics is the result of the nationalization of political media, there's regrettably not much we can do, apart from propping up as much local journalism as possible. Still, most people in most places will continue to get their news online from nonlocal sources. So we'll need to articulate a philosophy of freedom and responsibility that maps onto the political realities of today. The emphasis on individual choice may seem at odds with the collective aims of democracy; on the contrary, a reengagement with our individual responsibilities as small-*d* democrats is the only way forward. The digital environment isn't going away, which means the hazards of groupthink, of curated news feeds, of algorithmic thinking supplanting actual thinking, aren't going away either. The individual citizen will have to choose to act democratically *and* ethically. We all have a little bad faith in us, and though we can never stamp that out, awareness of it is a precondition for meaningful engagement.

The existentialist turn at the end of this book is therefore purposeful. For the bad faith problem goes well beyond media pathologies and partisan warfare. One of the ambitions of this project is to force us to think a little more deeply about the tragic ambiguity of the democratic condition. The rise of digital culture presents both an opportunity and a realization: an opportunity to confront the burden of a truly open culture and the concomitant realization that we must live with the illiberalism that that culture has unleashed. Democracy allows for—and even encourages—all these encroachments, and the loss of gatekeepers limits our capacity to check them. The best we can do is construct a culture of communication that fosters the sort of engaged freedom democracy demands. We're thrown into this situation, and we're responsible for the choices we make, the choices that shape our shared situation. Democracy is worth the price so long as it affords the freedom of expression and the opportunity to curtail power, but whether it does either of those things depends partially on the health of our communicative environment.

The beauty of the Sisyphus myth is that it offers a metaphor for democratic action. Camus wrote his famous essay on Sisyphus and absurdity against the backdrop of World War II. He likened awareness of the absurd to the collapse of a stage set. It was like waking up and realizing that the world doesn't fit any of your conceptual schemes. Facing absurdity in 1942 meant acknowledging that all our grand narratives, all our totalizing ideologies, were not only false constructions but dangerous delusions. This was a good thing as far as Camus was concerned. For him, any form of teleological thinking was a kind of betrayal. It was an attempt to make life coherent by imposing an order on it. The ideologies of communism and fascism, in his view, were essentially frustrated religions. Our current moment lacks the epic violence of Camus's era, but there are some important parallels. The erosion of liberalism means a forced collision with the existential reality of democratic life. But that doesn't have to be a cause for despair. Just as Sisyphus chooses to find meaning in his fate, so we democrats must decide what to make of our own boulder. It's just as likely to tumble in the direction of dictatorship as it is liberal democracy.

Thinking all this through against the backdrop of the coronavirus pandemic has been instructive. For one thing, the lack of a shared reality has crippled our capacity to deal with a public health crisis. But a pandemic is also such a clear illustration of the limits of using media to bend reality. You can't mediate a virus away; it has to be confronted through the ethical choices of information and conduct. The striking thing about a pandemic is that it foregrounds what's already true of our condition. It forces us to think about our responsibilities to the people around us, to fellow citizens. Camus's novel *The Plague* is so clarifying here, because it draws out the conflict between individual happiness and moral obligation. The hero of the story is a committed doctor named Rieux. From the very beginning, Rieux devotes himself to resisting the plague and achieving solidarity with its victims. His sense of purpose is wrapped up in the struggle and sacrifice demanded by the scourge. The model of ethical action that Rieux represents is apt not only for our conduct during a pandemic but also in any democratic society. The practices of democracy demand a similar existential commitment. To put it another way: the freedom and openness of democracy run on a kind of honor system. The grounds for ethical communication are never secured and are always being contested. And the overall health of a democratic culture is nothing but the sum total of choices made by the people who make it up.

There's always a temptation with books like this one to conclude with a grand plan to "fix" democracy. But the point of this book is to say that no such plan is possible. Democracy can't be "fixed" if by that we mean stripped of its inherent contradictions. There is some consolation in knowing that the turmoil we're experiencing now is different but not new. Democratic cultures have been upended by novel media technologies and demagogic rhetorical styles repeatedly, each time in a familiar cycle of innovation, disruption, and adaptation. Democracy remains an existential burden for all who inherit it. It's disappointing and worthwhile at the same time. It affords freedom of expression, going all the way back to *isegoria* and the Greeks, and it provides opportunities to confront power in all its forms. But democracy can never guarantee anything permanent, least of all good governance. This is the eternal dynamic of every democracy that has ever existed. But when we recognize that democracy is an open culture of communication guided by persuasion and defined by its tools of connection, the importance of engagement, of education and media savvy, becomes obvious. We can plainly see that democracy is a story being written in the present by citizens, activists, corporations, and politicians who are bound only by their capacity to persuade each other.

But the precariousness of our situation persists. There's no clearing space beyond the chaos of democracy. In the end, we must perceive the existential opportunities in the frenzied flows of discourse, and that comes down to the individual choices of individual citizens to form groups, movements, and political parties. Sartre famously said that the French were never freer than under Vichy rule, because they all had to make a choice: compromise or resist. The situation today is not all that different. We can choose to engage, or we can fold up our democratic tents and wait for the apocalypse. But no matter what we do, power is always committed, always ready to exploit communication and buttress itself. Democracy hangs in the balance today, just as it always has. Democracy has no destiny, no ground, and what it *is* at any moment depends on how hard and how long we push that boulder. And we can't know the outcome in advance. All we can do is make the choice to share in rolling our boulder up that democratic hill again and again. That is the only way to continually re-achieve democracy.

EPILOGUE

On January 6, 2021, a group of patriots stormed the US Capitol, a building last raided by the British during the War of 1812. Some in the group were spangled with face paint and wore military garb. Some were toting Confederate flags. Many were taking selfies or live-streaming the rebellion. They roamed the halls of Congress, screaming, "Stop the steal!" Offices were vandalized. Windows were broken. Statues were toppled. A woman was shot and killed. Four others died, including a Capitol Police officer. It was a remarkable assault on the foundation of American democracy, staged at the very moment a peaceful transfer of power was under way.

The events of January 6 were ugly, embarrassing, and seditious, but they weren't surprising. This was a subversion of democracy in defense of democracy. We can now add the United States to the list of Athens, Rome, France, Spain, and Peru, among others, as democracies that have experienced a self-coup attempt. The men and women who invaded the Capitol did so because they believed—truly believed—that President Donald Trump had won a landslide victory which subsequently was stolen. He had raised over $200 million in the two months after the election by alleging voter fraud, an established Big Lie that gained widespread purchase in our fragmented information space by conservative media across radio, cable television, and social networking. Dozens of lawsuits echoing these charges struggled to so much as gain standing in state and federal courts. Trump then suggested the possibility that Vice President Mike Pence and Congress could overturn the election on January 6, whereupon he instructed his supporters to march on the Capitol, telling them to "fight like hell."

We're fortunate that the insurrection failed, but that it happened at all is instructive. This book is about a paradox at the center of every democratic culture, a paradox that runs in opposite directions at the same time. Because of the open communication it offers, a democracy can't protect itself from all the consequences of unfettered expression. The incentives born out of this circumstance can be perverse. It means that anything is possible, because anyone can say anything, and therefore anyone can be convinced of anything. To suggest that everything is permitted in a democracy is not to say that everything is justified. It means that persuasion, not truth, is the master variable in a democratic society. What people believe is true is more important than what is actually true because what people do in the world is a function of what they believe about the world.

The assault itself was illegal, and those who breached the Capitol found themselves subject to criminal prosecution. The president who had encouraged such behavior, while impeached, was not convicted for incitement to insurrection. His acquittal is somewhat fitting for the paradox of democracy. When political speech is free, it makes use of all available media and can be harnessed for antidemocratic purposes. For that reason, President Trump could openly deny the election results. His former national security advisor, Lieutenant General Michael Flynn, could call for the imposition of martial law. Another supporter, Senator Mike Lee of Utah, could insist on Twitter that the United States is not a democracy. These are all affronts to democracy, but a democracy tolerates them all because it must. Politicians are allowed to persuade their supporters, and supporters can persuade others. Persuasion is indeed the dividing line between protected expression and illegal action. Those insurrectionists had a right to suspect election fraud, even if their suspicions were wrong—and even if they were knowingly operating in bad faith. Charging the Capitol was something different, an act that sought to upend democracy by physical force, not communication.

The only way to transcend the paradox is to abolish the freedom that creates it. Had the events of January 6 broken differently—a captured vice president, an executed Speaker of the House, a vote held at gunpoint—President Trump need only have issued a proclamation of national emergency to invoke section 706 of the Communications Act. Doing so would have taken offline every radio and television station, all internet access, and every phone. American democracy could have been over, just like that. By comparison, less than a month after the Capitol insurrection a far more serious and successful coup took place in Myanmar as the military expunged the election results from the previous November. The new leadership had no compunction about shutting off communications such as public Wi-Fi while assemblies of protesters were proscribed and then actively harmed. Democracy melted away overnight. In India during this time, the government cracked down on protests against new farming legislation and arrested the journalists who covered them. It also threatened to jail Twitter executives for not eliminating online profiles at the government's request.

India, the world's largest democracy, appears headed in the direction of the China model, the most prominent example of an antidemocratic political system. China has erected a sprawling censorship apparatus supplemented by a Great Firewall that filters the internet and an online, state-run "cheerleading" content mill that eclipses bad news by diverting attention from actual problems. Traditional state-run media glorify China's leader, Xi Jinping, as "The Ultimate Arbiter." Power is concentrated and exercised absolutely. The goal, observes a jailed Chinese dissident professor, Xu Zhangrun, is "stability maintenance."[1] For the China model to work, such a society requires the outright stifling of free expression, without which democracy is impossible. Yet this model, like all authoritarian systems, leads inexorably to corruption and oppression. The Chinese government not only exacerbated the pandemic through its obfuscations in 2020 but continued the systemic mass detention of Uighur Muslims and eradicated the democratic independence of Hong Kong. For what? To sustain the considerable privilege and arbitrary power of the regime by eliminating threats, the ultimate of which is the freedom of expression. The protester, the journalist, the minority, the professor: none shall use their voice to object, to report, to petition, to theorize, and citizens shall not use sight, sound, and touch to get informed (let alone vote).

The temptation to flee the challenges of democracy is alluring, a promise to do away with the paradox. For its part, China does not pretend to care about democracy. What's trickier is that others do. There was, in fact, a rigged 2020 election, but it was in Belarus, where Alexander Lukashenko had served as the country's only president for over a quarter century. Threatened by the popularity of his electoral opponent, the social media activist Siarhei Tikhanovskaya, Lukashenko had him jailed. When that man's wife, Svetlana Tikhanovskaya, decided to run and coalesced the opposition parties, Lukashenko based his campaign on sexist tropes. He then claimed a popular victory with 80 percent of the vote that August, a figure met with widespread mockery and disgust by election observers. Hundreds of thousands of Belarussians protested in Minsk while Svetlana Tikhanovskaya fled into exile and stands accused of terrorism. Can democracy emerge in Belarus? We can't know.

What we can tell you is that the promises of stability and wise rule imagined by antidemocratic rhetoric can't be guaranteed. This applies within actual democracies as much as totalitarian systems. In 2018, Brazil elected a populist president, Jair Bolsonaro, who once famously insisted, "You won't change anything in this country through voting—nothing, absolutely nothing."[2] He had benefited from an anticorruption revolt that impeached a sitting president, Dilma Rousseff, and imprisoned a former president, Lula da Silva. In office, Bolsonaro continued to play the populist heel, undermining his own government's responses to emergencies such as fires that razed the Amazon rain forests and a pandemic that has killed hundreds of thousands of Brazilians. Public corruption hasn't fared much better. In fact, as investigative reporting from the *Intercept Brasil* demonstrated, Operation Car Wash (Lava Jato), the probe that supported Bolsonaro's political fortunes, was itself corrupt. The magistrate in charge, whom Bolsonaro later elevated to minister of justice, had secretly worked with prosecutors to drum up charges against Lula and spy on his defense team. Much of the money recovered from Lava Jato had been funneled to a private foundation overseen by the investigators rather than returned to the public. Lula was released from prison and his conviction overturned, paving a return to politics. Round and round we go: democracy facilitates political expression and the ability to check power, but the opportunities for expression can abuse and exploit power as much as resist it.

So where does that leave us? We'd like to say that democracy's destiny is equality and everlasting peace. We'd like to say that safer shores are just a few legislative achievements away, or that our communicative follies will resolve themselves. But that's nonsense. The Tower of Babel is always crumbling. Democracy is always free speech and its consequences. Which brings us back to Sisyphus and his boulder. The existentialist dilemma is about choice and responsibility. The individual confronts a world of uncertainty and has to take responsibility for that freedom. The ontological condition of democracy is no different. Collectively, we face a choice, not unlike the one presented to Alyosha by Dostoevsky's "Grand Inquisitor": which do we prefer, the uncertainty of democratic freedom, or the predictability of authoritarianism? The power of Dostoevsky's famous scene lies in its stone-cold depiction of human nature. The Inquisitor is a tyrant and a liberator all at once. His gift to humanity is to relieve it of the burden of choice. He wagers that people don't want freedom so much as order and subsistence. But human life can never be made coherent because the world we inhabit is absurd. We transcend our need for mere bread by communicating with one another. Totalitarian regimes and antidemocratic politicians are blind to this fact. They can only offer, as the Inquisitor slyly suggests, the illusion of stability at the expense of freedom itself.

Democracy offers no such illusion. It is the best form of politics precisely because it grants freedom of expression and the possibility of challenging unjust power in all its forms. While it may not depend on truth as much as we'd like, democracy inheres a robust communicative culture and a willingness to embrace the contradictions of human life. But communication is only as reliable as the media on which it relies. Amid a transition from the convergence of all media to a more fully digitized society, the ground will continue to shift beneath us. That will require another radical adjustment of our expectations. The communicative culture that sustained democracy in the previous century is dead, and it's not coming back. If the power of the gatekeepers is gone, so, too, is the impact of pseudo-events. For President Trump in 2020, his daily televised press conferences about the pandemic, his

Bible-waving photo-op after the removal of protesters, his Republican National Convention speech at the White House, his outrageous performance at the first presidential debate with Joe Biden, and his fist-pumping recovery from COVID-19 were all intended as terrific moments in presidential communication to capture attention and land an impression. They failed. Biden, a candidate who neither campaigned with in-person rallies nor offered any visible media strategy, won by more than seven million votes. As a final blow, even the January 6 insurrection struck Trump, who watched it on television, as a "'low-class' spectacle of people in ragtag costumes rummaging through the Capitol."[3] American democracy didn't die that day, but the televisual age came to a close. As if to herald the change, social networking giants Facebook and Twitter removed Trump's accounts soon after the Capitol was stormed.

Our hopes ought not rest with the tech industry exercising editorial control over its platforms. It's a welcome shift, but too late. Frankly, contemplating the politics of a truly digital age is an event horizon beyond our grasp. As artificial intelligence evolves, the problem may no longer be persuasion but the absence of persuasion. That should scare us. Nothing should be taken for granted, least of all political liberty. While open communication allows for public expression and mobilization, corporate and state actors continue to possess data collection, facial recognition, and other surveillance technologies. Governments still retain control of servers to shut off internet access. Satellite internet could expand connectivity across the entire globe, but such constellations are only as good as the private entities who send them into orbit. And even if we could install a global communications network free from corporate and state control, we would still be thrown back into a state of tension that defines every democracy: the freedom on which we depend, open communication, remains our deepest existential threat.

Ultimately, democracy is only a clearing space. Ideas and arguments and rhetorical styles clash through various media. Good governance and good faith are not guaranteed in advance. Truth rarely prevails. The best or most logical arguments do not always triumph. There's no telos or direction. Whoever persuades, by whatever means, wins. We can no more eliminate the tugs of human emotion than the sophistic techniques that appeal to them. Sometimes you wind up with leadership that exercises power to reflect the will of the people, and sometimes that power rewards only itself. That some would destroy democracy to sustain their power is always in the offing. The open communication of such a culture means that it can be pushed in either direction. We'll never quite get the democracy we want, and that's okay. That's the paradox. We all have work to do, then, in making the most of the democracies we have.

ACKNOWLEDGMENTS

The germ for the idea of this book was planted on a muddy hiking trail outside of Pocatello in October 2016. We had briefly met playing pickup basketball at the Louisiana State University rec center over a decade before, only to reconnect when Sean was invited to give a talk at Idaho State University.

We approached the project from different perspectives. Thankfully, we had a number of opportunities to refine our thinking. Vox permitted Sean the space to explore the works of Plato and Walter Lippmann and the connections between politics and media in his essays for the site. We were also fortunate that Zac could present our ideas at an important conference on fascism hosted by Texas A&M University in 2018. Nathan Crick edited the resulting volume, *The Rhetoric of Fascism* (University of Alabama Press, 2022), and his guidance helped shape our contribution, "The Spectacle of Fascism," which offers a more theoretical take on the subject than what you'll find in chapter 5, though it draws from similar literature. Then in 2019, Sean delivered a public lecture at LSU on the challenges of liberal democracy in the digital age.

We continually benefited from the encouragement and support provided by Zac's department at ISU and its chair, Jim Disanza. We'd also like to credit our agent, Ted Weinstein, for helping us find our voice. Our conversations with our editor, Charles Myers, were invaluable, and we consider ourselves lucky to have had Sandra Hazel edit the manuscript.

NOTES

Introduction

1. Steven Levitsky and Daniel Ziblatt, *How Democracies Die* (New York: Penguin Random House, 2018).
2. Yascha Mounk, *The People vs. Democracy* (Cambridge, MA: Harvard University Press, 2018).
3. Anne Applebaum, *Twilight of Democracy* (New York: Penguin Random House, 2020).
4. Norberto Bobbio, *The Future of Democracy*, trans. Roger Griffin (Minneapolis: University of Minnesota Press, 1987), 26.
5. Plato, *The Dialogues of Plato*, trans. B. Jowett, vol. 1 (New York: Bigelow, Brown, 1914), 158.
6. Walter Lippmann, *Public Opinion* (New York: Harcourt, Brace, 1922), 269.
7. Lippmann, 73.
8. John Dewey, "Review of *Public Opinion* by Walter Lippmann," *New Republic*, May 3, 1922, 288.
9. John Dewey, *Democracy and Education* (New York: Jovian, 2016), 95.

Chapter One

1. Umberto Eco, *The Search for the Perfect Language*, trans. James Fentress (Cambridge, MA: Blackwell, 1995), 353.
2. Friedrich Nietzsche, *The Gay Science*, trans. Walter Kaufmann (New York: Vintage Books, 1974), 298.
3. R. I. M. Dunbar, "Coevolution of Neocortical Size, Group Size and Language in Humans," *Behavioral and Brain Sciences* 16, no. 4 (December 1993): 681–94.
4. Brooke Gladstone, *The Trouble with Reality* (New York: Workman, 2017), 2.
5. Ron Suskind, "Faith, Certainty and the Presidency of George W. Bush," *New York Times*, October 17, 2004, https://www.nytimes.com/2004/10/17/magazine/faith-certainty-and-the-presidency-of-george-w-bush.html.
6. Lee McIntyre, *Post-Truth* (Cambridge, MA: MIT Press, 2018), 10.

7. Elizabeth L. Eisenstein, *The Printing Press as an Agent of Change* (New York: Cambridge University Press, 1982).

8. Nicholas Carr, *The Shallows: What the Internet Is Doing to Our Brains* (New York: W. W. Norton, 2011).

9. Joshua Meyrowitz, *No Sense of Place* (New York: Oxford University Press, 1985), 331.

10. Marshall McLuhan, *Understanding Media: The Extensions of Man* (Cambridge, MA: MIT Press, 1994),16.

11. Harold Innis, *The Bias of Communication* (Toronto: University of Toronto Press, 2003), 188.

Chapter Two

1. Plato, *Apology*, trans. G. M. A. Grube, in *Complete Works*, ed. John M. Cooper (Indianapolis: Hackett, 1997), 18a.

2. Plato, *Gorgias*, trans. Donald J. Zeyl, in *Complete Works*, ed. Cooper, 521c–d.

3. Herodotus, *The Histories*, trans. David Greene (Chicago: University of Chicago Press, 1987), 5.78.

4. Yohio Nakategawa, "Isegoria in Herodotus," *Historia* 37, no. 3 (1988): 270.

5. S. Sara Monoson, *Plato's Democratic Entanglements: Athenian Politics and the Practice of Philosophy* (Princeton, NJ: Princeton University Press, 2000), 53.

6. Thucydides, *The Peloponnesian War*, trans. Steven Lattimore (Indianapolis: Hackett, 1998), 2.35.

7. Thucydides, 2.37.

8. I. F. Stone, *The Trial of Socrates* (New York: Anchor Books, 1989), 197.

9. Debra Hawhee, *Bodily Arts: Rhetoric and Athletics in Ancient Greece* (Austin: University of Texas Press, 2009).

10. Gorgias, in *The Older Sophists*, ed. Rosamund Kent Sprague (Columbia: University of South Carolina Press, 1972), 49.

11. Plato, *Sophist*, trans. Nicholas P. White, in *Complete Works*, ed. Cooper, 231e.

12. Richard Weaver, *Ideas Have Consequences* (Chicago: University of Chicago Press, 1948), 154.

13. Plato, *Phaedrus*, trans. Alexander Nehamas Paul Woodruff, in *Complete Works*, ed. Cooper, 267 A–B.

14. John Adams, letter to John Taylor, December 17, 1814, https://founders.archives.gov /documents/Adams/99-02-02-6371, accessed July 12, 2021.

15. Plato, *Protagoras*, trans. Stanley Lombardo and Karen Bell, in *Complete Works*, ed. Cooper, 319d.

16. Roslyn Weiss, *The Socratic Paradox and Its Enemies* (Chicago: University of Chicago Press, 2006), 26.

17. Plato, *Sophist* 231d.

18. Gorgias, quoted in Sprague, *The Older Sophists*, 52–53.

19. Thrasymachus, quoted in Sprague, *The Older Sophists*, 90.

20. Plato, *Theaetetus*, trans. M. J. Levett and Myles F. Burnyeat, in *Complete Works*, ed. Cooper, 161c.

21. Plato, *Phaedrus* 275e.
22. *Politics*, in *The Complete Works of Aristotle: The Revised Oxford Translation*, ed. Jonathan Barnes, vol. 2 (Princeton, NJ: Princeton University Press, 1984), 4.2.
23. Cicero, *On Oratory and Orations*, trans. J. S. Watson (Carbondale: Southern Illinois University Press, 1986), 1.8.
24. Paul Veyne, *Bread and Circuses: Historical Sociology and Political Pluralism*, trans. Brian Pearce (New York: Penguin Books, 1990), 292.
25. Longinus, *On the Sublime*, trans. D. A. Russell, in *The Rhetorical Tradition*, ed. Patricia Bizzell and Bruce Herzberg, 2nd ed. (Boston: Bedford/St. Martin's, 2001), 7.4.

Chapter Three

1. *The Tryal of John Peter Zenger* (London: J. Wilford, 1738), 29, https://history.nycourts.gov/wp-content/uploads/2018/11/History_Tryal-John-Peter-Zenger.pdf.
2. Frederic Hudson, ed., *Journalism of the United States, 1690–1872* (New York: Harper and Brothers, 1873), 44–48.
3. Brittney Washington, "A Pamphlet War in England, 1641–1643," *Collation*, June 19, 2018, https://collation.folger.edu/2018/06/pamphlet-war-in-england-1641-1643/.
4. In Andrew Pettegree, *The Invention of News* (New Haven, CT: Yale University Press, 2014), 237.
5. *Areopagitica*, in *Complete Prose Works of John Milton*, vol. 2, *1643–1648*, ed. Ernest Sirluck (New Haven, CT: Yale University Press, 1959), 487.
6. John B. Blake, "The Inoculation Controversy in Boston, 1721–1722," *New England Quarterly* 25, no. 4 (1952): 505.
7. Mitchell Stephens, *A History of News* (New York: Viking, 1988), 192.
8. In Hudson, *Journalism of the United States*, 113.
9. In Paul Starr, *The Creation of the Media* (New York: Basic Books, 2004), 67.
10. *The Papers of Thomas Jefferson*, vol. 26, *11 May to 31 August 1793*, ed. John Catanzariti (Princeton, NJ: Princeton University Press, 1995), 444.
11. Michael Durey, *With the Hammer of Truth: James Thomson Callender and America's Early National Heroes* (Charlottesville: University Press of Virginia, 1990), 93.
12. Leonard Levy, *Emergence of a Free Press* (New York: Oxford University Press, 1985), xvii.
13. Jeremy Popkin, *Revolutionary News: The Press in France, 1789–1799* (Durham, NC: Duke University Press, 1990), 5.
14. Robert Darnton, *Revolution in Print: The Press in France, 1775–1800* (Berkeley: University of California Press, 1989), 27.
15. Popkin, *Revolutionary News*, 180.
16. Edmund Burke, *Reflections on the Revolution in France* (New York: Oxford University Press, 1999), 69.
17. "Letter to a Member of the National Assembly," in *The Works and Correspondence of the Right Honourable Edmund Burke*, vol. 4 (London: Gilbert and Rivington, 1852), 360.

Chapter Four

1. In Bell Gale Chevigny, "To the Edges of Ideology: Margaret Fuller's Centrifugal Evolution," *American Quarterly* 38, no. 2 (1986): 175.

2. In *Margaret Fuller, Critic: Writings from the* New-York Tribune, *1844–1846*, ed. Judith Mattson Bean and Joel Myerson (New York: Columbia University Press, 2000), 11.

3. *Margaret Fuller, Critic*, 131.

4. Margaret Fuller, *These Sad but Glorious Days*, ed. Larry J. Reynolds and Susan Belasso Smith (New Haven, CT: Yale University Press, 1991), 166.

5. Heinrich von Kleist, *Michael Kohlhaas*, trans. Michael Hoffman (New York: New Directions, 2020), 7.

6. In T. G. Steward, *The Haitian Revolution, 1791 to 1804; or, Side Lights on the French Revolution*, 2nd ed. (New York: Thomas Y. Crowell, 1914), 240.

7. *The Political Thought of Bolívar: Selected Writings*, ed. Gerald E. Fitzgerald (The Hague: Martinus Nijhoff, 1971), 57, 60.

8. *Works of Fisher Ames*, ed. Seth Ames (Boston: Little, Brown, 1854), 394.

9. Nancy Isenberg and Andrew Burstein, *The Problem of Democracy: The Presidents Adams Confront the Cult of Personality* (New York: Viking, 2019), 380.

10. Frances Wright, *Course of Popular Lectures, as Delivered by Frances Wright* (New York: Free Enquirer, 1829), 174–75.

11. In Dan Schiller, *Objectivity and the News: The Public and the Rise of Commercial Journalism* (Philadelphia: University of Pennsylvania Press, 1981), 30.

12. In Helen Woodward, *The Lady Persuaders* (New York: Ivan Obolensky, 1960), 23.

13. Trish Loughran, *The Republic in Print: Print Culture in the Age of U.S. Nation Building, 1770–1870* (New York: Columbia University Press, 2007).

14. Alexis de Tocqueville, *Democracy in America*, trans. Arthur Goldhammer (New York: Library of America, 2004), 207.

15. Tocqueville, 205.

16. Tocqueville, 265.

17. Michael Schudson, *Discovering the News: A Social History of American Newspapers* (New York: Basic Books, 1978), 22–23.

18. In James L. Crouthamel, *Bennett's* New York Herald *and the Rise of the Popular Press* (Syracuse, NY: Syracuse University Press, 1989), 21.

19. Andie Tucher, *Froth and Scum: Truth, Beauty, Goodness, and the Ax Murder in America's First Mass Medium* (Chapel Hill: University of North Carolina Press, 1994), 40–41.

20. Fuller, *These Sad but Glorious Days*, 165.

21. Fuller, 277–78.

22. In Priscilla Robertson, *Revolutions of 1848: A Social History* (Princeton, NJ: Princeton University Press, 1952), 53.

23. Jonathan Israel, *The Expanding Blaze: How the American Revolution Ignited the World, 1775–1848* (Princeton, NJ: Princeton University Press, 2017), 562.

24. In T. A. B. Corley, *Democratic Despot: A Life of Napoleon III* (Westport, CT: Greenwood, 1974), 56.

25. Elizabeth Cady Stanton, *Eighty Years and More, 1815–1897* (New York: European Publishing Company, 1898), 149.

26. Samuel F. B. Morse, *Foreign Conspiracy against the Liberties of the United States*, 7th ed. (New York: American and Foreign Christian Union, 1855), 30.

27. Sigmund Freud, *Civilization and Its Discontents*, trans. James Strachey (New York: W. W. Norton, 1961), 39.

28. Daniel Walker Howe, *What Hath God Wrought: The Transformation of America, 1815–1848* (New York: Oxford University Press, 2007), 7.

29. James Carey, *Communication as Culture: Essays on Media and Society* (New York: Routledge, 2009), 162.

30. Carey, 162.

31. "A Word about Ourselves," *New York Times*, September 18, 1851.

32. In Edward Cook, *Delane of the Times* (New York: Henry Holt, 1916), 277.

33. In Cook, 277.

34. John Stuart Mill, *On Liberty* (New York: Oxford University Press, 1924), 28.

35. In Benjamin Evans Lippincott, *Victorian Critics of Democracy* (Minneapolis: University of Minnesota Press, 1938), 64.

36. Karl Marx, *The Eighteenth Brumaire of Louis Bonaparte*, trans. Daniel DeLeon (Chicago: Charles H. Kerr, 1913), 55–56.

37. In Saul K. Padlover, *Karl Marx: An Intimate Biography* (New York: McGraw-Hill, 1978), 133.

38. Thomas R. Whitney, *A Defence of American Policy, as Opposed to the Encroachments of Foreign Influence, and Especially to the Interference of the Papacy in the Political Interests and Affairs of the United States* (New York: De Witt and Davenport, 1856), 34.

39. *Select Speeches of Kossuth*, ed. Francis W. Newman (London: Trubner, 1853), 185.

40. *Political Speeches and Debates of Abraham Lincoln and Stephen A. Douglas, 1854–1861*, ed. Alonzo T. Jones (Chicago: Scott, Foresman, 1896), 211.

41. *Political Speeches and Debates of Abraham Lincoln*, 65.

42. In Phillip Knightley, *The First Casualty: The War Correspondent as Hero and Mythmaker from the Crimea to Iraq* (Baltimore: Johns Hopkins University Press, 2004), 23.

43. In David T. Z. Mindich, *Just the Facts: How "Objectivity" Came to Define American Journalism* (New York: New York University Press, 1998), 71.

44. E. L. Godkin, "The Newspaper and the Reader," *Nation*, August 10, 1865, 165–66.

45. In Brenda Wineapple, *The Impeachers: The Trial of Andrew Johnson and the Dream of a Just Nation* (New York: Random House, 2019), 83.

46. In Joe Gray Taylor, "New Orleans and Reconstruction," *Louisiana History* 19, no. 3 (1968): 195.

47. In James McGrath Morris, *Pulitzer: A Life in Politics, Print, and Power* (New York: Harper Collins, 2010), 161.

48. Paul Collins, *The Murder of the Century: The Gilded Age Crime That Scandalized a City and Sparked the Tabloid Wars* (New York: Broadway, 2011), 55.

49. Adolph S. Ochs, "Business Announcement," *New York Times*, August 19, 1896.

50. "Vociferous Detectives," *New York Times*, June 30, 1897.

51. Rodger Streitmatter, *Mightier Than the Sword*, 3rd ed. (Boulder, CO: Westview, 2012), 76.

52. In David Wetzel, *A Duel of Giants: Bismarck, Napoleon III, and the Origins of the Franco-Prussian War* (Madison: University of Wisconsin Press, 2001), 120.

53. In Wetzel, 160.

54. W. E. B. Du Bois, "The African Roots of War," *Atlantic*, May 1915, https://www .theatlantic.com/magazine/archive/1915/05/the-african-roots-of-war/528897/.

55. In Ruth Harris, *Dreyfus: Politics, Emotion, and the Scandal of the Century* (New York: Metropolitan Books, 2010), 34.

56. In Jeanne Humphries, "The Dreyfus Affair: A Woman's Affair," *Historical Reflections* 31, no. 3 (Fall 2005): 437.

57. In Mary Louise Roberts, "Acting Up: The Feminist Theatrics of Marguerite Durand," *French Historical Studies* 19, no. 4 (Autumn 1996): 1123.

58. In Daniel Balmuth, "Origins of the Russian Press Reform of 1865," *Slavonic and East European Review* 47, no. 109 (1969): 370.

59. Louise McReynolds, *The News under Russia's Old Regime: The Development of a Mass-Circulation Press* (Princeton, NJ: Princeton University Press, 1991), 32.

60. In Robert E. McMaster, "Danilevsky and Spengler: A New Interpretation," *Journal of Modern History* 26, no. 2 (1954): 160.

61. Christopher Clark, *The Sleepwalkers: How Europe Went to War in 1914* (New York: HarperCollins, 2013), 380.

62. Imanuel Geiss, ed., *July 1914, the Outbreak of the First World War: Selected Documents* (New York: Charles Scribner's Sons, 1967), 117.

63. Laurence Lafore, *The Long Fuse: An Interpretation of the Origins of World War I*, 2nd ed. (Philadelphia: J. P. Lippincott, 1971), 210.

64. Edmund von Mach, ed., *Official Documents Relating to the Outbreak of the European War* (New York: MacMillan, 1916), 515–16.

65. Geiss, *July 1914*, 260.

66. Geiss, 261.

67. *In These Great Times: A Karl Kraus Reader*, ed. Harry Zohn (London: Carcanet, 1984), 77.

68. William James, "Remarks at the Peace Banquet," *Atlantic*, December 1904, https:// www.theatlantic.com/magazine/archive/1904/12/remarks-at-the-peace-banquet /307802/.

69. James, "Remarks."

70. In Jill Lepore, *These Truths: A History of the United States* (New York: W. W. Norton, 2018), 274.

71. Carrie Chapman Catt, "Open Address to the U.S. Congress," November 1917, https://awpc.cattcenter.iastate.edu/2017/03/21/address-to-congress-november -1917/.

Chapter Five

1. Melvyn Stokes, *D. W. Griffith's "The Birth of a Nation"* (New York: Oxford University Press, 2007), 112.

2. In Mark E. Benbow, "Birth of a Quotation: Woodrow Wilson and 'Like Writing History with Lightning,'" *Journal of the Gilded Age and Progressive Era* 9, no. 4 (2010): 515.

3. Thomas Dixon Jr., *The Clansman: An Historical Romance of the Ku Klux Klan* (New York: A. Wessels, 1907), 86.

4. Dixon, 269–70.

5. Dixon, 325.

6. Dixon, 327, 341, 342–43.

7. Richard J. Evans, *The Coming of the Third Reich* (New York: Penguin, 2004), 451.

8. Edward Bernays, *Propaganda* (New York: Ig, 2005), 52.

9. Roger Griffin, *The Nature of Fascism* (New York: Routledge, 1993), 32.

10. Amy Louise Wood, *Lynching and Spectacle: Witnessing Racial Violence in America, 1890–1940* (Chapel Hill: University of North Carolina Press, 2009), 159.

11. Felix Harcourt, *Ku Klux Kulture: America and the Klan in the 1920s* (Chicago: University of Chicago Press, 2017).

12. Schenck v. United States, 249 U.S. 52 (1919).

13. Abrams v. United States, 250 U.S. 630 (1919).

14. Walter F. White, "The Eruption of Tulsa," *Nation*, June 29, 1921, https://www.thenation.com/article/tulsa-1921/.

15. Whitney v. California, 274 U.S. 375 (1927).

16. Fred W. Friendly, *Minnesota Rag* (New York: Random House, 1981), 179.

17. Stromberg v. California, 283 U.S. 369 (1931).

18. Dorothy Thompson, "Mr. Welles and Mass Delusion," *New York Herald Tribune*, November 2, 1938.

19. F. T. Marinetti, *Critical Writings*, ed. Gunter Berghaus, trans. Doug Thompson (New York: Farrar, Straus and Giroux, 2006), 13.

20. In Herbert W. Schneider, *Making the Fascist State* (New York: Howard Fertig, 1968), 58.

21. Benito Mussolini, *My Autobiography* (Westport, CT: Greenwood, 1970), 122.

22. Robert O. Paxton, *The Anatomy of Fascism* (New York: Knopf, 2004), 78–79.

23. Benito Mussolini, "Fascism's Myth: The Nation," in *Fascism*, ed. Roger Griffin (reprint, Oxford: Oxford University Press, 2009), 44.

24. Giacomo Matteotti, *The Fascisti Exposed: A Year of Fascist Domination*, trans. E. W. Dickes (New York: Howard Fertig, 1969), 74.

25. In George Seldes, *Sawdust Caesar* (New York: Harper and Brothers, 1935), 400.

26. Matteotti, *The Fascisti Exposed*, 149–50.

27. Mauro Canali, "The Matteotti Murder and the Origins of Mussolini's Totalitarian Fascist Regime in Italy," trans. Antony Shugaar, *Journal of Modern Italian Studies* 14, no. 2 (2009): 143–67.

28. In Seldes, *Sawdust Caesar*, 179.

29. Antonio Gramsci, *Selections from the Prison Notebooks*, ed. and trans. Quintin Hare and Geoffrey Nowell Smith (New York: International, 2003), 150.

30. Winfried Lerg, "Media Culture of the Weimar Republic," *Journal of Communication Inquiry* 13, no. 1 (1989): 94–110.

31. Harold Gordon Jr., *Hitler and the Beer Hall Putsch* (Princeton, NJ: Princeton University Press, 1972), 365.

32. Adolf Hitler, *Mein Kampf*, trans. Ralph Manheim (Boston: Houghton Mifflin, 1971), 583.

33. Ernest K. Bramsted, *Goebbels and National Socialist Propaganda, 1925–1945* (East Lansing: Michigan State University Press, 1965), 9.

34. Nicholas O'Shaughnessy, *Selling Hitler: Propaganda and the Nazi Brand* (London: Hurst, 2016), 26.

35. Hannah Arendt, *The Origins of Totalitarianism* (New York: Meridian Books, 1958), 349.

36. Martin Heidegger, "German Students," in *The Heidegger Controversy: A Critical Reader*, ed. Richard Wolin (Cambridge, MA: MIT Press, 1993), 46–47.

37. Carl Schmitt, *The Concept of the Political*, trans. George Schwab (Chicago: University of Chicago Press, 1996), 26.

38. Susan Sontag, *Under the Sign of Saturn* (New York: Farrar, Straus and Giroux, 1980), 87.

39. Jules Levey, "Georges Valois and the Faisceau: The Making and Breaking of a Fascist," *French Historical Studies* 8, no. 2 (1973): 280.

40. Stanley Payne, *Fascism: Comparison and Definition* (Madison: University of Wisconsin Press, 1980), 116.

41. Walter Benjamin, *Illuminations*, ed. Hannah Arendt, trans. Harry Zohn (New York: Schocken Books, 1969), 241.

Chapter Six

1. Joe McGinniss, *The Selling of the President 1968* (New York: Trident, 1969), 39.

2. McGinniss, 65.

3. Edward J. Epstein, *Between Fact and Fiction: The Problem of Journalism* (New York: Vintage Books, 1975), 225.

4. *In Our Own Words: Extraordinary Speeches of the American Century*, ed. Robert Torricelli and Andrew Carroll (New York: Kodansha International, 1999), 286–87.

5. Lewis F. Powell Jr., *Powell Memorandum: Attack on American Free Enterprise System*, 1971, 3. https://scholarlycommons.law.wlu.edu/powellmemo/1/.

6. Daniel Boorstin, *The Image: A Guide to Pseudo-Events in America* (New York: Vintage Books, 1992), 22.

7. Oliver North, "Opening Statement to Joint Iran Contra Congressional Committee," July 9, 1987, https://www.americanrhetoric.com/speeches/olivernorthfrancontrahearing.htm.

8. Chaim Perelman and Lucie Olbrechts-Tyteca, *The New Rhetoric: A Treatise on*

Argumentation, trans. John Wilkinson and Purcell Weaver (South Bend, IN: University of Notre Dame Press, 1969), 32.

9. Walter Fisher, *Human Communication as Narration: Toward a Philosophy of Reason, Value, and Action* (Columbia: University of South Carolina Press, 1987), 147–53.

10. C. W. Anderson, Leonard Downie Jr., and Michael Schudson, *The News Media: What Everyone Needs to Know* (New York: Oxford University Press, 2016), 56–57.

11. A. J. Liebling, "Do You Belong in Journalism?," *New Yorker*, May 14, 1960, 108.

12. Max Horkheimer and Theodor W. Adorno, *Dialectic of Enlightenment*, trans. John Cumming (New York: Seabury, 1969).

13. Daniel Bell, "The Cultural Contradictions of Capitalism," *Journal of Aesthetic Education* 6, no. 1 (1978): 26.

14. Armand Mattelart, *Networking the World, 1794–2000*, trans. Liz Carey-Libbrecht and James A. Cohen (Minneapolis: University of Minnesota Press, 2000).

15. Marvel Cooke, "The Bronx Slave Market," in *The Art of Fact*, ed. Ben Yagoda and Kevin Kerrane (New York: Touchstone, 1998), 255.

16. Agis Salpukas, "Suspect, to Neighbors, Was Withdrawn Loner," *New York Times*, May 17, 1972.

17. Edward D. Berkowitz, *Something Happened: A Political and Cultural Overview of the Seventies* (New York: Columbia University Press, 2006), 161.

18. Barbara Leaming, *Orson Welles: A Biography* (New York: Viking, 1985), 522.

19. Javier Cercas, *The Anatomy of a Moment: Thirty-Five Minutes in History and Imagination*, trans. Anne Mclean (New York: Bloomsbury, 2011), 25.

20. "Vaclav Havel's Radio Appeals from 1968," trans. Paul Wilson, Vaclav Havel Library Foundation, https://www.vhlf.org/news/vaclav-havels-radio-appeals-from-august-1968/, accessed July 1, 2021.

21. Gyan Prakash, *Emergency Chronicles: Indira Gandhi and Democracy's Turning Point* (Princeton, NJ: Princeton University Press, 2019), 376.

Chapter Seven

1. John Keane, *Democracy and Media Decadence* (New York: Cambridge University Press, 2013), 2.

2. Neil Henry, *American Carnival: Journalism under Siege in an Age of New Media* (Berkeley: University of California Press, 2007), 183.

3. Floyd Norris, "Time Inc. and Warner to Merge, Creating Largest Media Company," *New York Times*, March 5, 1989, 1, 39.

4. Telecommunications Act of 1996, 110 Stat. 56 (1996).

5. Andrew Jay Schwartzman, Harold Feld, and Pauril Desai, "Section 202(h) of the Telecommunications Act of 1996: Beware of Intended Consequences," *Federal Communications Law Journal* 58, no. 3 (2006): 586.

6. C. Edwin Baker, "The Media That Citizens Need," *University of Pennsylvania Law Review* 147, no. 2 (1998): 388–89.

7. James Fallows, *Breaking the News: How the Media Undermine Democracy* (New York: Vintage Books, 1997), 31.

8. Kathleen Hall Jamieson, *Dirty Politics: Deception, Distraction, and Democracy* (New York: Oxford University Press, 1992), 10.

9. Henry, *American Carnival*, 190.

10. Zizi A. Papacharissi, *A Private Sphere: Democracy in a Digital Age* (Malden, MA: Polity, 2010), 52.

11. Mark Andrejevic, *Infoglut: How Too Much Information Is Changing the Way We Think and Know* (New York: Routledge, 2013), 2.

12. Marshall McLuhan, "Playboy Interview," in *The Essential McLuhan*, ed. Eric McLuhan and Frank Zingrone (New York: Basic Books, 1995), 249.

13. R. S. Foa, A. Klassen, M. Slade, A. Rand, and R. Collins, *The Global Satisfaction with Democracy Report 2020* (Cambridge: Centre for the Future of Democracy, 2020), 2.

14. Fareed Zakaria, "The Rise of Illiberal Democracy," *Foreign Affairs*, November/December 1997, 42.

15. John McMillan and Pablo Zoido, "How to Subvert Democracy: Montesinos in Peru," *Journal of Economic Perspectives* 18, no. 4 (2004): 69.

16. Catherine M. Conaghan, *Fujimori's Peru: Deception in the Public Sphere* (Pittsburgh: University of Pittsburgh Press, 2005), 29.

17. Kai Schultz, "Modi Defends Indian Citizenship Law amid Protests," *New York Times*, December 22, 2019, https://www.nytimes.com/2019/12/22/world/asia/modi-india-citizenship-law.html.

18. "Binyamin Netanyahu's Obsession with the Press," *Economist*, January 26, 2019, https://www.economist.com/middle-east-and-africa/2019/01/26/binyamin-netanyahus-obsession-with-the-press.

19. Tim Johnson, "Coup Leader Elected President," *Miami Herald*, December 6, 1998, https://www.miamiherald.com/news/nation-world/world/americas/venezuela/article222712665.html.

20. Rachel Nolan, "The Realest Reality Show in the World," *New York Times*, May 4, 2012, https://www.nytimes.com/2012/05/06/magazine/hugo-chavezs-totally-bizarre-talk-show.html.

21. Madeleine Albright, *Fascism: A Warning* (New York: Harper, 2018), 130.

22. Benjamin Moffitt, *The Global Rise of Populism: Performance, Political Style, and Representation* (Stanford, CA: Stanford University Press, 2016), 57.

23. Bethan McKernan, "From Reformer to 'New Sultan': Erdoğan's Populist Evolution," *Guardian* (US edition), March 11, 2019, https://www.theguardian.com/world/2019/mar/11/from-reformer-to-new-sultan-erdogans-populist-evolution.

24. In Ergin Bulut and Erdem Yoruk, "Digital Populism: Trolls and Political Polarization of Twitter in Turkey," *International Journal of Communication* 11 (2017): 4105.

25. Soner Cagaptay, *Erdogan's Empire: Turkey and the Politics of the Middle East* (New York: I. B. Tauris, 2020), 298.

26. "Hungary PM: We Lied to Win Election," *Guardian* (US edition), September 18, 2006, https://www.theguardian.com/world/2006/sep/18/1.

27. Viktor Orbán, "I love this country," Cabinet Office of the Hungarian Prime Minister, https://miniszterelnok.hu/i-love-this-country-and-i-do-not-want-to-see-anyone-change-it-under-orders-from-outside/, accessed July 14, 2021.

28. Anna Szilágyi and Andras Bozóki, "Playing It Again in Post-Communism: The Revolutionary Rhetoric of Viktor Orban in Hungary," *Advances in the History of Rhetoric* 18 (2015): S164.

29. Arkady Ostrovsky, *The Invention of Russia: The Rise of Putin and the Age of Fake News* (New York: Penguin Books, 2017), 201.

30. Masha Gessen, *The Man without a Face: The Unlikely Rise of Vladimir Putin* (New York: Penguin, 2012), 181.

31. Martin Fletcher, "The Joke's Over—How Boris Johnson Is Damaging Britain's Global Stature," *New Statesman*, November 4, 2017, https://www.newstatesman.com/politics/uk/2017/11/joke-s-over-how-boris-johnson-damaging-britain-s-global-stature.

32. Sarah Lyall, "Conservative Is Elected as Mayor of London," *New York Times*, May 4, 2008, https://www.nytimes.com/2008/05/04/world/europe/04iht-boris.2.12550163.html.

33. Donald Trump with Tony Schwartz, *The Art of the Deal* (New York: Ballantine Books, 1987), 58.

34. Russell Muirhead and Nancy L. Rosenblum, *A Lot of People Are Saying: The New Conspiracism and the Assault on Democracy* (Princeton, NJ: Princeton University Press, 2019), 70.

35. Eli Stokols and Ben Schreckinger, "How Trump Did It," *Politico*, February 1, 2016, https://www.politico.com/magazine/story/2016/02/how-donald-trump-did-it-213581.

36. "Donald Trump Transcript: 'Our Country Needs a Truly Great Leader,'" *Wall Street Journal*, June 16, 2015, https://www.wsj.com/articles/BL-WB-55953.

37. "The Inaugural Address: Remarks of President Donald J. Trump—As Prepared for Delivery," January 20, 2017, https://trumpwhitehouse.archives.gov/briefings-statements/the-inaugural-address/.

38. "Trump CIA Speech Transcript," *CBS News*, January 23, 2017, https://www.cbsnews.com/news/trump-cia-speech-transcript/.

39. Jonathan Mahler, "CNN Had a Problem. Donald Trump Solved It," *New York Times*, April 4, 2017, https://www.nytimes.com/2017/04/04/magazine/cnn-had-a-problem-donald-trump-solved-it.html.

Chapter Eight

1. William Wan, "Inside the Republican Creation of the North Carolina Voting Bill Dubbed the 'Monster' Law," *Washington Post*, September 2, 2016, https://www.washingtonpost.com/politics/courts_law/inside-the-republican-creation-of-the-north-carolina-voting-bill-dubbed-the-monster-law/2016/09/01/79162398-6adf-11e6-8225-fbb8a6fc65bc_story.html.

2. Ezra Klein, "4 Political Scientists Are Tracking Whether Trump Is Damaging

American Democracy," *Vox*, October 5, 2017, https://www.vox.com/policy-and
-politics/2017/10/5/16414338/trump-democracy-authoritarianism.

3. In Sean Illing, "20 of America's Top Political Scientists Gathered to Discuss Our
Democracy. They're Scared," *Vox*, October 13, 2017, https://www.vox.com/2017/10
/13/16431502/america-democracy-decline-liberalism.

4. Pew Research Center, "Political Polarization in the American Public," June 12, 2014,
https://www.pewresearch.org/politics/2014/06/12/political-polarization-in-the
-american-public/.

5. Danielle Allen, *Education and Equality* (Chicago: University of Chicago Press,
2016).

6. Christopher Achen and Larry Bartels, *Democracy for Realists* (Princeton, NJ:
Princeton University Press, 2016).

7. Astra Taylor, *Democracy May Not Exist, but We'll Miss It When It's Gone* (New
York: Metropolitan Books, 2019).

8. Pew Research Center, "For Local News, Americans Embrace Digital but Still Want
Strong Community Connection," March 26, 2019, https://www.journalism.org
/2019/03/26/for-local-news-americans-embrace-digital-but-still-want-strong
-community-connection/.

9. Lee Shaker, "Dead Newspapers and Citizens' Civic Engagement," *Political Communication* 31, no. 1 (2014): 131–48.

10. Shanta Iyengar and Masha Krupenkin, "The Strengthening of Partisan Affect,"
Advances in Political Psychology 39, no. 1 (2018): 201–18.

11. Jeffrey L. Pasley, *The Tyranny of Printers: Newspaper Politics in the Early American
Republic* (Charlottesville: University Press of Virginia, 2001).

12. Sonja R. West, "Favoring the Press," *California Law Review* 106, no. 1 (February
2018): 91–134.

13. Whitney Phillips, "The Oxygen of Amplification," *Data and Society*, May 22, 2018,
https://datasociety.net/output/oxygen-of-amplification/.

14. Jacques Rancière, *Hatred of Democracy*, trans. Steve Corcoran (New York: Verso,
2006), 51.

15. Robert W. McChesney, *Rich Media, Poor Democracy: Communication Politics in
Dubious Times* (Urbana: University of Illinois Press, 1999), 285–86.

16. Chantal Mouffe, *The Democratic Paradox* (New York: Verso, 2005).

17. John Rawls, *Political Liberalism* (New York: Columbia University Press, 1996), 217.

18. Mouffe, *The Democratic Paradox*, 103.

Epilogue

1. Xu Zhangrun, "Viral Alarm: When Fury Overcomes Fear," trans. Geremie R.
Barmé, *China File*, February 10, 2020, https://www.chinafile.com/reporting
-opinion/viewpoint/viral-alarm-when-fury-overcomes-fear.

2. Eliane Brum, "How a Homophobic, Misogynist, Racist 'Thing' Could Be Brazil's
Next President," *Guardian* (UK edition), October 6, 2018, https://www.theguardian

.com/commentisfree/2018/oct/06/homophobic-mismogynist-racist-brazil-jair
-bolsonaro.

3. Phillip Rucker, Ashley Parker, and Josh Dawsey, "After Inciting Mob Attack, Trump
Retreats in Rage. Then, Grudgingly, He Admits His Loss," *Washington Post*, January 7, 2021, https://www.washingtonpost.com/politics/trump-rage-riot/2021/01/07
/26894c54-5108-11eb-b96e-0e54447b23a1_story.html.

INDEX

behavioral tracking, and geopositioning, 203
Being and Nothingness (Sartre), 266
Bell, Daniel, 173–74, 262
Benedetti, Vincent, 108–9
Benjamin, Walter, 153–54
Bennett, James Gordon, 85–87, 91
Berchtold, Count, 117–18
Berezovsky, Boris, 229–32
Berlin Wall, 184, 227
Berlusconi, Silvio, 219
Bernays, Edward, 126
Bernstein, Carl, 171
Bertillon, Alphonse, 112
bias: campaign against, 22; of digital, 23–24; and disruption, 10, 15–27, 52–53, 168; and fake news, 254; and fascism, 26–27; history of, 24–27; and knowledgeable voters, 255–56; liberal, 22, 161; media, 10, 21–24, 27, 51–52, 85, 161, 168–69, 200, 204, 254, 257; and news media, 22; and newspapers, 24–27; and news-print, 52–53; and open communication, 37; political, 85, 169; and politics, 85, 169
Bias of Communication, The (Innis), 24–27
Bible, 25, 52
Biden, Joe, 276
Bill of Rights, 66. *See also* US Constitution
bin Laden, Osama, 207–8
Birth of a Nation, The (Griffith film), 123–27, 151
Bismarck, Otto von, 76, 109
Black, Conrad, 235–36
Black Lives Matter, 205, 250
Blackshirt (fascist newspaper), 152
Blair, Jayson, 190
Blair, Tony, 265
Blanc, Louis, 89
Blanqui, Louis Auguste, 89
blaxploitation films, 181
blogospheres, 7, 202

Blum, Leon, 152
Bly, Nellie, 106
Bobbio, Norberto, 6
Bolívar, Simón, 77, 218
Bolshevik Revolution, 26, 75, 117, 119, 128, 135
Bolsonaro, Jair, 274
Bonaparte, Louis-Napoléon, 89–90, 94; as Napoléon III, 97, 108
Bonaparte, Napoléon, 70–71, 76–77; as Napoléon I, 90
books, 3, 4, 23, 42, 51, 52, 67, 78–79, 92, 178, 193
Boorstin, Daniel, 162
Boston Gazette, 57, 60–61, 65
Boston Globe, 191
Bowling Alone (Putnam), 12
Boyer, Pascal, 68
Bozóki, Andras, 227
Brady, Jim, 178
Brandeis, Louis, 129–30
Breitbart, 241, 244
Breivik, Anders Behring (Andrew Berwick), 207–8
Bremer, Arthur, 178
Breslin, Jimmy, 176
Brexit, 234–37, 265
bribery, 117, 213–14, 216–17. *See also* corruption
Brissot, Jacques Pierre, 68
British Union of Fascists (BUF), 152
broadsheets, 54, 116–17. *See also* newsprint
Brown, Helen Gurley, 176
Brown, John, 99
Brutus, 43
Brutus (pen name), 92
Buckley, William F., 177–78
BUF. *See* British Union of Fascists (BUF)
"Bulletins of the Republic," 89
Burke, Edmund, 69–70
Burke, Kenneth, 18
Burnett, Mark, 238
Burr, Aaron, 66

Grimké, Sarah, 81
Gül, Abdullah, 221
Gülen, Fethullah, 221, 223
gun control regulations, 180–81. *See also*
    Second Amendment (militia/arms)
Gutenberg, Johannes, 25, 51–52, 71
Gyurcsány, Ferenc, 224–25

Habermas, Jurgen, 263
hagiography, 66
Hale, Sarah Joseph, 81
Hamilton, Alexander, 63–66
Hamilton, Andrew, 49–50, 65
Hannity, Sean, 241
Hard Copy (TV newsmagazine), 201
Harding, Warren, 124
harmony: and communication, 93;
    cultural, 16; and purity, 264; and
    truth, 20; universal, 15
Harper's Magazine, 177, 260–61
Harper's New Monthly Magazine, 103
Hartford Courant, as longest-running
    newspaper in Americas, 59–60
Havel, Václav, 184
Hayes, Rutherford B., 104
Hearst, William Randolph, 106–8, 110,
    128, 141
Hébert, Jacques, 68
hegemony, 265
Heidegger, Martin, 149
Heighton, William, 80
Heinzen, Karl Peter, 98
Hemingway, Ernest, 172
Henry, Hubert-Joseph, 113
Henry, Neil, 200
Henry, Patrick, 60
Herodotus, 30
Herschel, John, Sir, 85
Hersey, John, 171–72
Hersh, Seymour, 170
Hierarchy (magazine), 137
Himmler, Heinrich, 148
Hinckley, John, Jr., 178
Hindenburg, Paul von, 147–48

Hitler, Adolf, 76, 131, 142–50, 153
Hofstadter, Richard, 92
Holmes, Oliver Wendell, 129–30
Hooker, Joseph, General, 101
Hoover, J. Edgar, 129
Horkheimer, Max, 173
Horthy, Miklós, 152, 225
Horton, Willie (William), 165–66
Houston, Sam, 83
How Democracies Die (Levitsky and
    Ziblatt), 5–6
Howe, Daniel Walker, 93
Hugenberg, Alfred, 143, 150
Hugenberg Trust, 143
Hughes, Charles Evans, 130
hysteria, and mass manipulation, 254

identity: and autocracy, 211; collective,
    265; and communication technology,
    208–9; cultural, 110; and data, 204;
    and discourse, 266; and emotion,
    39; and equality, 253; ethnic, 115;
    and ethnonationalism, 197, 207, 215,
    225, 232; and exploitation, 188; and
    information, 187; and infotainment,
    201; lost, and violence, 208–9; and
    meaning, 8; and nationalism, 110,
    115, 211; and partisanship, 256; and
    personal data, 204; and persuasion,
    215; and politics, 197, 201, 265, 267;
    and power, 188, 207, 209–10, 215, 233;
    and rhetoric, 110; social, 256
ideology: and broadsheets, 116–17; and
    communism, 227–28, 268; and con-
    sumerism, 173; and democracy, 266;
    as false and dangerous, 268; and fas-
    cism, 153, 268; and fusionism, 181; and
    global hegemony, 265; and knowl-
    edge, 209; and liberal democracy, 174;
    and media bias, 23; and nationalism,
    114; and open media, 174; and parti-
    sanship, 253; political, 74–75, 239; and
    politics, 74–75, 239; and publicity,
    52–53; and technology, 11